T0305248

The Economics of Adaptation and Long-term Relationships

Dean Victor Williamson

Independent researcher and formerly Antitrust Division, US Department of Justice, USA

Edward Elgar
PUBLISHING

Cheltenham, UK • Northampton, MA, USA

Cover image: *LS City* by Mariola Jaśko, 2018, oil on canvas, 110 × 160cm.
Reproduced by permission of the artist.

Published by
Edward Elgar Publishing Limited
The Lypiatts
15 Lansdown Road
Cheltenham
Glos GL50 2JA
UK

Edward Elgar Publishing, Inc.
William Pratt House
9 Dewey Court
Northampton
Massachusetts 01060
USA

A catalogue record for this book
is available from the British Library

Library of Congress Control Number: 2018960950

This book is available electronically in the **Elgar**online
Economics subject collection
DOI 10.4337/9781788979665

MIX
Paper from
responsible sources
FSC
www.fsc.org   FSC® C013056

ISBN 978 1 84980 037 2 (cased)
ISBN 978 1 78897 966 5 (eBook)

Typeset by Servis Filmsetting Ltd, Stockport, Cheshire

Printed and bound in Great Britain by TJ International Ltd, Padstow, Cornwall

Contents

Preface

Do institutions and organization matter, or is the economic analysis of institutions a distraction from the most important action? Indeed, does Vernon Smith's notion of the institution-free core of formal economic theory encompass that most important action? If so, does that render an economics of organization almost devoid of economic content? Do tradeoffs of little consequence obtain between the ways parties to long-run exchange organize their collaborations? Worse, are committed institution-alists, much like the monks of medieval Scholasticism busy cataloguing (only) those details from scriptures and commentaries that support their favored dogmas?

This book takes up questions of economic organization with neither the religious fervor of the inquisitor Saul of Tarsus (a proponent of orthodoxy) nor that of his alter ego, the apostate Paul (a great impresario of heterodoxy). The approach is more agnostic, opportunistic and even a little irreverent: What can theory do and not do? Theory can stimulate questions about how parties to complex exchange manage (sometimes competing) demands for commitment and flexibility in their relationships. It can frame ways of seeing. However, what blind spots persist?

The book opens with an informal tour of the economics of system design out of which an economics of adaptation in long-term relationships fitfully emerged. Five applications follow. The applications include explorations in both the law and economics relating to how parties manage relationships within the firm, within research and development (R&D) joint ventures, within the context of long-term contracts, and, most vividly, within the context of antitrust conspiracy. The applications make contact, in an accessible way, with the design of contracts, venture financing, and project finance.

HOW TO READ THIS BOOK

Each chapter is self-contained, although I recommend reading the opening chapter first. It sets up the themes of the book and situates each chapter with respect to those themes. I even recommend reading the chapters in order.

Some chapters feature some math and statistics. None of that math would be beyond the reach of the reader with training in calculus, but the exposition is generous in that you need not wend your way through the math to appreciate the propositions and empirical results. If you don't have time for the math, skip over it.

ACKNOWLEDGMENTS

The most important acknowledgment goes to an institution: the Society for Institutional and Organizational Economics (SIOE). The SOIE started out in 1996 as the International Society for the New Institutional Economics, and from the beginning it sponsored an annual conference. The annual conference has comprised an eclectic gathering of students of organization. That would include people in economics, the law, political science and a host of other fields. The SIOE conference remains an eclectic gathering, and it is a good laboratory for presenting formative material, whether theory or empirical research, relating to the design of institutions and the economics of organization more generally. At some point I presented most of the materials that comprise the body of this book at the SIOE or at the Corsican brother of SIOE, what is now the Institutional and Organizational Economics Academy.

The fifth chapter of the book makes contact with trade and financial contracting in the Middle Ages. The Gladys Krieble Delmas Foundation had an important hand in supporting two of my summer stints at the State Archives of Venice. The staff at the State Archives were also very generous. I showed up every day, six days a week at opening time and worked to the point of exhaustion. I think the staff respected that, and they helped me secure my documents.

I also acknowledge the support of my Caltech professors Phil Hoffman and Lance Davis. Lance was not even on my dissertation committee, but he was pleased to see someone venture forth into the (surprisingly physically demanding) work of archival research and come away with more than a few results. He looked eagerly for results that could illuminate the dynamics of institutional change. Admittedly, my work was more modest than that. I endeavored merely to understand how economic agents used the institutional tools available to them to adapt to changing circumstances. Work on Lance's larger project awaits.

I thank a host of people. Sally McKee gave me the inspired idea of exploring the Venetian contracting data from Crete. At one or more times, the following people gave me their concentrated attention and comments: Meir Kohn, Timur Kuran, Lynne Kiesling, Scott Masten, Lee Alston,

Benito Arruñada, Gary Libecap, Claude Menard, Giorgio Zanarone, Ann-Charlotte Dorange and F.X. LeDuc. I also benefited from lively seminar experiences including those at Berkeley, Michigan, Tilburg, Grenoble and the competition authority in Stockholm. Indeed, I thank Jens Prüfer and Stephane Robin for organizing those wonderful extended visits to Tilburg and Grenoble, respectively, where I managed to do a lot of the early writing and had the privilege of giving quite a number of seminar presentations spanning a diverse range of work. The tutorials in rock climbing in Grenoble were great fun, too. We may have been up on a ledge, but looking over my shoulder to see small farmhouses clustered far below in the valley did create the illusion of being suspended at a point of great elevation. Letting go of the rock face did, that first time, require more than a little concentration. Finally, I thank my brother Oliver E. Williamson, Jr. for allowing me to do much of the later writing over the course of two visits, each in excess of a month, at his house tucked away in the foothills of the Tatras Mountains.

This book is dedicated to Lauren S. Ziegler who, being a generous spirit, would have been thrilled to know this book was coming out.

1. The provenance of an economics of adaptation in long-term relationships

> When a law is made, the cunning that finds loopholes goes to work. One cannot deny that there is a certain slyness among younger players, a slyness which, when rules are written to prevent slyness, makes use of the rules themselves. (Kawabata 1951 [1981], p. 54, on the governance of *Go* tournaments)

When asked what the book is about, I say "long-term relationships". This piques everyone's interest. Everyone has experience with long-term relationships or with relationships that had the potential to persist for a long time. I then indicate that the book is about long-term commercial relationships – long-term contracts, partnerships, joint ventures, relationships within the firm, and implicit contracts. I also volunteer, however, that many of the concerns involved in maintaining personal relationships also show up in commercial relationships. A principal concern is exit: how do parties to an important relationship determine when to end a certain collaboration or to end their entire relationship? How do they manage the processes of wrapping up project-specific operations or their entire portfolio of operations? Insofar as parties can anticipate that breaking up can be hard to do, what processes might those parties commit to in advance for mitigating the costs of any prospective break-up? What processes can they set up for dividing assets, including intellectual properties, they had contributed to their collaboration or had developed through the course of collaboration, and how would they deal with knowledge assets to which it would be difficult to assign crisp property rights?

These are the types of questions that the designers of the long-running collaboration between Human Genome Sciences (HGS) and SmithKline Beecham (SKB) would have had to address. Human Genome Sciences was an early entrant in the business of identifying gene sequences. Indeed, HGS was established in 1992 in the same neighborhood as the National Institutes of Health in Rockville, Maryland, the same place where Craig Venter, a co-founder of HGS, had championed the development and application of particular, high-speed (shotgun) gene-sequencing technologies. Gene sequencing could advance genetic engineering – the engineering,

1

for example, of gene therapies that involve modifying DNA. Knowledge of gene sequences could also inform the design of drug therapies.

However, knowledge of gene sequences alone would not yield drug therapies or gene therapies. Human Genome Sciences would have to bring more capabilities into the firm – or be brought into another firm as when the pharmaceuticals firm GlaxoSmithKline absorbed HGS in 2012. Or HGS could do what it did before 2012: engage tight collaborations short of mergers with pharmaceuticals companies. Thus entered SKB in 1993, a large pharmaceuticals company that itself was ultimately absorbed in GlaxoSmithKline. The collaboration between HGS and SKB would join SKB's capabilities in designing and commercializing drugs with HGS's capabilities in identifying genes and characterizing gene expression.

The collaboration started in 1993 with a ten-year contract.[1] Making it work involved what amounted to a broad cross-licensing agreement by which each party would grant to the other rights of way to use technologies that were subject to patent or would be patented in the future. Such cross-licensing amounted to commitments not to sue for expropriation of intellectual property in the future. (Absent such commitments, one party might exploit threats to press claims of patent infringement or other expropriation of property rights as a way of gaining bargaining leverage over the counterparty. Anticipating such hazards, parties might be less likely to enter long-term collaboration in the first place.) Making the collaboration work also involved the delicate business of sharing know-how or tacit knowledge, for example, the artisanal knowledge in the heads of engineers, not amenable to patenting, with which engineers could abscond to another firm. More generally, the parties to collaboration would contemplate how to mitigate the leakage of know-how outside the bounds of their collaboration. On this count, the two parties agreed to impose some limits on personnel transfers. Specifically, SKB reserved the right to send two engineers to HGS facilities to work alongside HGS engineers. That is, the parties agreed that HGS would maintain a veto over proposals from SKB to send over more than two engineers. The parties also included a no-poaching clause according to which neither party would secure employment of former employees of the other party for at least a year after a given employee's departure. The parties set up production benchmarks (milestones) as well as deliberative processes, replete with voting mechanisms, for identifying and approving prospective research projects.

---

[1] All the information reported here derives from public versions of contracts HGS filed as exhibits to its Securities and Exchange Commission Form 10-Q dated August 20, 1996.

The prospect of approving projects, of course, contemplates the prospect of rejecting projects. More importantly, approval and rejection contemplates the prospect of (possibly bitter) disagreement. Hence, the principal purpose of deliberative processes: to enable parties to collectively make decisions and take action even in the face of messy, irreconcilable disagreement. Then there is the question of exit. Almost surprisingly, the contract contemplated very little in the way of a deliberative, bilateral process as regards the decision of one party or the other to exit. With some months' notice, one party or the other could exit. Rules were already in place to sort out the division of intellectual properties developed through the course of any one research project.

Whether or not HGS or SKB ever vigorously threatened exit to gain leverage in bilateral bargaining is not obvious, but, as it was, neither HGS nor SKB (nor SKB's successor, GlaxoSmithKline) exited the relationship. Even so, the original contract never exhausted its ten-year term. Instead, the agreement was periodically amended or superseded. It was amended mostly to enable the two parties to draw yet other parties into collaboration. These amendments pertained largely to extending rights of way to these other parties. Along the way, however, HGS entered bilateral relationships with other pharmaceuticals firms, but GlaxoSmithKline's acquisition of HGS in 2012 did more than a little violence to those relationships. It put an end to them, a result that may explain the lack of complete enthusiasm on the part of HGS management to merge with GlaxoSmithKline.

There will be much more of that in this book: violence to relationships, efforts to contain or channel that violence, and the intrinsic messiness of long-term relationships more generally. Indeed, Chapter 5 will take us to the Eastern Mediterranean in the fourteenth century, a time and place of much actual violence and dislocation. It was a time at which Venetian seafaring traders and their abundant competitors had to put up with war, plague, crusade, and piracy – in addition to the hazards that more ordinarily comprise the topics of economic research (agency hazards) – in order to generate the gains from trade that ultimately made Venice the queen of the Adriatic and a leading peer among peers in the Eastern Mediterranean. However, we are getting ahead of ourselves. The immediate purpose here is to ask, why the management of relationships has not been a more obvious and prominent topic of economic research until the last few decades? The broad answer advanced here is not new, but I assemble material not generally brought together in one place. The broad answer is that no role has yet emerged for a manager or management in formal economic theory. It is not obvious how to characterize what managers do. It gets worse. From the perspective of economic theory, it is not immediately obvious how parties to long-term collaboration or even to short-term exchange could find themselves mired in disagreement. Among other things, it takes a lot of work and technical sophistication to characterize how parties who appear symmetrically informed could agree to disagree about where opportunities to realize mutual gains from exchange might reside.[2] How is it that collaborators could not jointly examine opportunities and find themselves agreeing on what projects to pursue?

One answer is that parties to prospective exchange are not symmetrically informed. Indeed, one function of deliberative processes would be to induce them to share what they know about prospective projects and thereby induce a common understanding about prospective gains from exchange. Yet, if talking things out were all that there were to deliberative processes, then the study of collaborative ventures might not be that interesting. But we can imagine that parties might yet perceive strategic advantages to withholding private information. The strategic manipulation of private information is an important topic and shows up in the chapters of this book, but there are much deeper issues. Specifically, theory is good at characterizing gains from exchange, but (1) theory offers little guidance about how parties actually identify and engineer mutual gains, and (2) historically, not everyone, whether in the social sciences or not, has understood that exchange may afford opportunities for mutual gains. There is, for example, a long tradition of primitive economic thinking, which still prevails in public policy, that frames exchange as zero-sum rather than as capable of generating mutual benefits. In contrast, economic theory has a lot to say about gains from exchange, but it has had little to say about the role (if any) of institutions and collaborative arrangements in generating those gains. Instead, it offers a narrative that is too neat and clean: parties to exchange bring complementary assets and capabilities together, thereby enabling themselves to create value. The parties' interests will be aligned insofar as they each have an incentive to maximize the surplus (the "size of the pie") from collaboration. Disagreement might obtain regarding the sharing of surplus. (Who gets the largest slice of the pie?) And, yet, bargaining theory suggests that bargaining should be efficient in that parties should be able to sort out the sharing of surplus without jeopardizing the creation of surplus.

The idea that exchange could yield mutual gains is powerful and yet has been under-appreciated in policy debates. Nevertheless, it would be wrong

---

[2]   For a good introduction to the state of the literature on "agreeing to disagree", see Dominiak and Lefort (2015). Aumann (1976) is a good introduction to the fundamental questions.

to suggest that purely efficient bargaining should obtain spontaneously. On any one morning we can look out on to the world and easily find examples of parties occupied with destroying value and destroying each other rather than with bargaining their way to mutually beneficial exchange. As Farrell (1987, p. 115) observes, axiomatic bargaining theory (inspired by Nash 1950, 1953) does not help us understand how it is that bargaining can be inefficient in that one of the axioms of the theory is that parties will bargain their way to efficient outcomes. As Farrell (1987) further observes, making superficial appeals to the fiction of frictionless bargaining in the spirit of the Coase Theorem amounts to ignoring important action. The point of Coase (1960) was that bargaining is not seamless and frictionless. Insofar as any process for organizing exchange involves some dissipation of value owing to friction in the bargaining process, then any one set of messy processes and institutions (property rights, administrative processes embedded in firms or government, and even market processes) might have a role in enabling parties to engage in gainful (if not always purely efficient) exchange.

We develop friction further on, but for now we proceed to the zero-sum concept of exchange. The idea that gains from trade do not spontaneously obtain but must be engineered could go some way toward rationalizing a role for processes and personnel that look a lot like management and managers. These people could occupy themselves with making sure that they and their trading parties do a good job of recognizing opportunities for gainful exchange and then realizing those gains. However, if exchange is zero-sum, then the role of managers is diminished in that there are no gains from exchange to seek out and secure. Indeed, zero-sum, mercantilistic thinking has a lot of intuitive and enduring appeal. Here the idea is that exchange cannot yield mutual gain but, at best, involves zero-sum payoffs in that one party's gain entails another party's loss. If some party benefits, then some other party must have been exploited.[3] It can get worse in that parties to exchange may end up wasting resources fighting each other. Wasting resources may yield negative-sum payoffs.[4]

---

[3] For references, among many, that discuss zero-sum thinking, see Bagus et al. (2016), Ogilvie (2014) regarding medieval guilds, and Rubin (2003) on "folk economics". See also Verburg (2012) on the evolution from zero-sum conceptions of exchange to "gains from trade", and see Gordon (1978) on the zero-sum conception of capitalism in "Classical-Marxian" economics.

[4] Consider the following counter-example. Geologists speculated that large oil deposits would likely be found in a particular, poor country. The country's leadership understood that, at the time, no one in the country maintained the technical

The zero-sum concept of exchange is interesting for what it is not, that is, an affirmative theory of value. It is a theory – or more of a folk intuition – that exchange does not generate value, but we can at least credit people such as the Physiocrats of the French Enlightenment for asking the question about where value did come from. To do this, they had to conceive of an economic system. They then endeavored to develop an engineer's knowledge of the natural laws governing that system. An engineer's understanding of the system could enable some degree of control over the system. The program, presumably, would involve identifying control variables (the "levers and knobs" of the system) and then distinguishing the control variables from endogenously determined quantities that might otherwise have appeared as tempting control variables.

In the Physiocrats' conception of the system, value came out of the ground. It derived from agricultural production. That value was then fully realized and distributed across the system through vertical chains of exchange relations and other productive pursuits. "The physiocrats", Hannah Robie Sewall (1901, p. 81) observed, "maintained that manufacture and trade were sterile industries, in that they created no new wealth, but merely changed its form and carried from one place another that already created". Müller (1974, pp. 314, 320–21) made explicitly plain, however, that the Physiocrats did not dismiss "manufacture and trade" as unproductive but as ancillary to the realization and distribution of value.

François Quesnay emerges in the history of economic thought as one of the most prominent of the Physiocrats, and scattered across his writings are passages that anticipate and sound a lot like Adam Smith's "invisible hand" (Müller 1974, p. 314). Smith's own sparing references to an invisible hand have been heavily interpreted. Ultimately, the invisible hand has

---

competence to find, extract, refine, or commercialize that oil. The leadership appreciated, however, that it owned a resource of great potential value. It would be valuable, because the owners of the resource could contract with oil-field engineers and other parties who did maintain the competence and capabilities to develop the resource. The leadership also understood that it could induce teams of engineers to compete for contracts to develop the oil resource. After some time, the competition settled down to two parties, one party sponsored by the British government, and the other party, Standard Oil of Southern California (SoCal). SoCal eventually secured the contract. SoCal and the country's leadership set up an entity, the Arabian-American Oil Company (subsequently Aramco), to develop and commercialize the oil resource. SoCal subsequently became Chevron, and that poor country, which had not existed until 1932, was Saudi Arabia. See *Discovery! The Search for Arabian Oil* (Stegner 2007). In the early 1950s, Chevron contracted Wallace Stegner, the director of the creative writing program at Stanford, to consult its archives and compose an account of its early experience on the Arabian peninsula.

been set up as a metaphor for a proposition (the First Welfare Theorem) that atomistic, independent economic agents can collectively exhaust gains from trade in an economic system via market-mediated exchange. The proposition amounts to a glorious defenestration of the zero-sum concept of exchange. It is based on an underlying theory of value, according to which each instance of voluntary, market-mediated exchange yields value. That alone is important. The great surprise, however, is that (on paper, at least) economic agents can extract from the system all of the gains from trade that the system could yield in that no subset of agents could abscond with their own resources, trade among themselves and do better. Even more astonishing is the idea that market-mediated exchange could decentralize economic exchange between these agents in that they could collectively benefit from exchange without direction from a central authority.[5]

In discussing such results regarding a particular conceptualization of an economic system, Koopmans (1957, p. 148) observed:

> The main service [the conceptualization] renders is to show that value theory – that is, the theory of prices as guides to allocation of resources and of the relationships between these prices and the technology – is of such a fundamental character that it can be constructed without reference to institutional postulates regarding the existence and the behavior of firms and consumers.

Koopmans's comment anticipates Vernon Smith on the "institution-free core" of economics. (See, for example, Smith 2007, pp. 3, 100 or Crockett et al. 2009, although Oliver Williamson credits the "institution-free core" to Vernon Smith as early as Williamson 1990.) There are at least three interpretations of the "core". The most optimistic is that the core may make no accommodation for a manager or for institutional processes, because it does not have to. Institutions are just a distraction, and investing them with importance is delusional; the core spans the important action. A more catholic, agnostic view would be to see how much of the important action the core really does span. A role for the manager and for institutions in supporting exchange might yet become manifest. A more pessimistic view would be that the core misses the most important action in that exchange does not obtain spontaneously but instead requires institutional supports; it is the fiction of fully-efficient, frictionless exchange

---

[5] Decentralization lends itself to any number of metaphors beyond Adam Smith's "invisible hand". For example, in *Socony-Vacuum Oil v. United States* 310 U.S. 658 (1940) the Supreme Court of the United States recognized "the free play of market forces" as "the central nervous system of the economy".

that can be a distraction; cheap and easy appeals to free markets are far too glib.

We can imagine that Koopmans might have situated himself somewhere close to optimistic, that Smith would situate himself closer to catholic, and that Williamson might situate himself a touch more pessimistically than Smith. Notably pessimistic, however, might have been Adam Smith himself who, in Nathan Rosenberg's account (Rosenberg 1960) perceived a role for a host of processes and norms in enabling market-mediated exchange. Then there is the role of processes and norms to enable exchange within the firm or within other bodies (government, say) that are invested with administrative processes.

Meanwhile, neither optimistic, nor pessimistic but puzzled by the role of market-mediated processes in economic systems might have been, in Herbert Simon's telling, "[a] mythical visitor from Mars" (Simon 1991, pp. 27–8):

> Suppose that it (the visitor[,] I'll avoid the question of its sex) approaches the Earth from space, equipped with a telescope that reveals social structures. The firms reveal themselves, say, as solid green areas with faint interior contours marking out divisions and departments. Market transactions show as red lines connecting firms, forming a network in the spaces between them. Within firms (and perhaps even between them) the approaching visitor also sees pale blue lines, the lines of authority connecting bosses with various levels of workers . . .
>
> No matter whether our visitor approached the United States or the Soviet Union, urban China or the European Community, the greater part of the space below it would be within the green areas, for almost all of the inhabitants would be employees, hence inside the firm boundaries. Organizations would be the dominant feature of the landscape. A message sent back home, describing the scene, would speak of "large green areas interconnected by red lines." It would not likely speak of "a network of red lines connecting green spots." . . .
>
> When our visitor came to know that the green masses were organizations and the red lines connecting them were market transactions, it might be surprised to hear the structure called a market economy. "Wouldn't 'organizational economy' be the more appropriate term?" it might ask.

In 1938, Orson Welles's radio production of H.G. Wells's *The War of the Worlds* is purported to have convinced a number of radio listeners that actual Martians had landed on a farm in New Jersey – and these Martians had not presented themselves as curious students of organization. In 1937, however, a young Englishman posed questions and observations consistent with those of Herbert Simon's mythical Martian. In "The nature of the firm", Ronald Coase (1937) observed what would seem to have been unremarkable to the person on the street: the economy is populated with firms (many or even most of the "large green areas" in Simon's telling), and these firms interact with each other in markets (in the "network of red lines"). What was remarkable, however, was that economic theory was not equipped to accommodate firms. (Again, theory offered no role for a manager.) Instead, theory had been occupied with the program to which Koopmans (1957, p. 148) alluded: the development of "a theory of prices as guides to [the] allocation of resources and of the relationships between these prices and the technology". At the same time, the program of organizing an entire economy (that of the Soviet Union) as a single, all-encompassing firm had already been far advanced by 1937. Intellectuals in Western Europe enthusiastically hailed what appeared to them to be Joseph Stalin's successful effort to thrust Russia out of its anachronistic, agrarian past and into a mature, industrialized present.[6]

More generally, global economic depression in the 1930s induced policymakers to revisit the idea that a shift away from market-mediated exchange (capitalism) toward increasing statism and centralization of production and distribution could mitigate excess competition and promote cooperation in economic systems.[7] The United States, for example, may have established the Antitrust Division of the Department of Justice in 1933, but the real mission of the new administration of Franklin Roosevelt was to promote cartelization through such legislation as the 1933 National Industrial Recovery Act. By 1938, the Administration reversed course. Observing, among other things, that German conglomerates were busy organizing international cartels of munitions-relevant industries, the Administration assigned the Antitrust Division a new anti-cartel mandate.[8]

It was into these turbulent waters about the relative merits of market-mediated exchange and centralization that Coase tossed "The nature of

---

[6]　See, for example, Medvedev (2004) on "European writers on their meetings with Stalin". Also, "like a good totalitarian", George Bernard Shaw stands out as one of the most conspicuous admirers of the Stalinist–Leninist program. "I have advised the nations to adopt Communism", exclaimed Shaw, "and have carefully explained how they can do it without cutting one another's throats. But if they prefer to do it by cutting one another's throats, I am no less a Communist. Communism will be good even for Yahoos" (Letter to Kingsley Martin, 1942, cited in Schwartzman 1990, p. 123).

[7]　Concerns about excess competition had been around for some time. See, for example, Perelman (1994). Also, Seager and Gulick (1929, pp. 72–85), on the "advantages and disadvantages of trusts," illuminates some of the policy puzzles of the day.

[8]　See, for example, Borkin and Welsh (1943 [1960]). Joseph Borkin went on, in 1938, to become the chief of the Division's new Patent and Cartel Section. See also Franklin Roosevelt himself on excess competition and cartelization in Roosevelt (1942).

the firm" like a message in a bottle. It was a message ultimately retrieved, a world war and half a cold war later, from tamer waters by Ken Arrow (1969) and Oliver Williamson (1971). An economics of adaptation was slow to emerge, however, because economics had been preoccupied with much bigger things. For most of two centuries, it had been occupied with the design and implementation of economic systems. Yet, in the hands of some parties, the preoccupation with economic systems was directed at implementing heaven on earth in the here and now (as in the Soviet experience). In the hands of others (such as Koopmans), the preoccupation motivated a demanding but less exalted project: to sort out the allocative efficiency of alternative systems. In the hands of all parties, however, the management of economic relationships did not inform system design. By the early twentieth century, for example, the most enthusiastic practitioners perceived the design and implementation of an efficient system as a trivially accessible matter. "The whole of society will have become a single office and a single factory," Vladimir Lenin exclaimed in 1917 (Lenin 1917 [1970], p. 121). Technocrats and their experts would impose factory discipline on the whole of that single factory (society), and they would do it by applying the principles of the emerging scientific management as expounded specifically by Frederick W. Taylor in his slender 1911 tome, *The Principles of Scientific Management*.[9] If there were an implementation problem, it would amount to no more than sweeping aside entrenched interests. In Lenin's oratory, this would involve "defeating the capitalists" or, the same thing, "overthrowing the exploiters" (Lenin 1917 [1970], p. 121).

Taylor, the former president of the American Society of Mechanical Engineers, was interested in shop-floor efficiency, and Lenin's concept of the Bolshevik program was to organize the entire economy as a single shop floor. The program would elevate the shop-floor workers to collective management of the shop floor, and they would impose shop-floor efficiency. Implicit in the Taylor program, however, was the idea that the shop was a distinct entity (a firm, say) that would interact with other entities in market-mediated exchange. Specifically, Taylor contemplated a role for managers in procuring inputs from other firms and selling shop-floor outputs to other firms. In Taylor's telling, the shop floors that populate the economy emerge as something akin to Herbert Simon's "green areas" or to D.H. Robertson's "islands of conscious power in this

---

[9]   See Wren (1980) regarding scientific management in the Soviet Union. *The Principles of Scientific Management*, meanwhile, was published together with *Shop Management* in a more expansive tome titled *Scientific Management* (Taylor 1947).

ocean of unconscious co-operation [market-mediated exchange], like lumps of butter coagulating in a pail of buttermilk".[10] Mixing metaphors, Robertson continued:

> But even these patches [the shop floors that populate "the factory system"] are still small and scattered in comparison with the whole field of economic life. In the main the coordination of the efforts of the isolated business leaders is left to the play of impalpable forces – news and knowledge and habit and faith, and those twin elementals, the Law of Supply and Demand. (Robertson 1923, p. 86)

The Bolshevik program, meanwhile, seemed to contemplate the idea that shop-floor processes could be scaled up at no cost to encompass all exchange in the economy between erstwhile firms. There would be no need for markets. All procurement of inputs and distribution of outputs would be centrally coordinated.

In *The Economics of Control* (1946, p. 62), Abba Lerner could observe that the Bolshevik experience had yielded a "disastrous result", but enter Fred M. Taylor unto the breach. This other Fred Taylor expounded, in his presidential address to the American Economic Association in 1929, on a way of maintaining centralized control while preserving the autonomy of the "shop floors". The scheme would involve impressing an ambitious interpretation of the Second Welfare Theorem into service. (More on this below.) A central authority, rather than markets, could set prices for all commodities produced and exchanged in an economic system. Economic agents (firms and consumers) would take these prices as parameters in their internal calculus and determine inputs, outputs and consumption of commodities accordingly.

In this scheme, the fiction of the "Walrasian auctioneer" would become incarnate in the reality of a Central Planning Board, as in Lange (1937, 1938 [1964]). The Walrasian auctioneer, recall, posts prices, records excess demands, and adjusts prices in an iterative *tâtonnement* process, which is supposed to converge on a set of prices that balances supply and demand simultaneously across all markets for all commodities in the economic system. The prices that ultimately obtain are right in that no excess demand or supply in a given market persists. (The system achieves a Walrasian equilibrium.) The First Welfare Theorem implies that such prices might be doubly right in that they enable economic agents to exhaust gains from exchange across the entire economy. (The Walrasian equilibrium is Pareto optimal.) No potential gains end up being unrealized.

---

[10] Robertson (1923, p. 85). Some readers may recall that Coase (1937) cited this same passage from Robertson.

Vilfredo Pareto first advanced the Pareto optimality criterion (*ophélim-ité*) in the first volume of his *Cours d'Economie Politique* (Pareto 1896), and he first advanced a version of the First Welfare Theorem in sections 720–35 of the second volume (Pareto 1897). He advanced these theoretical developments as a way of suggesting how free, market-mediated exchange (*la libre concurrence*) could yield socially desirable outcomes. More pointedly, he advanced these results as a benchmark against which *l'Etat collectiviste* (or any system) would have to perform (Pareto 1909, ch. 6, paras 49–55; see also Pareto 1897, s. 837).

The proposition advanced by Taylor (1929), Lange (1937, 1938 [1964]), Lerner (1946) and others was that the collectivist state could meet and then exceed outcomes achievable by market-mediated exchange. For starters, the Central Planning Board could achieve the Walrasian benchmark (no excess demand across all markets) by implementing the computational program suggested by Walras himself, an iterative (and presumably convergent) *tâtonnement* process. They could then appeal to the theory inspired by Pareto (the First Welfare Theorem) to suggest that the result of the same computational program would meet the Paretian benchmark; having satisfied the Walrasian benchmark, they would not have to do more work to meet the Paretian benchmark.

Writing on "The computer and the market" Lange (1967, p. 158) explained that in 1938 he had demonstrated "how a market mechanism could be established in a socialist economy" which would secure the Walrasian benchmark "by means of an empirical procedure of trial and error". He elaborated:

> Starting with an arbitrary set of prices, the price is raised whenever demand exceeds supply and lowered whenever the opposite is the case. Through such a process of *tâtonnements*, first described by Walras, the final equilibrium prices are gradually reached. These are the prices satisfying the system of simultaneous equations. It was assumed without question that the *tâtonnement* process in fact converges to the system of equilibrium prices.

But, it was now 1967. Computing capability would render calculation of the "right" prices a trivial affair. "Let us put the simultaneous equations on an electronic computer," Lange (1967, p. 158) declared, "and we shall obtain the solution in less than a second. The market process with its cumbersome *tâtonnements* appears old-fashioned. Indeed, it may be considered as a computing device of the pre-electronic age."

The question of computing equilibrium prices did inspire important theoretical advances in general equilibrium theory. Among other things, Herbert Scarf and others demonstrated that more general computational algorithms could compute equilibrium prices for economic environments that were themselves more general than those contemplated by Pareto, Lange and other contributors. (See Scarf 1973 for a useful introduction.) The theoretical results were all the more powerful in that they yielded constructive proofs of the welfare theorems. They were constructive in that they established more than just the existence of equilibrium prices for a more general set of economic environments; they also yielded actual prices. A larger point, however, was that, having handily dispatched the problem of computing the right prices by whatever algorithm, the collectivist program could then exceed market-mediated exchange by appealing to dynamic considerations. Specifically, they argued that the Central Planning Board could end the plague of business cycles to which a system of free, market-mediated exchange was susceptible.

It is not obvious that any state, including the Soviet Union, had attempted to implement the program that Oskar Lange had advocated as late as 1967, but the Soviets had experimented with other schemes for centralizing control of the production and distribution of goods and services. Meanwhile, in 1978 the Ford Foundation had a hand in sponsoring a gathering in the Soviet Union of American and Soviet academics. The proceedings included a tour of a Soviet automobile factory. One of the Russian hosts explained how the Soviets managed the factory. One of the American participants, James March, inquired of his Russian counterpart something to the effect of, "Are there ever any problems?" After a pause, his Russian host declared, "No!" After another pause, all the Russians laughed.[11]

In 1985 the Soviets, under Mikhail Gobachev's leadership, began to fitfully introduce economic reforms and political reforms. These were presented as *Perestroika* (restructuring) and *Glasnost* (openness). Within six years, the Soviet Union dissolved.[12]

---

[11] My original source for this anecdote is Oliver Williamson who, along with James March, participated in the 1978 meeting. I thank James March for helping me pin down details, although we agree that recollections of a meeting after a span of 40 years may not be complete.

[12] Some authors contrast the Soviet experience with the still unfolding Chinese experience. The Chinese Communist Party eventually granted its imprimatur to a fitful program of economic reforms initiated in 1978. Authors credit Chinese success to introducing reforms without introducing political liberalization openness. Demands for political liberalization did emerge and climaxed, arguably, with the Tiananmen demonstrations. The authorities sent the tanks into Tiananmen Square on June 4, 1989, but China's economic growth continued unabated. The Chinese experience is interesting, because it complicates end-of-history narratives according to which political liberalization and economic liberalization (a shift away from centralized control to market-mediated exchange) are perceived as complementary processes.

We now take up two questions: (1) how did prescriptions of the sort advocated by Oskar Lange become heated topics of debate in the first place, and (2) how is it that problems of adaptation in economic relations only fleetingly informed the debate? That is, how did we get here? We begin where Karl Marx's great impresario, Friedrich Engels, opened his essay "Socialism: utopian and scientific" (Engels 1892 [1978]). Engels started with acknowledgment of Jean-Jacques Rousseau and "the great French philosophers" of the French Enlightenment more generally (Engels 1892 [1978], p. 681). It was in Rousseau's (1775, first published 1755) *Discours sur l'origine et les fondements de l'inégalité parmi les hommes* that the great philosophers first seriously identified private property as the principal obstacle to implementing their concept of heaven on earth. We also begin with another current common to the French, English and Scottish Enlightenments, the beginning of the emergence from its chrysalis of the concept of the economy. By the late nineteenth century the concept of the economy had evolved into a quantity susceptible to manipulation by economic policy.

From Rousseau in the mid-eighteenth century we flash forward to Pareto in the 1890s. The global economy had been mired in depression in the early 1890s, and, as with the economic depression of the 1840s or early 1870s, economic hardship may have inspired anew the expectation that Marx's chiliastic prediction of the final crisis of capitalism and the inevitability of socialism was about to unfold.[13] Capitalism would fall under the weight of its own internal contradictions and give way to the socialist revolution. The question was: should eager socialists patiently wait around for the inevitable revolution, or should they play an active role in inducing the revolution?[14]

---

[13]   In the afterword to the German edition of *Das Kapital* (1872, p. 822, English edition 2018, p. 15), Karl Marx confidently predicted just such an impending crisis of capitalism in Germany:

The contradictions inherent in the movement of capitalist society impress themselves upon the practical bourgeois most strikingly in the changes of the periodic cycle, through which modern industry runs, and whose crowning point is the universal crisis. That crisis is once again approaching, although as yet but in its preliminary stage; and by the universality of its theatre and the intensity of its action it will drum dialectics even into the heads of the mushroom-upstarts of the new, holy Prusso-German empire.

[14]   The failure of the 1848 revolutions in continental Europe appears to have convinced at least one eager socialist, the 30-year-old Karl Marx, that socialist revolution would require some active effort. In the *Neue Rheinische Zeitung*, the daily newspaper that he edited, Marx posted a piece titled "The victory of the

Pareto (1896, 1897) seems to suggest that socialist revolution may be all well and good, but the socialist program should be made to stand up to performance benchmarks. Hence his early sketch of the First and Second Welfare Theorems. These theorems suggest how markets can perform surprisingly well (on paper at least) in stylized, frictionless economic environments. However, that was merely preamble to Pareto's larger analysis. Pareto's contributions included ideas that anticipate Coase (1937), on the relative costs of organizing exchange in markets or by means of administrative processes in firms, and Arrow (1969), on "the costs of running the economic system" more generally. He deployed a metaphor from thermodynamics to suggest that exchange processes – whether centralized, decentralized or hybrid – are not frictionless but instead dissipate value much as a steam engine dissipates energy (in the form of heat) in its own operation (see Pareto 1897, s. 837). He went on to propose a type of comparative institutional analysis: decentralized processes (principally, *la libre concurrence*) and centralized processes (the socialist program) should be made to stand up against each other, and transaction costs, characterized much as a form of thermodynamic dissipation or friction (*frottements*), should be folded into the analysis. "*La machine à vapeur n'utilise qu'une petite fraction des calories produites par le combustible*" ("The steam engine uses only a small fraction of the calories produced by the fuel"), he observed, but, one "machine" may yet outperform another: "*[S']il existait une machine qui utilisât mieux la chaleur, il faudrait se hater de la substituer à nos machines à vapeur*" ("If there exists another machine that dissipates less energy as heat, then we should hasten to substitute our steam engines with it") (Pareto 1897, p. 187).

It was Enrico Barone (1908 [2009]), not Fred Taylor or Oskar Lange, who first advanced the idea that the welfare theorems identified how a central authority, "the Ministry of Production in the collectivist state", could implement a program that would satisfy Pareto's benchmarks. What really excited later proponents of such a program, however, was

---

counter-revolution in Vienna". He assigned blame for the failure of the revolutions on the members of the bourgeoisie. By his telling, the bourgeoisie had a pivotal role to play in toppling the established elites, but their interests proved to be too close to those of those same elites. They betrayed the October revolution in Vienna. An angry and frustrated Karl Marx closed his piece with a flourish: "The purposeless massacres perpetrated since the June and October events, the tedious offering of sacrifices since February and March, the very cannibalism of the counterrevolution will convince the nations that there is only one way in which the murderous death agonies of the old society and the bloody birth throes of the new society can be shortened, simplified and concentrated, and that way is revolutionary terror" (Marx 1848 [1977], pp. 505–6).

not the program itself but (1) the prospect of using the program to achieve the ultimate objective of socialist programming (the imposition and maintenance of economic equality), and (2) to do it in a way that would insulate the program from critics (principally, Ludwig von Mises and Friedrich Hayek) who had advocated decentralized, market-based solutions as superior alternatives to centralized, socialist solutions. They would do all of this by appealing to the Second Welfare Theorem as a kind of crude implementation theorem. Specifically, the state would impose a one-time redistribution of wealth, and then it would let economic agents trade in markets for which the state would have calculated prices. Lange (1937, pp. 134–5) did suggest that redistributing wealth without too much dislocation could involve something in the spirit of a surprise, economy-wide smash-and-grab "expropriation" by the state so that the victims of such expropriation would not have time to mount a defense. "Socialism", Lange (1937, pp. 135) averred, "is not an economic policy for the timid."

In his Nobel Prize lecture, Eric Maskin could observe that the "Planning Controversy" of the 1930s may have been "important and fascinating", but, not surprisingly, "for certain onlookers such as Leonid Hurwicz, it was also rather frustrating" (Maskin 2008, p. 571). Leo Hurwicz went on to be one of the most important developers of implementation theory. At first sight, we can distinguish implementation theory from the early "Utopian Socialism" and the later Marxist "Scientific Socialism" as a matter of verb tense. "Socialism" had made it into the lexicon by 1820, and it was the early socialists and proto-socialists such as Rousseau who had advanced a program for how the world *should* be made to work. The Marxist program was ostensibly scientific in that it advanced a prediction about how the world *would*, as a matter of course, be made to work by virtue of the historical inevitability of the socialist chiliasm. Implementation theory, however, has been occupied with how the world *could* be made to work. Indeed, Hurwicz expressed some frustration with the Marxist approach in that its theory of the "historical inevitability" of Socialism (and, ultimately, of Communism) induced "neglect of problems of resource allocation" (Hurwicz 1977, p. 4). In contrast, implementation theory situated itself to take up questions of comparative institutional analysis of the sort contemplated by Pareto (1897).

One of the great innovations of implementation theory is that it explicitly folds incentive constraints into the analysis of resource allocation problems. The theory has also been generalized to address matters smaller than the design of economic systems. It has been scaled down to accommodate richer, boutique applications as in contract theory and mechanism design theory more generally. This is where, finally, we might expect economic theory could situate itself to begin to recognize a role for a manager, for management, and for problems of adaptation over the course of long-term exchange, but it turns out that recognizing a role for management requires more than just folding incentive constraints into the theory. A larger theory has had to accommodate concepts such as incomplete contracting. I further submit that an adequate theory would have to complement incomplete contracting with a notion of transaction costs or friction. Ultimately, the combination of friction and incomplete contracting gives life to an economics of efficient adaptation in long-term relationships.

THE PROVENANCE OF EFFICIENT ADAPTATION: TAKE ONE

Let us revisit system engineering. Starting at least with eighteenth-century political economy, economics had become occupied with the engineering of economic systems rather than with the management of economic relationships. Indeed, management is not cognizable from an engineering perspective and, therefore, has not generally proven amenable to formal modeling. It gets worse. It is not obvious that there has been much appreciation that management was an important consideration, anyway.[15]

However, management aside, the concept of an economic system or of an economy, an entity susceptible to design and manipulation, was itself slow to emerge. (See, for example, Pribram 1937, 1951; Neill 1949; and Schabas 2007; on this count.) From Schabas (2007), I understand the emergence of the concept of a manipulable economy amounted to a shift from (1) a physics or biology perspective by which economic processes were understood as being exogenously governed by natural laws to (2) an engineering perspective according to which the economy could be controlled. Once notions of control became established, however, they became (and remain to this day) the subject of much debate.

The debates on system design and engineering did inspire theoretical developments germane to the analysis of relationships. Mechanism design and implementation theory, for example, may have been inspired by the

---

[15] On this count Demsetz (1995, 2011b) might rise to the defense, arguing that "[T]he task faced by neoclassical economics was to understand coordination in a decentralized economic system. Its firms and its presumption of a free price system serve this task well". (See Demsetz 2011b, p. S11. The first and second commentaries in Demsetz 1995 are also apposite.) Questions about adaptation and the management of relationships have their place, but that does not preclude inquiries that ignore such considerations.

big issues (system design), but they yielded abundant results that have since inspired the development of a distinct body of contract theory. (Maskin makes parallel points. See, especially, Maskin 2008, pp.571–2 on "a brief history of mechanism design".) The theory went far towards operationalizing the idea that incentives matter and can inform the design of contracts (or institutional processes more generally). Relatedly, the theory accommodated the prospect that parties to exchange might privately hold information that would be relevant to the payoffs they and their counterparties might realize from that same exchange. The Revelation Principle went far toward folding problems involving privately held, payoff-relevant information (hidden information) into the design of contracts.

Folding incentives and private information into the design of contracts has greatly enriched microeconomics as a theory of the second best. (See Hoff 1994 for some pointed examples.) Everyone has a (generally negative) idea about what it means to "game the system". The mechanism design approach endeavors to factor the way parties can be expected to "game" the system into the design of the system. The results of factoring in such behaviors are formidable, because they constitute an important check on what Demsetz (1969) might recognize as the nirvana approach to design problems. (See also Williamson 1996a on remediableness.) In general, incentive constraints and informational constraints can do just what they are advertised to do: constrain the outcomes that parties to a contract can secure. Absent such constraints, parties might be able to secure what poet-economists would recognize as first-best outcomes. Incentive constraints might not always bind, but, if they do bind, expectations of achieving the first best amounts to magical thinking. Instead, parties might only be able to secure second-best outcomes.

One manifestation of the nirvana approach would be to confuse first-best outcomes with implementable outcomes. That is the magical thinking. Another manifestation would be to condemn second-best outcomes as inefficient because a hypothetical, ideal (yet infeasible) first-best outcome would appear to dominate. Again, things can be much worse, in that becoming mesmerized with the magical thinking and endeavoring to secure nirvana can yield outcomes that are (possibly far) inferior to the second best. Policymakers can find themselves instituting Rube Goldberg schemes that never secure their idealized policy outcomes. However, were that informing contract design (and design problems more generally) with incentive constraints and informational constraints all that remained, then the engineering approach to contract design might nearly have exhausted further development of contract theory. Absent further development, however, the theory is silent on how parties to exchange manage their relationships after they have designed and implemented their contract. However, if the design of a contract factors in all relevant considerations – that is, if contracting is complete – what eventualities would require management? An easy answer is that it is not obvious that parties can program all relevant contingencies into their contract. Even if they feasibly could do so, it is not obvious that leaving out some contingencies would be uneconomical – hence the appeal to "uncontracted-for" contingencies as in Hart (1995, p. 32) or Hart (2003, p. C70). It could make sense to leave contracts endogenously incomplete. Either way, incompleteness can generate demands to design and institute processes to manage uncontracted-for contingencies when and if they arise.

Such questions begin to illuminate even deeper questions about what Oliver Williamson recognizes as *ex post* governance in the context of incomplete contracting. In Williamson's early work, he appealed to bounded rationality as a motivation for the incompleteness of contracts. Williamson further argued that incompleteness mattered to contracting parties in that it could yield opportunities for mischief (opportunism). Having stumbled into a contingency not contemplated in a contract, one party might, for example, find its bargaining position improved vis-à-vis a counterparty, and might exploit the opportunity to impose renegotiation and extract more favorable terms of exchange. (See Williamson 1971, 1973, 1975 on bounded rationality and opportunism, as well as Williamson 1976 for a case study.) Opportunism makes *ex post* governance an important economic problem in that the prospect of mischief could influence decisions to invest resources in exchange relations in the first place. To mitigate such hazards, parties to exchange might set up processes for governing their relationships as they unfold over time – hence the "*ex post*" and "governance" in *ex post* governance. Finally, the economic problem is all the more interesting in that *ex post* processes might themselves be costly to design and operate. Parties to prospective exchange can be expected to factor such costs into their *ex ante* decision to invest in the relationship. Such decisions might amount to no investment and forgoing any exchange at all.

Opportunism, I would suggest, is short-hand for the compound proposition that (1) parties to exchange might behave opportunistically as (2) uncontracted-for contingencies arise. Further, (3) such hazards could inform the design and implementation of contracts and *ex post* processes, and (4) the costs of operationalizing and operating such processes can inform *ex ante* decisions to engage in exchange in the first place. The proposition has much intuitive appeal, but I would suggest that much of its appeal is that it inspired important theoretical developments, especially regarding control rights and financial structure. The main question is deceptively simple: if a party were to behave opportunistically, could not a counterparty simply exit the relationship, and would not the threat of exit be sufficient to discourage opportunistic behavior in the first place? (We will shortly get to Alchian and Demsetz 1972 on just this question.) If so, who needs to worry about designing (potentially costly) *ex post* processes (much less contracts) if the threat of exit alone enables parties to exchange to police their relationships? That is, if investments in a relationship could be seamlessly and costlessly redeployed (possibly in a relationship with a different party), then should not the threat of exit be sufficient?

An answer could be that the threat of exit would be sufficient but that the prospect of seamless and costless redeployment is a degenerative, hypothetical case. *Ex ante* investments in a relationship may be specific to that relationship insofar as redeployment involves dissipation of value. In the extreme, assets may have zero salvage value outside a specific relationship but much value were parties to persist in deploying those assets within that relationship even after some uncontracted-for contingency were to obtain. Knowing this, one party might hold up a party that had sunk an investment in relationship-specific assets by threatening exit from the relationship. Threatening exit amounts to imposing renegotiation of the terms of exchange. It amounts to a demand to be paid off to not exit. Knowing that there is more value to continuing the relationship than ending the relationship, the investing party can be expected to pay off the party imposing hold up.

One manifestation of opportunism amounts to exploiting opportunities to impose hold up. Even so, paying off a party to remain in a relationship is not obviously a source of economic inefficiency. Inefficiency arises if the party contemplating relationship-specific investments dials back those investments so that it may mitigate hold up. However, should not the parties be able to factor the prospect of hold up into the design of a contract and thereby preserve *ex ante* incentives to invest? The parties might, for example, commit to exchange over a long term, thereby granting the investing party some assurance that assets specific to the relationship would be deployed over a long term without the threat of hold up. A more general proposition might be that, were it both feasible and economical to craft complete contracts, then parties could neutralize the hold-up problem. The incompleteness of contracts leaves open the prospect that some contingency might yet arise in which some party to exchange perceives an opportunity to threaten exit as a way of imposing renegotiation and walking away with a payoff. (See Klein et al. 1978, especially p. 301, for a parallel formulation of this proposition.) So far, incomplete contracting matters, because hold-up hazards may yet obtain.

Grossman and Hart (1986) and Hart and Moore (1990) took the hold-up problem and framed it in a way that opened a line of inquiry into what Robert Gibbons and co-authors would come to recognize as contracting for control. (Baker et al. 2011 would be a good place to start.) Grossman, Hart and Moore made control rights an explicit focus of analysis. Parties might be able to resolve hold ups by writing clever contracts. The incompleteness of contracts matters, however, because it might restrict how clever parties can be. They might not be able to secure performance along all payoff-relevant dimensions of exchange, in which case hold ups may yet obtain if and when uncontracted-for contingencies arise. A question then arises about how assets (over which property rights are presumably well defined) are to be redeployed in just such contingencies. An important idea here is that ownership implies control in these contingencies; the owner of an asset may assign to other parties rights to determine how to deploy the asset. However, insofar as these control rights or decision rights do not span all contingencies, and when such contingencies obtain, control reverts to the owner.

In the Grossman–Hart–Moore framework, the allocation of property rights matters, because it influences the magnitude of hold ups that could yet obtain in uncontracted-for contingencies. (For the most accessible introductions, see Moore 1992 and chapter 2 of Hart 1995.) Indeed, judicious allocations of property rights could potentially mitigate hold ups, and it is just such an idea that motivated what Hart (1995) recognizes as the Property Rights Approach to the theory of firm boundaries. The theory suggests how firms may correspond to judicious agglomerations of assets and attending property rights. The main point I want to indicate is that the framework invests ownership and control with much operational significance. (We revisit this point in the next chapter.) "Given that a contract will not specify all aspects of asset usage in every contingency, who has the right to decide about missing usages?" (Hart 1995, p. 30). According to the property right approach, "it is the owner of the asset in question who has this right . . . [T]he owner of an asset has *residual control rights* over that asset, the right to decide all usages of the asset in any way not inconsistent with a prior contract, custom, or law" (Hart 1995, p. 30, original emphasis). Hart further observes that characterizing ownership this way contrasts "to the more standard definition of ownership, whereby an owner possesses the residual income from an asset rather than its residual control rights" (Hart 1995, p. 30).

The property rights approach provided a way of formalizing the hold-up problem – that is, it rendered a mathematical formulation of problems involving relationship-specific investment that could (and did) yield analytical results. The early results inspired a prodigious stream of formal modeling, and some contributors subsequently observed that such formalization subsumed, or nearly subsumed "the intuitions of transaction cost economics, as created by Coase and Williamson" (Salanié 1997, p. 176). Effectively, these authors identified Williamson's economics of *ex post* governance with the hold-up problem. Indeed, Robert Gibbons could observe that "one still sometimes hears the claim that 'Grossman and Hart (1986) formalized Williamson (1979)'" or "Grossman–Hart *merely* formalized Williamson, and '*Finally*, someone formalized Williamson" (Gibbons 2005, p. 1, original emphases). However, note what is missing. Adaptation remains missing in action. The formal modeling has yet to fold the "*ex post*" into "*ex post* governance". That is, the formal theory identified no overlap between problems involving underinvestment in relationship-specific assets (the hold-up problem) and problems of managing relationships in the future. Hold up did not inform adaptation; adaptation did not inform hold up.

To some observers, divorcing hold up from adaptation might be puzzling. One reason is that authors such as Klein et al. (1978) and Williamson (1979) explicitly appealed to the hold-up problem in order to motivate demand for efficient adaptation. One version of the general proposition might be: assets are specific to a relationship to the degree that they are less amenable to redeployment outside that relationship without significant dissipation of value; parties contemplating ventures involving investment in highly specific assets are more likely to concentrate the management of such ventures within a single entity (the firm). The single entity is better situated to absorb and respond to demands to adapt terms of exchange.

How we get from relationship-specific investment to the vertical integration of assets and capabilities within a single firm remains an important topic of research, but to motivate this proposition, let us first recap: ventures involving relationship-specific investment would be most susceptible to hold up. Hold up could distort or even jeopardize investment. That alone would invite parties contemplating complex exchange to commit to processes that could mitigate or even neutralize hold up. Remedying hold up would preserve investment incentives. That, however, is not the end of the story. Investment (relationship-specific or not) may contemplate exchange that would have the potential (and even the expectation) of unfolding over the course of a long term. Investment may even be predicated on the expectation of long-term exchange. Yet, the fact that relationships unfold over time may leave open the prospect that contingencies arise over which contracting parties would perceive mutual gain to revisiting and realigning their terms of exchange. Where investments are seamlessly redeployable (possibly outside the relationship), adaptation becomes a degenerative non-problem. Parties simply redeploy assets, no value is lost, and that is that. But where relationship-specific investment is involved, assets cannot be redeployed without some dissipation of value. The prospect of dissipation invites parties to exchange to contemplate processes that give them some capacity to identify, craft and implement adaptations. "How to effect these adaptations poses a serious contracting dilemma" (Williamson 1979, p. 241). Among other things, how can parties invest themselves with just such capacity?

It is about here that discussion shifts to modes of governing exchange, in that different modes differentially invest parties with capacity to identify, craft and implement adaptations. Would a long-term contract afford parties sufficient capacity to implement out adaptations, or would haggling between the various parties undermine efforts to work things out? Could a more tightly integrated relationship obviate some of the haggling and serve their purposes more efficiently? For example, could it make sense to create a separate legal entity, a (finitely lived) joint venture, and invest the joint venture with the authority and processes to implement adaptations? Or should parties effectively transform themselves into a single, indefinitely lived entity by integrating all assets and capabilities within a single firm?

The crafting of more tightly integrated relationships by contract or joint venture, or even by fully integrating parties into a single party (the firm), gets us into deep questions about what it means to be a distinct party to exchange in the first place. (Alternatively, what does it mean to be integrated?) For certain purposes, perceiving the firm as a single entity can make sense. Firms assume the role of juridical persons (individuals) all the time as when, say, they individually contract with other juridical persons. However, within the firm, actual persons or teams of individuals may constitute distinct parties in intra-firm exchange, and those same persons will contract with the firm itself. This is, for example, the business of employment contracts.

The degree to which relationships can be integrated by a given mode of governing exchange may constitute one dimension over which modes of governance can be differentiated. The degree to which a mode of governance enables parties to integrate may be understood as a governance output, but what of the inputs, the various discrete features of various modes of governance that enable them to generate such outputs? Long-term contracts, for example, can be differentiated from short-term contracts by longer terms, and we may argue that, other things equal, longer terms integrate parties together more tightly. However, these same contracts may be differentiated along other dimensions. Some contracts may have more the spirit of a joint venture in that they feature voting mechanisms or other deliberative processes for enabling parties to work things out over the course of (possibly) long-term exchange. More generally, we could differentiate modes of governance by mapping the various dimensions of governance inputs into a taxonomy of governance structures. N dimensions might plausibly map into M modes with $M <$ N. We can go the next step and endeavor to map modes of governance into governance outputs such as an index that ostensibly measures the degree to which modes of governance induce integration. This is an ambitious exercise, but a less ambitious exercise might order modes of governance from those that induce the lowest degrees of integration to those that induce the highest degrees. (See Oxley 1997a and Majewski and Williamson 2004 for applications.) Then there is the last step: mapping outputs into performance. Do increasing degrees of integration, for example, invest parties to complex exchange with more capacity to work things out over the course of long-term exchange? If so, why is all exchange not integrated within a single entity? Or are there tradeoffs between governance structures that enable tighter integration and structures that maintain arm's-length relationships?

Such questions about the properties and performance of alternative modes of governance bring us not so much to a fork in the road as to a junction of paths radiating out in several directions. I indicate a few paths, one which this book spends most of its time exploring and another which it occasionally traverses, but the book makes little contact with a third path that pertains to the employment relation. The employment relation harkens back to Herbert Simon's (1951) seminal contribution on how we might operationalize in formal economic theory what it can mean to be someone's boss by means of the exercise of authority within the firm. Simon observed that "traditional economic theory" had little to say about management and "administrative process, i.e., the process of actually managing factors of production, including labor" (Simon 1951, p. 293). Administrative process matters, presumably, because it is just such process that justifies qualifying the firm as a single entity.

Simon's contribution is an early effort to formally characterize integration. It was an effort to characterize in formal economic theory the tradeoffs between (1) enlisting a boss or (vertical) hierarchy of bosses within the firm to manage relationships and (2) allowing parties to be their own bosses and to manage their (horizontal) relationships boss to boss. When it comes to governing exchange, what can the firm do that parties to exchange cannot do absent integration? Meanwhile, economic theory gadflies Alchian and Demsetz (1972) argued that it was not obvious why any tradeoffs should obtain insofar as managing relationships within the firm is no different than managing relationships between independent economic agents. "It is common to see the firm characterized by the power to settle issues by fiat, by authority, or by disciplinary action superior to that available in the conventional market", they exclaimed (Alchian and Demsetz 1972, p. 777). "This is delusion" (Alchian and Demsetz 1972, p. 777). They seemed to argue that the threat of exit remained the principal instrument parties could use for managing their relationships whether inside or outside the firm. "I can 'punish' you", they wrote,

> only by withholding future business or by seeking redress in the courts for any failure to honor our exchange agreement. That is exactly all that any employer can do. He can fire or sue, just as I can fire my grocer by stopping purchases from him or sue him for delivering faulty products.

Williamson (1996b, pp. 97–100) compactly discusses the issues and offers a pointed rejoinder to critiques of the sort advanced by Alchian and Demsetz (1972). This book, however, does not explicitly take up the employment relation or explicitly take up theory that endeavors to sort out what the firm can do that parties cannot achieve absent integration. I note, for example, that Grossman and Hart (1986) and Hart and Moore (1990) explicitly advanced their Property Rights Approach as a way of demonstrating tradeoffs between integration and non-integration, but this book makes contact with the property rights theory only insofar as it imposes structure on how to think about ownership and control more generally.

This book does take up a question that parallels the integration question. In place of the integration question (what can the firm do that parties to exchange cannot do absent integration?), it takes up a question that might appear to the uninitiated to be less demanding: what can parties achieve by long-term contract that they cannot achieve by a sequence of short-term contracts, or vice versa? A potential advantage of short-term contracts is that they allow parties to revisit their terms of exchange and adapt them to new circumstances after nothing more than a short term. Parties are thus less likely to find themselves committed for a long time to terms of exchange that are poorly adapted to prevailing circumstances – if and when circumstances change in a manner not explicitly contemplated by their contract. After being thrust into a state of maladaptation, they can anticipate soon having the opportunity to realign terms of exchange.[16]

Absent further development, short-term contracts would seem to dominate long-term contracts, but then why would parties ever commit to

---

[16]   One way of conceptualizing the idea of maladaptation is that it corresponds to being knocked off the contract curve, which is language suggesting that perturbations may have rendered prevailing terms of exchange Pareto inferior even though they had been statically Pareto optimal.

long-term contracts? If shorter terms always dominate, then why should parties to exchange commit to contracts of any duration greater than zero? Should not parties find themselves organizing otherwise complex exchange by means of simple spot contracts, bolt by bolt, nut by nut, and byte by byte? Should not the complexity of exchange extend to little more than the fact that exchange could involve a large number of atomized, instantaneous spot transactions?

An economy organized entirely on the basis of atomized, instantaneous spot transactions would correspond to exchange in classical or (depending on whose rendition you are reading) neoclassical environments in the theory of general equilibrium. Much theory had been occupied with identifying conditions (if any) under which Adam Smith's "invisible hand" of the market place would be operable. Specifically, Smith posed the intuition that an economic system that is decentralized in that it is based on free exchange between independent economic agents, with each pursuing his own private interests, could yield socially desirable outcomes. Theorists endeavored to identify the most parsimonious set of conditions they could think of under which Smith's intuition would constitute a coherent vision of economic performance. The classical environment identifies such conditions – principally the absence of nonconvexities in preferences and production, as well as the absence of indivisibilities in production.[17]

The classical conditions do not explicitly say much about the nature of transactions, but the model of decentralized exchange is most intuitively accessible insofar as it involves the frictionless, instantaneous exchange of commodities. The analytically convenient feature of stylized commodities is that they can be atomized. Exchange of atomized commodities between atomized economic agents would correspond to the most extreme version of what Ian MacNeil (1974, 1978) could recognize as transactional contracting. MacNeil characterized exchange as transactional insofar as the contracting that attended it is "sharp in by clear agreement" and "sharp out by clear performance" (MacNeil 1978, p. 902). Absent further development, the classical assumptions would seem poorly situated to accommodate what MacNeil was really interested in, that is, relational contracting. Here individual transactions may involve performance, which itself may be very elaborate, that unfolds over some non-trivial interval of time. Indeed, time might be an essential input in production, and the dimension of time alone may draw parties to exchange into a relationship. In the future, that relationship may support further exchange.

---

[17]   See, for example, Hurwicz (1972, p. 298), Hurwicz (1969, pp. 513–14), and Koopmans (1957, pp. 35–7) on the role of convexity assumptions.

Given the classical model of decentralized exchange is essentially static, we have to apply some imagination verging on willful suspension of disbelief in order to suggest how it could accommodate time. Neoclassical adaptations to the model include such abstractions as the fiction that economic agents trade in the present in markets for commodities that they consume in the future. We may further assume that these markets are complete in that they contemplate consumption at any place and at any time in the future. We might, for example, contemplate a market for ice cream the July after the next July on the corner of 34th and Lexington in New York.[18]

Then there is the question of transaction costs. In the view of Coase (1937) and Coase (1960, pp. 15–19), organizing transactions via market-mediated exchange is not free, but involves incurring some volume of transaction costs. (Again, see Pareto 1897, s. 837 on this count.) These costs could inspire an active role for the firm in that parties to exchange might finesse the costs of market-mediated exchange by organizing exchange within the firm – although this would also generate transaction costs. Yet, in the classical model, the firm is merely a mathematical construct, a production function that seamlessly takes prices as inputs and generates some volume of commodities. Transaction costs, however, could begin to motivate the integration question in that economic agents might organize transactions within the firm rather than execute them in markets. Coase seemed to further imply that it was not obvious that Smith's intuition would entirely hold up once the model of decentralized exchange was made to accommodate a more elaborate concept of firms. Demsetz (2011a) went on to argue, however, that the model of decentralized exchange could accommodate transaction costs (insofar as costs are costs) without upsetting Smith's intuition, but Demsetz (2011b, p. S11) also made the point that "the task faced by neoclassical economics was to understand coordination in a decentralized economic system. Its [abbreviated concept of] firms and its presumption of a free price system serve this task well".

> Transactors are characterized by their cleverness, to the point of deviousness, in circumventing rules, discovering loopholes, or otherwise exploiting strategic advantages. (Masten 1988, p. 182)

This passage from Masten (1988) is reminiscent of the passage from Kawabata's (1981) *The Master of Go*. Masten opens with a passage from Williamson (1985, pp. 41–2) on the "comparative institutional assessment

---

18 See, for example, Koopmans (1957, pp. 60–62) on how the model may be adapted to accommodate time. More generally, see "Arrow-DeBreu assets".

of *discrete institutional alternatives*". *The Master of Go* itself was a literary exploration of institutional alternatives. Kawabata enlisted changes implemented after World War II in the governance of *Go* tournaments as a metaphor for changes in governance more generally. He explored rules-versus-discretion tradeoffs between traditional modes of governance (that depended more on deference to age and rank) and rules-based, democratic modes (that depended on "modern rationalism" and "regulation") (Kawabata 1981, p. 52). Lost in the transition from traditional modes to rules-based modes was "the fragrance of Go as an art" in that "One conducted the battle only to win" (Kawabata 1981, p. 52). "[T]he finesse and subtlety of the warrior's way [the chivalric code of *Bushido*, 武士道], the mysterious elegance of an art" was sacrificed (Kawabata 1981, p. 54). Alas, "[t]he Master was accustomed not to this new equality but to old-fashioned prerogatives . . . and so it would seem that . . . his juniors had imposed the strictest rules to restrain his dictatorial tendencies" (Kawabata 1981, p. 55). More generally, "the Master could not [be permitted to] stand outside the rules of equality" (Kawabata 1981, p. 54).

Masten (1988), meanwhile, explores equity (if not strictly equality) in exchange relations. He does this in order to provide a context within which to introduce transactional frictions. Up to this point, transaction costs had mostly remained little more than metaphorical (as in Pareto 1897) or broadly hypothesized (as in Coase 1937). However, Masten (1988, p. 184) could observe that the hypothesis that bargaining is costly had been implicit in much literature in law and economics. He made the hypothesis explicit in a model in which two parties may perceive opportunities to strategically impose renegotiation of their terms of exchange as uncontracted-for contingencies arise, but not any and all contingencies. Given renegotiation is costly, it can make sense to impose renegotiation only on those contingencies that involve perturbations of sufficient magnitude that the party demanding renegotiation could expect to realize a net gain. "Haggling, strikes and litigation are generally costly to both sides and benefit the party that initiated them only if they result in a more favorable transfer to that party"[19] (Masten 1988, p. 186).

---

[19]   The proposition in Masten (1988) is actually a little more specialized. The more specialized proposition is that "contracts serve to secure the terms of trade *ex ante* and thereby prevent costly repetitive haggling over the distribution of rents once transaction-specific investments are in place" (Masten 1988, p. 186). I would be tempted to suggest that the proposition can be generalized by excluding the premise that "transaction-specific investments" are implicated. So long as the redeployment of assets, whether specialized or generic, incurs costs much as any "transactional frictions," then some degree of generic lock-in attends all assets,

The principal value of the appeal to uncontracted-for contingencies is that it helps motivate a role for efficient adaptation in that perturbations may induce maladaptation. Absent revision of the terms of exchange, parties may fail to realize full value in the future. It would be no surprise, then, that one or both parties to bilateral exchange would then demand renegotiation. In contrast, equity identifies perturbations that may not implicate efficiency in the future. Instead, one party or the other may realize an unexpected windfall, or one party or the other may find itself bearing an unexpected expense, but in neither case would an unexpected windfall nor an expected expense necessarily induce maladaptation. Instead, one party may find itself aggrieved in that it had not been situated to share the windfall or had found itself bearing the cost. The aggrieved party may impose renegotiation not to restore efficiency but merely to impose a more equitable distribution of unexpected windfalls and costs.

This chapter opened with the faint suggestion that contracting parties may appear more adult than some adults in that they take care to antici-pate and manage conflict in long-term relationships. Concerns for equity, however, have more the flavor of unnecessary drama in relationships. Among other things, fighting over equitable distributions of unexpected windfalls and costs can destroy value insofar as renegotiation merely generates costs. Equity is interesting, however, as concerns about it do inform exchange relations (see Goldberg 1985). It was Goldberg from whom Masten (1988) picked up the language of one party being aggrieved. This is all the more interesting in that Hart (2008) picked up on the phe-nomenon of aggrievement and used it to motivate his concept of reference points. Hart (2008) introduces reference points for much the same reason Masten (1988) recruited equity: "We need to bring back haggling costs!" (Hart 2008, p. 406).

Hart and Moore (2008) elaborated. The literature that Grossman and Hart (1986) and Hart and Moore (1990) inspired (literature which they recognized as *the* "literature on incomplete contracts") "generated some useful insights about firm boundaries, [but] it has some shortcomings" (Hart and Moore (2008, p. 2):

> First, the emphasis on noncontractible ex ante investments seems overplayed: although such investments are surely important, it is hard to believe that they are the sole drivers of organizational form. Second, and related, the approach is ill suited to studying the internal organization of firms, a topic of great interest

---

and all of them then have the appearance of being quasi-specialized. Later litera-ture on long-term contracting with respect to non-specific assets such as Masten 2009 would be apposite.

and importance. The reason is that the Coasian renegotiation perspective suggests that the relevant parties will sit down together ex post and bargain to an efficient outcome using side payments: given this, it is hard to see why authority, hierarchy, delegation, or indeed anything apart from asset ownership matters. (Hart and Moore (2008, p. 2)

Hart and Moore (2008, p. 4) sketch an environment in which a "trade-off between rigidity and flexibility" in contractual relations becomes cognizable and amenable to analysis. In their environment, "[a] flexible contract has the advantage that parties can adjust the outcome to the state of the world, but the disadvantage that any outcome selected will typically cause at least one party to feel aggrieved and shortchanged". The aggrieved party may then behave opportunistically. Thus, can parties to exchange commit to terms of contract that effect an economizing balancing between inflexibility and opportunism?

Note that, (1) demands for adaptation in long-term relationships illuminate tradeoffs between flexibility and rigidity, and (2) empirical research on such tradeoffs had already taken off by the middle of the 1980s. Masten and Crocker (1985), for example, observed that commitments secured under the terms of a long-term contract may preserve incentives to sink relationship-specific investments – that is, long-term commitments mitigate hold up[20] – but a long-term commitment is rigid in that it renders the relationship susceptible to maladaptation in the future. It would be incumbent on contracting parties to engineer mechanisms that would enable them to reduce the costs of adapting terms of exchange (when and if demands for adaptation were to arise). Implementing such mechanisms would enable them to preserve an otherwise rigid, long-term contract.

The problem of engineering flexibility in long-term contracts motivated other contemporaneous research. This included Libecap and Wiggins (1984), Hubbard and Weiner (1991), Goldberg and Erickson (1987), Crocker and Masten (1988, 1991), and Crocker and Reynolds (1993). Succeeding research took up friction or sources of friction (complexity) more broadly, but the problem of enabling flexibility remained. (See, for example, Lyons 1995, Tadelis 2002, and Zhu 2003.) Regarding all of this, however, I again suggest that a paradigmatic question would be: what can parties achieve by long-term contract that they cannot achieve by a sequence of short-term contracts, or vice versa? Why do not short-term contracts strictly dominate long-term contracts in that short-term contracts afford adaptation, as a matter of course, after a short term?

---

[20]   Empirical research by Joskow (1985, 1987) firmly established this idea in the literature.

Why, for that matter, does contract duration matter at all? Should not all exchange collapse into the degenerative case of extreme transactional contracting (as in MacNeil 1974, 1978) or into the same thing, spot market exchange? Should not markets decentralize all exchange? What is missing?

THE PROVENANCE OF EFFICIENT ADAPTATION: TAKE TWO

A traditional place to have started this book would have been Ronald Coase's "The nature of the firm" (1937). Instead, we introduced Coase (1937) by way of Simon (1991) and situated Coase (1937) in a larger context about system design. That helped us to appreciate points of contact and points of deviation between theories of system design and outstanding questions about governance in long-term relationships. We now make contact with Coase (1937) one more time and introduce it in a more traditional way. A more traditional approach would have been to suggest that Coase's paper introduces the make-or-buy decision – or, much the same thing, identifies the boundaries of the firm as a subject worthy of examination. Should a firm secure a given input internally (make), or should it secure that same input via market-mediated exchange with other firms (buy)? A given beer-brewing company, for example, might not bottle its own beer but might contract with another firm (a bottling company) to do just that. That same brewing company might not even brew its own beer. The firm may consist of little more than some intellectual property: uncodifiable know-how about brewing built-up in heads of a few beer enthusiasts-turned-entrepreneurs as well as a codified beer formulation. Our entrepreneurs could source ingredients from a number of firms, contract out beer production with a contract brewer, and organize distribution and sales through yet other entities. The nexus of contracts that encompasses the entire endeavor may end up spanning a number of distinct entities or firms. Why not coordinate all of those activities within a single firm?

Coase's principal issue was that there could be tradeoffs between coordinating activity within a firm and coordinating much of that same activity by means of market-mediated exchange between firms. Coase framed activity as transactions and posed the tradeoffs as a matter of comparing the costs of coordinating transactions within the firm with the costs of coordinating those same transactions outside the firm. We might then expect the boundaries of the firm to conform with the assignment of transactions – transactions assigned to the firm and transactions assigned to external exchange – that minimizes the sum of transaction costs realized by the firm.

All well and good, but a great difficulty is that it was not obvious (and remains not obvious) what coordination within the firm would entail.[21] Moreover, what is a transaction and what are transaction costs? Before revisiting such questions, let us situate questions about the boundaries of the firm and coordination in the debates about the relative merits of economy-wide decentralization and centralization. Coase motivated the question about firm boundaries by juxtaposing firms and markets. Orthodox economic theory elaborated how market-mediated exchange could secure an efficient allocation of resources, but made no accommodation for the idea that much allocation of resources might be coordinated within firms. As Demsetz (2011b, p; S8) suggested, "Coase's view of neoclassical theory's theory of the firm, expressed quite early in his career, is simple enough – it has no theory of the firm".

Theory or no theory, 1937 would have been a better year than most in which to pose questions about coordination within the firm, for there had been a resurgence of interest in central planning – that is, in the idea of organizing an entire economy almost as one large firm. In the United States, 1937 marked the beginning of the second, steep dip of the Great Depression. Economic depression, if not the double-dip feature, was a global phenomenon, and global depression had prompted a resurgence of interest in questions about the optimal role of government (if any) in tempering the business cycle. Hansen et al. (1936, p. 53) could, for example, observe that a "voluminous literature on business-cycle theory [had] appeared during the last two years". Interest resurged in questions about how to measure business cycles and, ultimately, in questions about how government might design and implement stabilization policies to moderate business cycles.

The socialist prescription for controlling business cycles was to dispense with partial measures (stabilization policy) and to impose a direct, fundamental solution, that is, eliminate business cycles by fiat. Capitalism had been identified with market-mediated exchange between independent entities (firms and consumers), and yet it had been understood for most of a century that capitalism was endogenously subject to periodic downturns.[22] The prescription was to concentrate control of an entire economy within a Central Planning Board. Lange (1937, p. 126), and others,

---

[21] Demsetz (1997) advances a few ideas about this. Simon (1951) introduced the "employment relation" as a way of characterizing coordination. Again, see Alchian and Demsetz (1972), especially the quip about what it would mean to "fire my grocer".

[22] In the afterword to the second German edition of *Capital*, Volume I (1873, for which see Marx 2018), Karl Marx identifies the financial crisis of 1825 in

appeared to argue that business cycles amounted to individually rational but collectively irrational outcomes. One private party's over-optimistic expectation of demand, for example, could encourage over-production. Over-production would inflate that same party's demands for others' inputs, which, in turn, would encourage other parties to over-produce. Firms operating in markets injected with over-demands would perceive price signals encouraging them to over-produce. Markets could induce a contagion, transmitting signals to markets spanning the economy. The economy would enter the boom of the boom-and-bust business cycle. Eventually, the reality of a demand insufficient to sustain inflated levels of production would become manifest, in which case markets would transmit a reverse contagion. Markets would transmit signals to cut production. Firms would cut back, some would close, and the economy would enter the bust phase of the boom-and-bust business cycle.

Two advantages presumably obtained to centralization (coordination of economic activity by means of administrative processes concentrated in the Central Planning Board) over decentralization (coordination of economic activity by means of market-mediated exchange between autonomous economic agents). The Central Planning Board would have the competence to identify collectively rational outcomes as well as the capacity to implement collectively rational outcomes. It would, for example, enjoy degrees of freedom to act not afforded to any single private party. "A private entrepreneur has to close his plant when he incurs grave losses", Lange (1937, p. 126) observed. However, the Central Planning Board, unencumbered with the parochial perspective, the parochial interest, or the parochial constraints of a given entrepreneur, could identify efficient adjustments in productive capacity (plant closures or expansions) and identify efficient levels of production in the future.[23]

We might understand extreme centralization as concentrating all make-or-buy decisions spanning the economy in the hands of the central planner,

---

Britain (the "Panic of 1825") as the first manifestation of the downside of an endogenous business cycle.

[23] Enrico Barone maintained some skepticism about the capacity of the central authorities to efficiently manage the expansion or withdrawal of production capacity.

Some collectivist writers, bewailing the continual destruction of firms (those with higher costs) by free competition, think that the creation of enterprises to be destroyed later can be avoided, and hope that with *organized* production it is possible to avoid the dissipation and destruction of wealth which such *experiments* involve, and which they believe to be the peculiar property of "anarchist" production. (Barone 1908 [2009], p. 288, original emphases)

but note what Coase (1937) did not do. He may have stood up firms next to what Demsetz (2011a, p. 2) recognized as "extreme decentralization", but he did not explicitly situate the firm between the two poles of extreme decentralization and extreme centralization. That is where the economics literature lost track of Coase (1937) – between the poles. It got lost in debates about the proper place of decentralization (market processes) or centralization (administrative processes) in ordering economic activity across entire economies.

Coase himself did not explicitly take up questions about economy-wide performance, but his ideas could have inspired deep questions. Would it be efficient to populate the economy with pockets of administrative ordering – that is, with firms? Could assigning transactions in a discriminating way to firms and to markets minimize what Arrow (1969) might have recognized as the costs of running the economic system? Should firms be permitted to organically emerge, or should a central authority direct that process? Specifically, should a central authority dictate the assignment of make-or-buy decisions to firms and markets?

The socialist prescription would appear to have been that the economy should be organized as one big firm – end of debate. The proponents of centralization could not admit room for debate, because they did not recognize any tradeoffs between centralization and decentralization. Whatever decentralization could achieve, centralization could do better. However, for parties who were willing to attribute costs to centralized, administrative processes – whether transaction costs of the sort contemplated in Coase (1937) or other costs – it would not have been obvious that centralization would dominate decentralization.

On this count, Ludwig von Mises demonstrated himself to be one of the more articulate and entertaining commentators. Writing, for example, on "socialism under dynamic conditions" (von Mises 1951 [2009], pp. 196–210) and on (he argued) the consequent "impracticability of socialism" (von Mises 1951 [2009], pp. 211–20), von Mises observed that the proponents of centralization recognized no role for management – that is, for the capacity to deal with considerations less amenable to programming. (In particular see von Mises 1951 [2009], pp. 196–7, 213–16.) These considerations would include "such questions as dissolving, extending, transforming and limiting existing undertakings and establishing new undertakings" (von Mises 1951 [2009], p. 215) in the face of demands for adaptation. The proponents instead seemed to perceive that economic activity would not require active adaptation in the future and was therefore amenable to strict programming. Indeed, Lenin himself, von Mises (1951 [2009], p. 214) observed, suggested that "Capitalism has simplified to the utmost and has reduced to extremely simple operations of superintendence and book-entry within the grasp of anyone able to read and write". Yet, the principal role of administrative process, by which centralization would dominate decentralization, extended beyond such clerical functions. It was to bring the expertise of properly trained bureaucrats to craft the programs by which the economic system would operate. Such a view derived from "the bureaucratic mind: that is to say it comes from people for whom all human activity represents [nothing more than] the fulfilment of formal, official and professional duties" (von Mises 1951 [2009], p. 215).

Explicit questions about how problems of adaptation relate to economic organization would have to await Williamson (1971) on "The vertical integration of production: market failure considerations" – vertical integration being a more technical term for make-or-buy. Moreover, by 1969, no one had managed to advance the Coasean program of 1937. That program would include developing an analysis that would yield testable hypotheses about the endogeneity of firm boundaries or (the same thing) the assignment of make-or-buy decisions. Arrow (1969, p. 60) could only elaborate marginally on the Coasean proposition in more modern terms: "An incentive for vertical integration is replacement of the costs of buying and selling on the market by the costs of intra-firm transfers; the existence of vertical integration may suggest that the costs of operating competitive markets are not zero, as is usually assumed in our theoretical analysis,"[24] and yet, "The identification of transaction costs in different contexts and under different systems of resource allocation should be a major item on the research agenda of the theory of public goods and indeed of the theory of resource allocation in general".

The socialist controversy involving von Mises, Lange and a host of others in the 1920s and 1930s constituted only one episode of debates relating to systems of resource allocation. Indeed, in the introduction to *Studies in Resource Allocation Processes*, Leo Hurwicz suggested that "The idea of searching for a better system is at least as ancient as Plato's *Republic*" (Hurwicz 1977, p. 3). For our purposes, however, it can make sense to put the wisdom of the ancients aside and to take up the tale of system design starting with the musings of Jean-Jacques Rousseau in his *Discours sur l'Origine et les Fondements de l'Inégalité parmi les Hommes* (Rousseau 1755) and *Discours sur l'Economie Politique* (Rousseau 1765), for Rousseau provided ideas relating to property rights, free exchange

---

[24]   The elaboration involves the bit about "intra-firm transfers" in contrast to inter-firm transfers. The elaboration presages Arrow (1977) on decentralization within firms. If decentralization is not relegated to exchange between firms but can inform coordination within firms, then does make-or-buy lose operational significance? See also Baker et al. (2001), "Bringing the market inside the firm?".

and social choice to which the early socialists and then Marx and his impresario Engels appealed.[25]

"The bourgeois is Rousseau's great invention", declared Allan Bloom (1990, p. 214). "He is the individualist in society, who needs society and its protective laws but only as means to his private ends." The bourgeois (townsman) contrasts with man in his natural state (natural man or savage man). Rousseau may have understood natural man as something of a myth in the actual development of human societies, but the institutions that support social interactions did not always exist. They may have organically and spontaneously developed, but societies had to invent them. These institutions, the laws to which Bloom refers, include property rights. Property rights may have facilitated certain exchange, but Rousseau opens part two of the *Discours sur l'Origine et les Fondements de l'Inégalité parmi les Hommes*, with a soliloquy about how the institutions of exchange (most notably property rights) merely gave people something to fight over. "The first person," Rousseau (1755, p. 95) declared,

> who, having enclosed a plot of land, took it into his head to say, "This is mine," and found people simple enough to believe him, was the true founder of civil society. What crimes, wars, murders, what miseries and horrors would the human race have been spared, had someone pulled up the stakes or filled in the ditch and cried out to his fellowmen, "Do no listen to this imposter. You are lost if you forget that the fruits of the earth belong to all and the earth to no one!"? (English trans., Cress 2011, p. 69)

Rousseau argued that, in his natural state man does not require social interactions to happily support himself. Thus, unencumbered with the demands of society and its oppressive institutions, he "is at peace with all nature and the friend of all his fellowmen" (Cress 2011, p. 101).[26]

---

[25]   Hurwicz (1977, p. 4) also volunteered that he perceived these early socialists, the "Utopians and Utopian socialists in particular . . . as the first system designers in the social sphere".

[26]   The very entertaining film *The Gods Must Be Crazy* (1980) explicitly dramatizes a Rousseauian perspective on private property, natural man and the bourgeois (or civilized man). (Much the same perspective is also presented, albeit rather more darkly, in the film *Walkabout*, 1971.) The first 15 minutes of *The Gods* presents the Bushmen of the Kalahari Desert as proto-typical specimens of natural man. They live off of the land, taking only what they need, and as their numbers are few and their needs modest, the land can serve their needs inexhaustibly. However, "One day, something fell from the sky." (A bush pilot had dropped an empty, glass Coke bottle from his plane.) "[The Bushman] Xi had never seen anything like this in his life. It looked like water, but it was harder than anything else in the world. He wondered why the gods had sent this thing down to the

The bourgeois, the civil man, the man of the *civitas*, the man of the city, is all about exchange. He is wheeling and dealing in the market square or in the coffee house – think Lloyd's Coffee House in London in 1698 – all for personal gain. The bourgeois perceives private advantage, and only private advantage, to social interaction. Moreover, social interaction provides opportunity for private gain. Without society, he would yield less private gain. We can imagine, however, that a society comprised of people who were merely pursuing private gain would ultimately yield less advantage to society as a whole. Society could perform better if individuals dedicated themselves not to pursuing private gain but to pursuing collective gain. Indeed, there is much intuitive appeal to the idea that greater gain across society as a whole could be secured were everyone in society prepared to work toward securing the common good or what Rousseau himself might have recognized as the common interest.

Insofar as one person's concept of the common good is another person's concept of arbitrary government, then it might not be obvious what common good means at all. If members of society cannot agree on what is good for society, then what is commonly understood to be commonly good? However, Rousseau's concept of the common interest or general will resolves such ambiguity by positing that each person maintains a (possibly) latent yet common understanding of what constitutes the common good. Moreover, each person commonly maintains a preference (also latent) to secure the common good. Whether or not he or she knows it, even the egoistic bourgeois maintains such a preference. On this count, none other than Ken Arrow himself advanced some ideas in *Social Choice and Individual Values* (1951 [2012]). Among other things he observed that, "There may, indeed, be wide divergences between the individual will, corrupted by the environment, and the true general will, which can never err . . . But the existence of the general will as a basis for the very existence of society is insisted on" (Arrow 1951 [2012], pp. 81–2).

---

earth." But Xi's clan of Bushmen soon discovered that "It was the most useful thing the gods had ever given them, a real labor-saving device. But the gods had been careless. They had sent only one." Alas, the Bushmen discovered something new to their experience: scarcity. "A thing they had never needed before became a necessity. And unfamiliar emotions began to stir, a feeling of wanting to own, of not wanting to share." A desire to assign private ownership began to corrupt them. "Other new things came: anger, jealousy, hate and violence. Xi was angry with the gods. He shouted, 'Take back your thing! We don't want it!'" Xi then resolved to "take it to the end of the earth and throw it off." He and his clansmen anticipated that his trek to the edge of the world could take many days.

Having insisted that the general will exists, Rousseau then moves on to the matter of ascertaining the general will (for it may not be obvious what the general will is) and then operationalizing the general will. Ascertaining the general will seems to contemplate administrative processes that involve well-intentioned government and leadership of central authorities who appreciate that "the general will is always on the side most favorable to the public interest, . . . so that it is necessary simply to be just to be assured of following the general will" (Cress 2011, p. 131). Free exchange, and the institutions that support free exchange, do not appear to have any role in securing the common interest, for, after all, free exchange merely enables and encourages the egoistic, parochial pursuits of the bourgeois. Arrow himself averred that decentralized processes (the market mechanism) could not be expected to have much, if any, role in securing the common interest. Specifically, he suggested that, "Any view which depends on consensus as the basis for social action certainly implies that the market mechanism cannot be taken as the social welfare function since the mechanism cannot take account of the altruistic motives which must be present to secure the consensus" (Arrow 1951 [2012], p. 86).

Arrow's conclusions suggest that a decentralized system of market-mediated exchange may not be able to implement the Rousseauian program in the kind of environment that Rousseau had contemplated. However, that is a special environment in that, in it, all parties share the same preferences. As Rousseau explains, "Men always love what is good or what they find to be so; but it is in this judgement that they make mistakes" (Cress 2011, p. 241). Individuals may be differentially informed, but they can talk things out, agree to censor incorrect (and potentially corrupting) opinion, and thereby dispel the prospect of agreeing to disagree. From the Rousseauian perspective of Woodrow Wilson's book *The State* (Wilson 1889, p. 659), the object of governance then becomes reduced to bringing "the individual with his special interests, personal to himself, in complete harmony with society with its general interests, common to all".

In the remaining nine pages of his book, Wilson (1889, p. 659) suggests that a program could be "formulated . . . without too great vagueness" that would secure the objective of "complete harmony with society". He was vague in that he did not suggest anything about what the program would be, except to advocate that central government would have much to do with it. In contrast, Rousseau and then the early Socialists, then the Marxists, and then the Bolsheviks were more explicit about where the program would begin. It would begin by excising the corrupting influence of that greatest of egoising institutions, private property. Pareto (1896, pp. 408–9) observed:

Les socialistes étaient fort portés à défendre la théorie, que la propriété du sol avait partout commencé par être collective. Ils en tiraient la conséquence que la propriété individuelle avait été une usurpation sur la propriété collective, et qu'il serait convenable que la communauté reprît les biens qu'elle s'était laissé enlever. (The socialists were very apt to defend the theory that the earth everywhere had originally been collectively owned. They concluded that the innovation of private property had constituted a usurpation of collective property and that, accordingly, it would be proper for the community to reassert collective ownership.)

Von Mises quipped that the program could be formulated as, "Once upon a time there were good times when private property did not exist; good times will come again when private property will not exist" (von Mises 1951 [2009], p. 53). Not to be outdone, the young Marx and Engels exclaimed in *The Communist Manifesto* (1848 [1969]) that, "[M]odern bourgeois private property is the final and most complete expression of the system of producing and appropriating products, that is based on class antagonisms, on the exploitation of the many by the few. In this sense, the theory of the Communists may be summed up in the single sentence: Abolition of private property" (Tucker 1978, p. 484).

THE PATH TAKEN THUS FAR

The Rousseauian program and its successors were occupied with ascribing the emergence of economic inequality to free exchange and to the institutions supporting free exchange – principally private property. Pareto (1896, 1897) developed a defense of *la libre concurrence* (free exchange) by establishing performance benchmarks against which any system of resource allocation (centralized, decentralized or hybrid) could be compared. Successive authors elaborated on Pareto's contributions to reconfigure how a central authority could (on paper) organize an economy. In their telling, centralized processes could mimic decentralized processes (free, market-mediated exchange) but could yet outperform an economy organized around free, market-mediated exchange.

The debates in the first half of the twentieth century about the relative merits of centralization and decentralization inspired great innovations on system design. Implementation theory and subsequent developments in mechanism design theory and contract theory folded incentive constraints and informational constraints into microeconomic theory and elevated it into an elegant and formidable theory of the second best. That body of theory, however, corresponds to Vernon Smith's institution-free core of economics. The question remained about whether the core encompassed all of the important action or if the analysis of problems of *ex post* governance in economic relations would require parallel theoretical developments.

Coase (1937) and Simon (1951, 1991) suggested where parallel development might start when they made the seemingly obvious observation that much exchange in the market economy is not organized by market-mediated exchange but is organized within institutions (firms and government bodies) that are invested with administrative processes. In "The nature of the firm", Coase (1937) offered the outline of an explanation for the coexistence of markets and firms. He suggested that there could be tradeoffs between organizing activity by means of administrative processes or by means of market-mediated exchange. He seemed to advocate an incipient economics of organization by which alternative modes of organizing activity are compared. Coase contemplated a binary choice: decentralized market exchange or a kind of centralization (integration within the firm). Williamson (1971) took up the binary choice but introduced adaptation as an important problem. By this time the binary choice was framed with such language as "vertical integration" or "make-or-buy" decision or "boundaries of the firm". There was a long wait for such contributions as Williamson (1985), or Williamson (1991) on "The analysis of discrete structural alternatives", for a generalization of the research program to other modes (joint ventures, long-term contracts, and so on). Even so, a host of authors (Goldberg, Masten, Crocker, Libecap, Joskow, and others) did not need to wait and had already launched a vigorous body of research on alternative modes of organizing activity. Their work set up efficient adaptation in long-term relationships as an important paradigm. Much of their work took up the question of how to set up commitments to collaborate while maintaining flexibility sufficient to enable efficient adaptations in the future without undermining those same commitments. Asset-specificity (relationship-specific or transaction-specific investment) was often important, but sometimes friction alone was the driver of action. Douglas Gale and Dean Lueck make a parallel point in their very accessible tome *The Nature of the Farm* (2003): we can characterize a lot of important action without having to recruit asset-specificity.

THE PATH IN THE FUTURE

The next chapter on "The single-entity question in antitrust" takes up a legalistic exploration of the nature of the firm and firm boundaries. By the time a young Ronald Coase was composing "The nature of the firm" (1937), litigation had already started wending its way through American courts that took up questions that really anticipated Grossman, Hart and Moore on control rights and Simon and Williamson on adaptation, vertical integration and hierarchy in organizations. Imagine two firms, erstwhile competitors, begin to collaborate. They might even formalize their collaboration by forming a legal entity to govern their collaboration, and they may call the entity a joint venture. The two parties might even dispense with partial measures and opt for full-on merger. Either way, a merger or joint venture would neutralize competition between the two firms. Were the antitrust authorities to come calling, however, the parties might claim that they effectively constitute a single, integrated enterprise. As a single entity, they would claim, there can be no question of there being a conspiracy to fix prices or otherwise neutralize competition, for it takes more than one distinct entity to form a conspiracy. An integrated entity cannot conspire with itself.

In a world that did not support some type of merger review process, the parties gambit would seem to insulate their collaboration from any effective antitrust scrutiny. Knowing this, the idea that divisions of a single firm could conspire with each other may have had some appeal. Indeed, without investing itself with some type of intra-corporate conspiracy doctrine, how else could the law rationalize some scope for antitrust scrutiny? The law did end up innovating just such a concept, but it then spent much of the next four decades trying to unravel it and replace it with something more sophisticated. That effort yielded what looks a lot like an informal and formative theory of the firm.

The third chapter takes up the problem of managing very special types of relationships: conspiracies that involve collaboration and repeated interaction between conspirators over a time interval of indefinite duration. It is one thing to manage a relationship over the course of long-term exchange. It is another to manage that relationship while having to keep the fact of the relationship hidden from other parties. In the former case, parties to collaboration might be able to design a contract and set up processes for governing their relationship. The problem of having to maintain the secrecy of a conspiracy, however, may complicate the design of a governance structure. Conspirators might not, for example, be able to appeal to legal processes. They might not be able to use formal contracts and court-ordered processes to help them govern what could well be an illegal arrangement. Instead, conspirators may find themselves having to set up processes that are doubly secret in that the processes themselves would have to be hidden from the view of outsiders.

Conspiracy has something of the flavor of non-contractability as in Baker et al. (2002) on relational contracts. Parties to exchange (conspiratorial or not) might not be able to formally enforce dimensions of performance or information reporting that would be relevant to their payoffs. They might find themselves having to rely on informal processes. They might, for example, find themselves having to enlist the prospect of exchange in the future (and the threat of withdrawing such exchange) to secure commitments to perform in the present.

Conspiracies that involve conduct that unfolds over time have some advantage and disadvantage over conspiracies that involve one-shot inter-actions. A one-and-done interaction might involve a plot to assassinate the king. In such a case, conspirators may have less scope for enlisting the prospect of exchange in the future to induce performance in the present, but once the deed is done, there is no question of having to manage performance of a stream of such deeds in the future. (Getting conspirators to remain quiet may be another matter.) In contrast, conspiracy that does involve a stream of performance over time may involve a stream of costly efforts to monitor and police performance over time. Yet the prospect of enlisting the future to police the present becomes an option. However, enlisting the future to police the present is what parties to long-run exchange may find themselves having to do when they have no other options for governing their relationship. It is the kind of desperate action parties take, for example, when they start off as antagonists rather than as natural parties to collaboration. An antitrust conspiracy, for example, to fix prices over time would involve parties who might naturally be disposed to compete with each other rather than to collaborate. Similarly, warring factions may find themselves enlisting a norm of tit-for-tat retaliation as a way of mitigating violence over time. (Israeli–Palestinian relations come to mind.) Specifically, the expectation of measured retaliation may encourage parties to throttle back or even forgo violent provocations in the first place. Observers may yet bemoan instances of retaliation, but absent some norm of retaliation, the violence might well be worse. Observers might further bemoan the fact that a stream of tit-for-tat retaliation appears interminable. ("Will it ever end?") They may have in mind some type of definitive denouement as in, say, the Manichaean script of a Hollywood film by which antagonists arrive at a chiliastic resolution – for example, a "war to end all wars" – whereas the hard reality might be that conduct that appears to persist indefinitely should be expected to persist indefinitely. Relationships may be messy in that there may never be a clean, definitive resolution.

This third chapter takes up the Apple ebooks antitrust litigation of 2013. In that matter, the district court understood that Apple had played a pivotal role in organizing a conspiracy among major, rival book publishers to raise the prices of ebooks. The chapter makes a point that the court failed to make: in any antitrust context, evidence that parties had set up some type of secret scheme to police performance could go far toward establishing an agreement to conspire (to fix prices, to fix output, to allocate customers or to otherwise neutralize competition). The chapter also makes contact with reputation effects in that Amazon, a party that had lobbied the government to look into the ebooks matter, had cultivated a reputation for exercising its wrath on trading partners, such as book publishers, who fail to commit to terms of contract that it favors.

The fourth chapter directly takes up the question of what parties to exchange can achieve by long-term contract that they could not achieve by a sequence of short-term contracts.

The research illuminates the role of financial structure (debt or equity financing) and contract renegotiation in enabling efficient adaptation over the course of long-term exchange. The chapter then lays out evidence from a dataset of electricity marketing contracts about how electricity generators and electricity marketers use four instruments – contract duration, risk-sharing schemes, financial structure, and veto provisions – to channel investment incentives and to address both programmable and unprogrammable demands for contract adjustments. Among other things, veto provisions invest contracting parties with some capacity to impose renegotiation. The capacity to impose renegotiation invests the relationship with some flexibility. A measure of flexibility makes it easier for contracting parties to commit to longer terms of contract, and that, in turn, can facilitate efforts to line up financing for big projects.

The fifth chapter takes up a debt-versus-equity question again, but this time it takes it up in an environment in which reputation effects might have been expected to inform much of the action. The context involves overseas trade emanating from Venice during 1190–1220 and trade emanating from Crete (which Venice then ruled) in the fourteenth century. The historiography of the Late Middle Ages assigns a lot of weight to the significance of the equity-like financing of trade ventures obtained under the terms of *commenda* contracts. A merchant might send a trading agent off to Egypt to acquire pepper. The parties might resell the pepper stocks at a trade fair in Venice, and they might then agree to share the proceeds from the entire venture according to the terms of a *commenda*. Parties to *commenda* generally shared profits by linear sharing rules: half-and-half, two-thirds/one-third, three-quarters/one-quarter. Knowing this, why would not the trading agent misrepresent the costs of acquiring the pepper in Egypt and thereby enable himself to abscond with the unreported share of the profit?

The reality is that it was debt, not *commenda*, that financed commerce on the informational frontiers of the trade economy. A merchant might give his trading agent five gold coins and instruct him to return in six months with six gold coins. Such a loan would relieve the merchant of having to know details of transactions conducted out of view at sites overseas. Debt would thus require little in the way of institutional supports. In contrast, an equity-like scheme such as a *commenda* contract might require some type of (costly) monitoring or auditing mechanism to support it.

The reality is also that trade between Venice and Egypt during 1190–1220 was not on the informational frontiers of the trade economy. It was in an information-rich core. Specifically, the Venetian Republic sponsored convoys of trading agents to selected sites. These trading agents would end up trading in common commodities at commonly visited ports. Information about prices of commodities would become commonly dispersed. The reality was also that most interactions between merchants and their trading agents were one-shot affairs. They did not occupy themselves with enlisting the prospect of future collaboration to police performance in the present. Moreover, it is not obvious that most trading agents or even merchants would participate in more than one trade venture. They would make their money and get out. Thus, it is not obvious that reputation effects could have much bearing on how merchants and their trading agents mobilized investment for trade.

The study illuminates a result that is something of the converse of Williamson (1988) on "Corporate finance and corporate governance". Williamson argues that equity-like financing can require costly supports such as costly monitoring or auditing mechanisms. Debt, in contrast, requires little in the way of costly supports. The main thing the lender needs to know is whether or not the borrower has paid up a particular fixed sum. Why, then, would parties ever use equity? One reason is that equity does not grant to some outside party (the bank) a foreclosure right. It does not allow a third party to march in and demand liquidation. Parties will use equity where much relationship-specific value is at stake. It allows them to work things out in the face of uncontracted-for contingencies without having to worry about a third party forcing them into foreclosure.

In Williamson (1988), equity shows up as the mode of financing of last resort. In the context of long-distance trade in the Late Middle Ages, debt shows up as the mode of financing of last resort. Where contracting parties could exploit features of the institutional landscape to support equity-like schemes, *commenda* could prevail. However, in environments that offer no such supports, parties would find themselves having to resort to debt financing or to forgo investment entirely.

The final chapter takes up a matter that I suggest can only be understood if we are willing to accept how messy and imprecise the governance of relationships can be. How do parties to collaborative research and development (R&D) police the disclosure to third parties of intellectual properties that they may have contributed to the collaboration or that they may have innovated within the context of the collaboration? A party to a former collaboration may engage a third party in a new collaboration. Should a counterparty to the former collaboration be able to hold up the new collaboration by marching in and asserting claims of the misappropriation of intellectual property?

We can imagine the tradeoffs. On the one hand, parties may want to contain the spillover of intellectual properties to third parties. Restrictions on the disclosure of intellectual properties may go some way toward containing unintended spillovers. On the other hand, disclosure restrictions may enable former partners to hold up new collaboration, especially regarding intellectual properties that are unavoidably subject to some non-trivial degree of spillover anyway. Contracts governing collaborative R&D may include – and, it seems, generally do include – restrictions on the disclosure of intellectual properties. What is interesting is that the duration of these disclosure restrictions varies widely. Parties tend to assign restrictions of long (and possibly indefinite) duration to intellectual properties that are less susceptible to unintended spillover. They assign restrictions of shorter (and possibly zero) duration to intellectual properties that are highly susceptible to unintended spillover.

A policy result comes out of the research. The Advanced Technology Program (ATP) hosted by the National Institute of Science and Technology endeavored to subsidize collaborative R&D which would yield intellectual properties that would be highly susceptible to spillover. High spillover would yield high social benefits, but, as a matter of course, high spillover would also frustrate the private appropriability of costly R&D. It was just such R&D that private parties could not be expected to pursue absent subsidies.

Analysis of the duration of disclosure restrictions from a dataset of contracts suggests that the ATP ended up subsidizing projects which tended to yield intellectual properties that were less susceptible to spillover and thus more amenable to appropriation – just the sort of intellectual properties that private parties could have been expected to develop without subsidies. The results suggest that the ATP was not able to do a good job of identifying R&D collaborations most worthy of subsidization. It subsidized the wrong R&D ventures.

2. The single-entity question in antitrust: ownership, control and delegation in organizations*

Can a parent company conspire with its subsidiaries? Is not the central point of integrating otherwise independent units within a single corporate entity to enable a parent company to coordinate with its subsidiaries on a whole host of matters, and could not coordination extend to pricing and production decisions? Yet, from the perspective of antitrust law, could an integrated, corporate structure be construed as the means of governing an illegal conspiracy among the various units to fix prices or output?

From a modern perspective, the answer would seem to be obvious: intracorporate entities can coordinate with each other; is this really a serious question? It turns out that, from the perspective of 1890 or 1947, it was a serious question, and not without reason. Indeed, one reason might be that, before 1978, the antitrust authorities in the United States did not maintain a robust merger review process.[1] The antitrust authorities may have learned about a merger, proposed or consummated, in much the same way most people did: by reading about it in the newspaper. However, merger review provides an answer to the following type of question: what is the difference between two competing firms agreeing to fix prices and the same two firms forming a new corporate entity, calling it the parent, calling themselves subsidiaries, and investing the parent with authority to coordinate the two subsidiaries' pricing? The latter arrangement may

---

* This chapter elaborates and expands on Williamson (2009) published in the *Journal of Competition Law & Economics*.

[1] In 1978 the federal government instituted the Premerger Notification Program. The program was authorized by the Hart–Scott–Rodino Antitrust Improvements Act of 1976. It requires parties to merger transactions that exceed certain valuation thresholds to notify the antitrust agencies, the Federal Trade Commission and the Antitrust Division of the Department of Justice, before consummating their mergers. The agencies then get 30 days to decide whether or not to investigate a merger more thoroughly. Parties to a proposed merger commit to holding off consummating their merger for the entire course of investigation or successive litigation.

correspond to a merger, but would not such coordination post-merger also amount to illegal price fixing?

With a mature merger review process in place, the answer may very well be "No". Had the antitrust authorities already scrutinized a proposed merger and declined to oppose the merger, then the merged firm would be free to coordinate in the future. However, absent merger review, merger would enable firms to finesse the trouble of secretly conspiring to fix prices. Instead, the firms would be able to coordinate pricing in plain view. It was concern over just this kind of result that may have prompted the Supreme Court of the United States to observe in *United States v. Yellow Cab* 332 US 218, 228 (1947) that the Sherman Antitrust Act 1890 was "aimed at substance rather than form". Specifically, when viewed from the perspective of 1890 or 1947, intracorporate entities could be understood as parties to an antitrust conspiracy.

The *Yellow Cab* case is understood to have launched an "intracorporate conspiracy doctrine" into the case law, but we can only imagine the limits of such thinking. Could any and all agglomerations of intracorporate entities be potentially characterized as conspiracies? A great deal of confusion persisted post-*Yellow Cab* about what would constitute an antitrust-cognizable conspiracy, but the confusion had been building for some time. Consider, for example, the experience of General Motors in 1938. General Motors Corporation (GMC) incorporated itself in 1916. In 1919 it set up a new unit, the General Motors Acceptance Corporation (GMAC) to facilitate access for both auto dealers and buyers to automobile financing. Yet, in 1938 GMC, GMAC and two other GMC subsidiaries found themselves identified as defendants in "a criminal prosecution for a conspiracy to restrain interstate trade and commerce in violation of Sec. 1 of the Sherman Anti Trust Act".[2] A jury rendered a verdict finding the four "corporate defendants" guilty of conspiracy. General Motors Corporation and the three subsidiaries were each fined the princely sum of $5,000.

The argument was that General Motors, GMAC and the other two subsidiaries had conspired with each other "to monopolize and control the business of financing the trade and commerce in new and used General Motors automobiles" with the effect of "unduly" restraining "the interstate trade and commerce in General Motors automobiles".[3] In 1919 few if any companies were offering automobile financing, but by 1939 there was

---

[2]   *United States v. General Motors Corporation*, 121 F.2d 376 (7th Circuit 1941) at 382.

[3]   *United States v. General Motors Corporation*, 121 F.2d 376 (7th Circuit 1941) at 383.

a host of entities offering such services. Some of these entities must have complained that General Motors sometimes required auto dealers to use financing from GMAC when procuring General Motors vehicles.

General Motors argued that GMC and its subsidiaries collectively comprised "a single enterprise" and that the single enterprise, comprised as it was of "non-competing units", should be able "to condition the sale of their product and to restrain their own product by selling it to whom they please".[4] The Seventh Circuit Court of Appeals disagreed. Anticipating *Yellow Cab*, the court opined that, "The test of illegality under the Sherman Act is not so much the particular form of business organization effected, as it is the presence or absence of restraint of trade and commerce".[5]

A more modern approach to the General Motors matter would have been to frame it as a tying arrangement by which a dealer's purchase of an automobile is tied to the financing that supports the automobile purchase. The prospectively illegal purpose of the tie would have been for General Motors to deny business to other financing firms with the expectation that it could then proceed to monopolize a market for automobile financing. (Section 7.6c of Hovenkamp 2005 is apposite.) More importantly, a modern approach would dispense with the appeal to conspiracy. Instead, insofar as a case would be framed at all, it would be framed as a matter of single-firm conduct, not multi-party conspiracy. From 1938, however, the courts seemed to perceive that they had to construe conduct as the product of a conspiracy in order to frame it in a way cognizable by the antitrust apparatus available to them.

The holding in *Yellow Cab* was narrow in that it ascribed the potential for conspiracy only to the vertical dimension of corporate structures (a parent entity could conspire with its wholly owned subsidiary). By 1951, however, subsequent case law extended the intracorporate conspiracy concept to horizontal aspects of corporate structures (subsidiaries could conspire with each other). It took another 33 years, some years after a robust merger review process had been implemented, for the Supreme Court in *Copperweld Corp. v. Independence Tube Corp.* 467 U.S. 752 (1984) to begin to articulate limits to intracorporate conspiracy doctrine, but lower courts had been setting up the Supreme Court to roll it back since at least the late 1960s. Moreover, the advent of free agency in professional sports in the 1970s concentrated interest on curious governance structures that had been around for some time:

---

[4]   *United States v. General Motors Corporation*, 121 F.2d 376 (7th Circuit 1941) at 404.

[5]   *United States v. General Motors Corporation*, 121 F.2d 376 (7th Circuit 1941) at 404.

professional sports leagues. Free agency invested players with bargaining power vis-à-vis their teams and their leagues, because free agents could induce teams to compete to contract with them.[6] Up to that point, leagues could take actions to suppress an individual player's bargaining power. They could, for example, restrict a player's capacity to defect from one team to another. Free agency would mean little were a league understood to constitute a single, monolithic entity with which a player would have to negotiate. In contrast, imposing free agency would amount to treating a league as a collection of distinct entities (teams), and these entities would have to compete with each other to secure any single free agent's contract.

The case law ultimately resolved the question about whether a professional sports league constituted a single entity by establishing that it could be understood as a single entity for certain purposes (promulgating certain league-wide standards and rules, say) but not for other purposes (regulating competition between teams in markets for player talent and coaching talent). Common to all of the case law, however, going back to at least *Yellow Cab*, were questions about how ownership and control could inform the ultimate question about what corporate relationships would constitute antitrust conspiracies. A conspiracy involves coordination between at least two distinct entities. The case law endeavored to use ownership and control to characterize conspiracies by sorting out what they are not: single entities. A difficulty is that the case law could never advance an operationally significant concept of control. What it did do, however, was advance legal tests that had much the flavor of "contracting for control" as in Baker et al. (2011). Over time, the tests built on concepts other than control. These concepts, which we might recognize as control rights, adaptation, and delegation, suggest how we can subsume the sometimes confusing array of single-entity tests proposed in the case law within a two-stage sequence of tests. The two-stage sequence came to be most crisply articulated in *Freeman v. San Diego Association of Realtors* 322 F.3d 1133, 1148-49 (9th Circuit 2003) nearly 60 years after *Yellow Cab*.

THE SINGLE-ENTITY QUESTION

This study was inspired by the following gambit. A cluster of hospitals forms a new entity, calls it the network, shares ownership in the new entity,

---

[6]   See Staudohar (1978) on "Player salary issues in Major League Baseball" with respect to the emergence of free agency as well as to the emergence of more potent collective bargaining.

and assigns to the entity control over many of the hospitals' activities. The prospect of appealing to a single-entity defense could enable parties to the network to finesse merger review by presenting the agglomeration of the network hospitals as a joint venture of distinct entities. Yet, when and if the antitrust authorities investigated, the parties could claim that the hospital network constitutes a tightly integrated single entity, and that, as a single entity, it would be free to coordinate the activities of its (non-competing) units.

Questions remain about whether courts should extend the status of single entity to such networks or should evaluate networks as clusters of distinct entities. They are questions that the framers of the Sherman Antitrust Act 1890 may have been well situated to appreciate. Explicit questions about the degree to which a governance structure is "tight" or "loose" (as in Thorelli 1955, p. 72) suggest that the framers appreciated what they were doing. Before getting into that, however, let us consider a sequence of structures parties have used to govern long-run relationships and order them from least integrated to most tightly integrated.

Governance Scenario 1: An Electricity Marketing Contract[7]

An electricity-generating firm sells to another firm, an electricity marketer, the exclusive rights to dispatch electricity from its generators over a 20-year interval. That is, when the marketer makes demands at any time over the next 20 years for the generator to fire up and produce electricity, the generator produces electricity, and when the marketer makes demands to cease generation, the generator stops production. The marketer compensates the generator by paying it a fixed monthly fee and by covering the generator's operating expenses. Thus, even if the marketer makes no dispatch demands in a given month, the generator still receives its fixed monthly payment. The generator maintains ownership of its generating units, but it also cedes to the marketer rights to veto proposals it might make over the course of the 20-year relationship to expand, upgrade, or to withdraw generation capacity at the generator's production sites.

It would be natural to label the relationship between the generator and marketer a long-term contract, and it might seem artificial to suggest that the generator and marketer collectively constitute a single entity. Note, however, how ownership does not strictly imply control of underlying assets. The generator may own the production capacity committed to the

---

[7]   We explore the structure of electricity marketing contracts more fully in Chapter 4 in this volume.

contractual relationship, but the contract assigns to the marketer important dimensions of control. The marketer controls the generator's output in wholesale electricity markets – that is the marketer's job – and the veto provision constitutes a way of assigning to the marketer some, but not all, control over investment in the generator's production capacity.

The point of the veto provision is not that the marketer would, as a matter of course, veto any and all proposals by the generator to expand, upgrade, or withdraw capacity. Instead, the marketer can use the threat of a veto to hold-up investment and force the generator to renegotiate terms of the contract, such as the level of the fixed monthly payment, in return for acquiescing to implement investment proposals. The marketer might also demand amendments to any one proposal. Either way, the veto provision gives the marketer influence over investment decisions by making it incumbent upon the generator to make it worth the marketer's while to go along with its proposals.

Governance Scenario 2: Two Electricity Marketing Contracts

Suppose that an energy marketer has secured long-term dispatch rights in separate contracts with each of two generators. Suppose, also, that these two generators are "actual or potential competitors"[8] in that they supply electricity to the same geographic market (load pocket). Finally, suppose that each contract includes a veto provision.

The suggestion that the marketer and two generators collectively constitute a single entity might, at best, seem audacious. More likely, antitrust authorities would perceive the arrangement as enabling two competitors (the generators) to neutralize competition between each other. The generators might, even, separately incorporate a third party and call it the marketer. When the antitrust authorities investigate, the parties might refer to the single-entity case law and tell the authorities to go away claiming that together they constitute a single entity.

What could constitute the basis for a claim to single-entity status? There does exist a single party, the marketer, which maintains exclusive control over each generator's output. It is not obvious, however, that this single party constitutes an independent center of decision-making with respect to all decisions that are central to the functioning of the candidate single entity. The veto provisions enable the marketer to assume some non-trivial

---

[8]   The concept of "actual or potential competitors" shows up in such matters as *City of Mt. Pleasant v. Associated Electric Cooperative, Inc.* 838 F.2d 268 (1988) at 276.

share of control over each generator's investment plans. Note, however, that the nexus of parties that maintains control over one generator's investment plans is different from the nexus of parties that maintains control over the other generator's investment plans. The marketer and one generator maintain control over that one generator's plans, and the marketer and the other generator maintain control over that other generator's plans. These nexuses of control intersect, but might a court use the fact that neither of these nexuses of control encapsulates the other to suggest that the business arrangement features more than one independent center of decision-making?

Governance Scenario 3: Hospital Networks[9]

A number of hospitals form a network by incorporating a new entity and assigning governance of the new entity to a board of directors. Each hospital reserves the right to appoint a number of directors to the new entity's board as well as the right to replace those same directors. Each hospital also maintains ownership of all its assets, and member hospitals do not transfer title to any property that they own to the new entity. However, the member hospitals assign to the new entity rights to veto proposals by any one hospital to expand, upgrade or withdraw services or capacity

---

[9]   The scenario is inspired by letters three different hospital networks submitted to the Premerger Notification Office of the Federal Trade Commission memorializing guidance they had received from Commission staff concerning the potential reportability of transactions with respect to rules and regulations implemented under the Hart–Scott–Rodino Antitrust Improvements Act 1976. I reference three letters posted at http://www.ftc.gov/bc/HSR/informal/opinions/9804005.htm, http://www.ftc.gov/bc/HSR/informal/opinions/0010003.htm, and http://www.ftc. gov/bc/HSR/informal/opinions/9908002.htm (all three websites accessed November 27, 2018). The last of these pertains to the Network Affiliation Agreement that laid out the structure of the governance of the Evanston Northwestern Healthcare Network. This network is interesting, because the hospitals constituting the network secured from the Commission an informal opinion that indicated that the merger through which the parties formed the network "would not constitute a reportable transaction under the HSR Act". In 2004, four years after formation of the network, the Commission challenged the merger, and in 2005 the Commission secured a favorable initial decision from Administrative Law Judge Stephen J. McGuire which is posted at https://www.ftc.gov/sites/default/files/documents/cas es/2005/10/051021idtextversion.pdf (accessed November 27, 2018). The member hospitals argued that not having to report their merger transaction constituted evidence that together they already constituted a single entity before the merger. The judge disagreed, indicating, among other things, evidence that the parties had not constituted a single entity at the time of the formation of the network.

(for example, hospital beds). The new entity aggregates profits from each hospital so that it may propose and finance plans to expand, upgrade or withdraw service capacity. The new entity restores to the hospitals profits it has not earmarked for investment. Each hospital maintains a veto over proposals by the new entity to expand, upgrade, or withdraw services or capacity at any of its sites.

Note that any proposal to expand, upgrade, or withdraw services or capacity at any single hospital's site requires the approval of both that member hospital and the new entity. Accordingly, the particular hospital and the new entity together constitute the nexus of parties that maintains authority over investment decisions at the single hospital. Investment decisions involving another hospital involve a different nexus – the nexus composed of that other hospital and the new entity – although the two nexuses intersect in that the new entity is party to both nexuses. Does the overlap imply that the two nexuses effectively constitute a single center of decision-making, in which case the new entity and all member hospitals might collectively constitute a single entity?

Even if we were to judge that the nexuses constitute distinctly enumerable centers of decision-making, we might suggest that they do not constitute independent centers. Member hospitals each maintain indirect influence over the new entity through their ability to appoint and replace directors. Does indirect influence imply the dependence rather than the independence of the various centers of decision-making, in which case the network might again be able to appeal to single-entity status?

Note also that hospitals' ownership of their assets does not strictly imply control over those assets. Hospitals share control with the new entity, and member hospitals indirectly influence how other hospitals' assets are disposed by virtue of their rights to appoint and replace directors.

Finally, note that the member hospitals pool proceeds. The pooling of proceeds is integral to the efforts of member hospitals to coordinate investment plans. Does pooling of itself indicate some degree of economic unity, or does it simply enable anticompetitive coordination among actual or potential competitors?

Governance Scenario 4: Delegation and Reserved Rights in a Traditional Corporate Hierarchy

Finally, let us consider the kind of governance structure contemplated in *Copperweld*: a hierarchy of wholly owned corporate subsidiaries and its parent. Traditional corporate hierarchy constitutes an obvious benchmark against which to contrast economic unity in other governance structures, and it constitutes a benchmark that *Copperweld* and succeeding case law inserted into the single-entity case law. This benchmark is interesting partly because it makes allowances for the prospect that some parties to a governance structure might delegate managerial functions to other parties. Does delegation amount to abdication of control, in which case single-entity status might be jeopardized, or does it reflect control, in which case single-entity status remains secure? The single-entity case law indicates the latter: delegating functions to other parties is consistent with single-entity status.[10]

Consider a parent corporation that wholly owns some number of separately incorporated subsidiaries. Suppose also that some of these subsidiaries themselves wholly own some other separately incorporated subsidiaries. These subsidiaries constitute "indirect subsidiaries" of the parent. Thus, the parent's subsidiaries are themselves parents to the indirect subsidiaries. Suppose that a parent anywhere in the hierarchy may delegate managerial functions to any its own subsidiaries or indirect subsidiaries and that any parent reserves the right to take back functions it had previously delegated. The pattern of delegation and reserved rights will illuminate a hierarchy of corporate entities. It turns out that this hierarchy corresponds exactly to the hierarchy that the pattern of ownership illuminates.

The complete agreement of these two hierarchies constitutes the benchmark case featured in *Copperweld*, and *Copperweld* extended single-entity status to this benchmark case. *Copperweld* did not, however, resolve the single-entity question for cases that deviate from this benchmark. How might the single-entity inquiry be resolved in cases in which the hierarchy mapped out by the pattern of ownership deviates in small or large measure from the hierarchy mapped out by the pattern of delegation?

The framers of the Sherman Antitrust Act of 1890 did not have access to the body of single-entity case law presented to the Supreme Court in *Copperweld*, but debate on the Senate floor in 1890 over how (and

---

[10]   The court of appeals in *Seagram and Sons v. Hawaiian Oke and Liquors* 416 F.2d 71 (9th Circuit 1969) observed that "sound management demands extensive delegation of authority within the organization" (p. 83). In overturning the lower court, the appeals court observed that "under the trial court's ruling, the more delegation there is, the more danger there will be that the holders of such delegated authority will be found by a court to be capable of conspiring with each other in carrying on the corporation's business", the conclusion being that "the doctrine [of intra-corporate conspiracy] hands to plaintiffs, on a silver platter, an automatically self-proving conspiracy" (pp. 83–4). *Copperweld* itself identifies control with the power to "delegate" managerial functions to otherwise "autonomous units" (p. 771) and with the power to take managerial functions back (pp. 771–2).

whether) to structure the first federal antitrust legislation suggests that they would have been situated to appreciate the single-entity question. Debate concentrated on concerns about how conspirators might exploit one organizational form or another to govern combinations that join erstwhile competitors under some degree of unified control. These combinations might be loose, such as those secured by joint ventures, long-term contracts, and the like, or they might be tight, such as those achieved by explicit, *de jure* merger.[11] Parties to the debate, however, appreciated that business interests might use these same governance structures to efficiently organize the production of goods and services.[12] It was thus not obvious, then, that they should outlaw any particular mode of organization per se. Instead, the problem, they perceived, was to enable a legal process by which particular, context-specific instances of combinations might be identified and outlawed. Context would matter in that illegal combinations would be those assembled "with a view to prevent competition, or for the restraint of trade, or to increase the profits of the producer at the cost of the consumer".[13]

Enabling a legal process amounted to situating the problem of identifying and characterizing illegal combinations in the common-law process. That is, leave it to the courts to develop a body of case law about what constitutes illegal combinations. Hovenkamp (2005) suggests just that and only that – that the Sherman Act ended up situating the problem in a common law process, if not in any particular body of common law. Pointing to Judge Taft's opinion in *Addyston Pipe & Steel Co. v. United States* 85 F.271 (6th Circuit 1898), for example, Hovenkamp suggests that the common law process started to innovate some important yet uncommon law to deal with antitrust issues, but it did so while outwardly maintaining a fiction that it was operating within some body of common law.[14]

It is, perhaps, in a similar spirit of fictionalization and innovation that the conclusion in *Yellow Cab* obtained: a parent company and its subsidiaries could potentially conspire to restrain interstate commerce in

---

[11] The trusts of the 1880s were the most infamous examples of tight combinations – hence the provenance of the term antitrust. Seager and Gulick (1929, pp. 1–9) catalogue governance structures, including trusts, that attracted legislators' attentions.

[12] See, for example, Thorelli (1955, pp. 182–3, 185) on this count. John Sherman himself elaborated at some length on this point, as Thorelli also notes, in an often quoted speech delivered on the Senate floor on March 21, 1890.

[13] Senator John Sherman in his speech, "Trusts," to the United States Senate (Sherman 1890, p. 6).

[14] See the discussion in Hovenkamp (2005, pp. 52–5, esp. p. 54).

ways deemed unreasonable (and thus illegal) when viewed through the lens of antitrust case law. If a parent entity and its subsidiaries were party to a single vertically integrated enterprise, this would not insulate them from scrutiny and sanction.

A difficulty was that intracorporate conspiracy doctrine invited all types of mischief in that it did not articulate limits on the concept – not until the Supreme Court started to unwind it in *Copperweld* (1984). *Copperweld* itself yielded a narrow result, specifically unwinding *Yellow Cab* in that it liberated the vertical relationship between a parent and its wholly owned subsidiaries from antitrust scrutiny. However, the objective of *Copperweld* and succeeding case law was to circumscribe the scope for mischief. The objective was to restrict prospective litigants from imposing demands on the courts to entertain the prospect that any combination of a corporate parent and its wholly owned subsidiaries could constitute an antitrust conspiracy.[15]

The most important efforts in the case law to impose structure on such questions have involved appealing to ownership and control in organizations.[16] It is intuitively appealing to suggest that ownership implies control. It is also intuitively appealing to suggest that a defining characteristic of a single entity is that control is concentrated in the hands of a single party. This still leaves open the question of extending single-entity status to business arrangements that feature less than completely concentrated control. *Copperweld* and the entire body of single-entity case law offers little guidance beyond the suggestion that ownership and control are related and that both inform analysis of the single-entity question. An outstanding problem is that none of the case law makes much progress sorting out what constitutes ownership and control, much less sorting out how they are related and how they inform analysis. It gets worse: the law does not have an operationally significant concept of "control", "authority", "fiat", or "power" to begin with. Surprisingly, neither does economics,[17] nor organization theory.[18]

---

[15] See Areeda (1983, pp. 451–2), Belsley (1996, pp. 726–7).

[16] See, for example, *Dagher v. SRI*, 369 F.3d 1108, 1118 (9th Circuit 2004); *HealthAmerica Penn. Inc. v. Susquehanna Health Sys.*, 278 F.Supp. 2d 423, 428 (2003); *Mt. Pleasant v. Assoc. Elec. Cooperative Inc.*, 838 F.2d 268, 276 (8th Circuit 1988); *Thomsen v. Western Electric Co.*, 512 F.Supp. 128, 133 (1981); *Murphy Tugboat Co. v. Shipowners & Merchants Towboat Corp.*, 467 F.Supp. 841, 859–60 (1979); *Knutson v. Daily Review Inc.*, 548 F.2d 795, 801 (1977); *Timken Roller Bearing v. United States*, 341 U.S. 593, 598 (1951).

[17] See, for example, Demsetz (1995, pp. 35–9), Alchian and Demsetz, (1972, p. 777). Nonetheless, control has recently made it back to economists' research agenda, as in Gibbons (2005).

[18] See Williamson (1995).

WHENCE THE SINGLE-ENTITY CONCEPT?

A sequence of Supreme Court opinions and lower court opinions between 1941 and 1951 established the antithesis of a single-entity concept, the intracorporate conspiracy doctrine, according to which commonly owned or controlled entities could conspire in ways cognizable under section 1 of the Sherman Act.[19] The "talismanic"[20] citation on this count came from *Yellow Cab*:

> [A] restraint [on interstate commerce] may result as readily from a conspiracy among those who are affiliated or integrated under common ownership as from a conspiracy among those who are otherwise independent. Similarly, any affiliation or integration flowing from an illegal conspiracy cannot insulate the conspirators from the sanctions which Congress has imposed. The corporate interrelationships of the conspirators, in other words, are not determinative of the applicability of the Sherman Act. That statute is aimed at substance rather than form.

In *United States v. General Motors* 121 F.2d 376 (7th Circuit 1941), General Motors attempted during the course of litigation to anticipate and neutralize reasoning of the sort applied in *Yellow Cab*. General Motors complained that jurors should have been instructed that:

> if they find that the defendant corporations [which were a selection of General Motors subsidiaries] together constitute a single co-operative enterprise, in the course of which defendants corporations do not compete with one another, that there is and can be no unlawful agreement among them to restrain trade and commerce among the states, in automobiles. (p. 409)

The Seventh Circuit Court of Appeals disagreed, indicating that,

> It has been shown as a matter of law that the appellants [the General Motors entities] are separate entities, even though as a matter of economics they may constitute a single integrated enterprise, and that they are not impotent to restrain the trade and commerce of the dealers in General Motors cars. Consequently, the Court was not obliged to give such an instruction [to jurors].

Building explicitly on *Yellow Cab*, the court in *Kiefer-Stewart Co. v. Joseph E. Seagram and Sons* 340 U.S. 211 (1951) observed that

---

[19] Note that intracorporate conspiracy can mean different things in different areas of the law. It has applications in criminal matters (for example, racketeering) and civil rights matters as well as applications in antitrust. See Smith (1996) on applications to civil rights and references to criminal and antitrust matters.
[20] Areeda (1983, p.458).

even if commonly owned or controlled units of a firm may constitute "mere instrumentalities of a single manufacturing merchandising unit . . . common ownership and control does not liberate corporations from the impact of the antitrust laws" (p. 261). Echoing its ruling in *Kiefer-Stewart*, the court in *Timken Roller Bearing v. United States* 341 U.S. 593 (1951) indicated that "The fact that there is common ownership or control of . . . contracting corporations does not liberate them from the impact of the antitrust laws" (p. 598).

Building, in turn, on *Kiefer-Stewart*, the Ninth Circuit Court of Appeals in *Joseph E. Seagram and Sons v. Hawaiian Oke and Liquors* 416 F.2d 71, 82 (9th Circuit 1969) explicitly identified a tension in the case law when it observed:

> It is now settled law that if a corporation chooses to conduct parts of its business through subsidiary or affiliated corporations, and conspires with them to do something that independent entities cannot conspire to do under section 1 of the Sherman Act, it is no defense that the corporations are, in reality a single economic entity. The Supreme Court has said that "common ownership and control does not liberate corporations from the impact of the antitrust laws." . . . [Yet] [t]he Court has never indicated what, if any, are the limits of this [intracorporate conspiracy] doctrine.

The *Hawaiian Oke* appeals court went on to suggest that authority to delegate managerial functions might illuminate some of those limits. The court observed that "sound management demands extensive delegation of authority within the organization" (p. 83). In overturning the lower court, the appeals court observed (pp. 83–4):

> [U]nder the trial court's ruling, the more delegation there is, the more danger there will be that the holders of such delegated authority will be found by a court to be capable of conspiring with each other in carrying on the corporation's business," the conclusion being that "the doctrine [of intra-corporate conspiracy] hands to plaintiffs, on a silver platter, an automatically self-proving conspiracy.

Paraphrasing the court of appeals in *Hawaiian Oke*, the court in *Murphy Tugboat Company v. Shipowners & Merchants Towboat Co.* 467 F.Supp. 841 (1979) identified a tension in intracorporate conspiracy doctrine between ownership and control. The court observed that, "Indiscriminate application of Section 1 to commonly owned or controlled corporations could therefore have absurd and counterproductive results, subjecting them to liability for 'an automatically self-proving conspiracy' on account of activity necessarily arising out of or inherently connected with common ownership or control" (p. 860).

The *Copperweld* court noted that the *Yellow Cab* court did not need to introduce an intracorporate conspiracy concept in order to characterize conduct in violation of section 1 of the Sherman Act. "Our point," the court observed in footnote 5, "is not that Yellow Cab found only the initial acquisition illegal; our point is that the illegality of the initial acquisition was a predicate for its holding that any post acquisition conduct violated the Act". The suggestion is that *Yellow Cab* could have spared much confusion in the case law had it ruled merely that the offending conduct it was examining stemmed from an acquisition of control that itself would have been judged illegal had it been subjected to scrutiny. (Unfortunately, the antitrust enterprise at the time was not equipped with a robust merger-review process – a process that could have adjudicated the question of illegality without elevating the matter to a court-ordered process.) The *Copperweld* court then proceeded to severely circumscribe intracorporate conspiracy doctrine when it held that "[defendants] Copperweld and its wholly owned subsidiary Regal are incapable of conspiring with each other for purposes of § 1 of the Sherman Act. To the extent that prior decisions of this Court are to the contrary, they are disapproved and overruled" (p. 777). The court went on to accept *Hawaiian Oke's* cue when it identified control with the power to "delegate" managerial functions to otherwise "autonomous units" (p. 771) and with the power to take managerial functions back (pp. 771–2).

Copperweld did not so much dismiss intracorporate conspiracy doctrine as create a single-entity safe harbor by screening out certain types of objectively identifiable governance structures. *Copperweld* expressly limited its inquiry to the "narrow issue" of "whether a parent and its wholly owned subsidiary are capable of conspiring in violation of § 1 of the Sherman Act" (p. 767). It explicitly left open for further consideration other types of business arrangements, such as those under which "a parent may be liable for conspiring with an affiliated corporation it does not completely own" (p. 767). Yet, the suggestion in *Copperweld* and in the entire body of single-entity case law is plain: ownership and control inform the single-entity concept, and control can be identified with the power to delegate managerial functions. An outstanding problem is that, beyond delegation, none of the case law makes much progress sorting out what constitutes ownership and control, much less sorting out how they are related and how they inform analysis. Fortunately, there is some economics that can tie ownership, control, and delegation together.

SOME LAW AND ECONOMICS OF CONFLICT AND CONTROL IN ORGANIZATIONS

Control Rights and Adaptation

Economic theory provides not so much an affirmative theory of control but a body of theory about when, where and to whom to assign control rights. We must ask, "Rights to control what?" An (admittedly abstract) answer is "assets", or, the same thing, the inputs parties contribute to the production of some good or service. Assets may include not merely the types of things to which it is easy to assign property rights, such as plant and equipment, but also intangibles such as trademarks and rights of way to commercialize patented technologies.[21]

It is important to note that most economic theory, including the theory that is traditionally applied to antitrust, need not make contact with control. Most theory is occupied with sorting out plans parties implement for deploying their assets and efforts. These plans may take the form of production plans implemented within the firm, formal contracts between firms, tacit agreements and so on. Insofar as a plan is nothing more than a set of scripted instructions, it is not obvious that it makes a difference whether parties implement a plan within the firm or between firms.[22] It makes no difference (yet) how parties organize production. Rather, parties contribute inputs, implement plans, and that is it. Questions about what governance structures constitute single entities are not cognizable within the framework. The key point is that nothing needs to be controlled as long as there is no demand to deviate from the plan. However, why deviate? What would induce demand to deviate? Control, it turns out, becomes a concern once demands for deviations arise – that is, when contingencies arise for which parties have not made allowances in their plans.

Questions about why parties would not have made allowances for certain contingencies indicate deep issues about how they adapt business arrangements to changing circumstances.[23] Why would parties have failed

---

[21]   Assets may also include things over which it is difficult to assign property rights, such as know-how or other inalienable human resources. Note again, however, the single-entity case law is occupied with corporate entities – juridical persons that are capable of assuming property rights.

[22]   In the language of game theory, a plan is a static strategy – a script indicating actions a party is to take at any contingency that might arise. The writer of the script could just as well seal it in an envelope, hand it to a technician to implement, and walk away.

[23]   See, for example, Williamson (1971, 1974, 2005) and Gibbons (2005).

to explicitly account for certain contingencies in their plans? Does the prospect that such contingencies arise motivate parties to find economical ways to adapt their plans?[24] Can it be economical to selectively leave plans incomplete? Finally, the control question: given demands for adaptation arise, who crafts the adaptations to be made and who implements the adaptations? That is, who gets to assume control?

The answer suggested in Grossman and Hart (1986), Hart and Moore (1990), Moore (1992) and Hart (1995) is the parties who own the assets get to assume and exercise control.

> Given a contract will not specify all aspects of asset usage in every contingency, who has the right to decide about missing usages? . . . [I]t is the owner of the asset in question who has this right. That is, the owner of an asset has *residual control rights* over that asset: the right to decide all usages of the asset in any way not inconsistent with a prior contract, custom, or law. (Hart 1995, p. 30, original emphasis)

This line of research imposes structure on the single-entity question in three ways. First, and most importantly, it suggests a way of understanding how ownership and control are related. Ownership implies control rights, which are the rights to decide how to redeploy assets in the event uncontracted-for contingencies arise. Ownership does not imply all control rights. Parties could (and often do) allocate control rights to non-owners – hence the qualification in Hart (1995) that ownership implies control rights that are "residual" in that other parties may have reserved some rights by "prior contract, custom, or law". (The first three governance scenarios are illuminating on this count.) Second, the appeal to residual control rights suggests a benchmark against which to judge economic unity: it is plausible to suggest that a candidate single entity may secure single-entity status on the basis of economic unity by demonstrating that it maintains all residual control rights. Maintaining all residual control rights amounts to owning all of the assets engaged in production. Finally, the appeal to residual control rights suggests a simple way of identifying single entities that satisfy this benchmark of economic unity. We can delineate the single entities that satisfy the test of economic unity simply by identifying the nexus of parties that collectively own the assets engaged in production.

---

[24] Research on adaptation in economic relationships is well established. Contributors include Masten and Crocker (1985), Crocker and Masten (1988, 1991), Crocker and Reynolds (1993), Joskow (1987, 1988), Goldberg and Erickson (1987). More recent contributors include Saussier (2000), Bajari and Tadelis (2001), Tadelis (2002), Zhu (1999, 2003), Zhang and Zhu (2000), and Gibbons (2005).

Thus, if two parties separately or collectively own assets engaged in production, we include those two parties in the single entity.

We should note that the appeal to residual control rights implies a concept of "economic unity" that is much more parochial than the concept the single-entity case law anticipates. *Copperweld* and succeeding case law anticipate a concept of economic unity that depends on centers of decision-making, not on centers of residual decision-making. Residual control rights, as opposed to control rights, may mean very little if the candidate single entity has signed away the most important control rights. Thus, we might want to include in any effort to delineate a single entity those parties that do maintain those most important control rights even if they own no assets and maintain no residual control rights. Instead, appealing to residual control rights alone might lead us to extend single-entity status to a party that is really no more than a component of a larger entity. In contrast, a concept of economic unity that depends on how parties allocate all control rights might provide a rationale for extending single-entity status to the relationship.

Conflict Within and Between Single Entities

Some of the case law seems to suggest that a defining feature of a single entity is a "unity of interest" between its constituent entities.[25] The law has been shy about defining what constitutes a unity of interest, but, even if we take it at face value, we can identify at least three immediate problems with the test. First, both economics and some of the single-entity case law recognize that conflict as well as mutual interests may characterize much of what goes on within single entities. In *Chicago Professional Sports LP v. National Basketball Association* 95 F.3d 593 (7th Circuit 1996), for example, Judge Easterbrook observed that "Even a single firm contains many competing interests . . . *Copperweld* does not hold that only conflict-free enterprises may be treated as single entities" (p. 598).[26] Indeed, the

---

[25]   *Copperweld* 467 U.S. 752 at 769, *Mt. Pleasant* 838 F.2d at 276, *Iain Fraser v. Major League Soccer, LLC* 284 F.3d 47, 58 (1st Circuit 2002).

[26]   The *Mt. Pleasant* court makes a parallel observation:

Even though the [defendant entities] may quarrel among themselves on how to divide the spoils of their economic power, it cannot reasonably be said that they are *independent* sources of that power. Their power depends, and has always depended, on the cooperation among themselves. They are interdependent, not independent. The disagreements we have described are more like those among the board members of a single enterprise, than those among enterprises which are themselves separate and independent. (p. 276, original emphasis)

prospect of conflict leads inexorably to the governance question that John R. Commons had posed: can the parties craft a governance structure that allows them to manage or even neutralize conflict and, in turn, to realize mutual gain that conflict had jeopardized?[27]

Second, even members of cartels may perceive both the prospect of mutual gain and conflict. Indeed, as the court in *Los Angeles Memorial Coliseum Commission v. National Football League* 726 F.2d 1381 (9th Circuit 1984) observed at 1389, "[A] commonality of interest exists in every cartel". Thus, we stumble upon John R. Commons's governance question again. Even cartel members may choose to design a governance structure that allows them to remedy conflict so that they may achieve mutual gains.

The third problem with the appeal to unity of interest is that the case law sometimes conflates it with tests pertaining to "actual or potential competition". (See, for example, *Mt. Pleasant* at 276.) The upshot is that unity of interest tests are a distraction from the real action. I now turn to that action.

A TWO-STAGE SEQUENCE OF SINGLE-ENTITY TESTS

The case law offers a sequence of two tests. The first test creates the safe harbor and the second amounts to the truncated rule-of-reason analysis. Courts have appealed to the second test when candidate single entities have failed the first test.

The sequence of tests implies a process mapped out in Figure 2.1. Corporate entities may find their relationships subject to antitrust scrutiny. These entities may forgo an option to appeal to single-entity status, in

---

[27]   This is an old, robust and important idea in economics. Oliver Williamson has paraphrased John R. Commons many times on this count:

Commons . . . recognized that economic organization is not merely a response to technological features – economies of scale; economies of scope; other physical and technical aspects – but often has the purpose of harmonizing relations between parties who are otherwise in actual or potential conflict (Commons 1934, p. 6). The proposition that economic organization has the purpose of promoting the continuity of relationships by devising specialized governance structures, rather than permitting relationships to fracture under the hammer of unassisted market contracting, was thus an insight that could have been gleaned from Commons. (Williamson 1985, p. 3; and see Commons (1934 [1989])

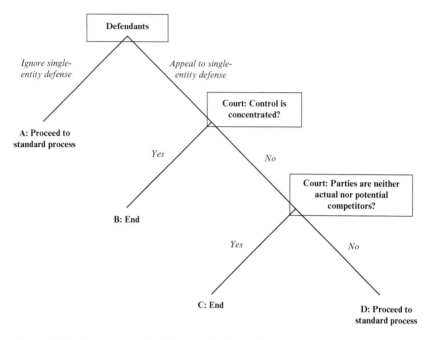

Figure 2.1   Process implied by the single-entity concept

which case court-ordered process will unfold in a standard manner. (The result corresponds to node A in Figure 2.1.) Alternatively, the entities may appeal to single-entity status and thereby force the court to evaluate it. The evaluation may "End" and relieve the parties of further scrutiny in either of two ways. (See nodes B and C in Figure 2.1.) Either the court accepts the proposition that "Control is concentrated" within the candidate single entity, or the court accepts that the parties to the candidate single entity are neither "actual nor potential competitors". Were the court to reject both propositions, court-ordering reverts to standard process (node D in Figure 2.1). I now elaborate.

Test 1: The Economic Unity Test

The first test, an economic unity test, inquires whether or not parties are already effectively integrated within a single entity.[28] It is a test of how concentrated control rights are. Evidence that control rights are frag-

---

[28]   *Copperweld* 467 U.S. 752 at 770, *Freeman* 322 F.3d 1133 at 1148, *Jack*

mented and distributed across constituent entities frustrates the appeal to single-entity status.

Both economics and the single-entity case law recognize affirmative control rights (rights to redeploy assets or impose initiatives) and negative control rights (rights to block other parties' proposed initiatives). Affirmative rights include the right to delegate managerial functions as well as the right to take those functions back. Negative rights include veto provisions or, the same thing, approval rights. First consider delegation. A single party within a single entity may not actively manage mechanical affairs such as setting prices but may delegate management functions to other parties. These other parties may in turn delegate functions to other units. In the prototypical corporate hierarchy, the pattern of delegation will trace out a hierarchical tree. That tree will have three features: (1) parties higher up the hierarchy may delegate functions to parties lower on the hierarchy; (2) parties lower down will not delegate functions to parties higher up; and (3) parties will reserve the right to take back management functions that they had delegated to others, which may amount to dissolving those parties further down the hierarchy. In contrast, we can distinguish less-integrated agglomerations of (possibly distinct) entities by distinguishing patterns of delegation that deviate from a hierarchical tree structure. Specifically, distinct entities may delegate no functions to each other. (They may be entirely independent.) Alternatively, two distinct entities may delegate functions to each other and may each reserve the right to recover those functions.

Now consider approval rights. Approval rights are more fundamental than affirmative rights, because affirmative rights can be characterized as the absence of other parties' approval rights.[29] While that may sound like little more than a pedantic observation, the observation illuminates some structure in the case law that an exclusive focus on the traditional hierarchy would miss. There are a few suggestions in the case law that we can make some progress characterizing the degree to which control is concentrated within the candidate single entity by identifying approval rights. For example, in *HealthAmerica Pennsylvania Inc. v. Susquehanna Health System* 278 F.Supp.2d 423 (2003) the court observed that hospitals and other entities that were parties to a formal "alliance agreement" could

---

Russell Terrier Network of Northern California v. American Kennel Club, Inc. 407 F.3d 1027 (US Circuit 2007) at 1034.

[29] Any party can propose an initiative. The ability to affirmatively impose an initiative derives from the absence of other parties' approval rights.

not redeploy assets without securing approvals from the board of directors of the alliance.[30] The court relied on these approval rights when, quoting *Copperweld*, it went on to conclude that "substantial authority is centralized in the Alliance and it is readily apparent that defendants' actions are guided 'not by two separate corporate consciousnesses, but one'" (p. 435). The court ultimately concluded that control was concentrated and that the structure governing the hospital alliance constituted a single entity. In *Chicago Professional Sports* Judge Easterbrook suggested that the absence of certain approval rights could frustrate an appeal to single-entity status. Judge Easterbrook focused on one of the most fundamental redeployment decisions: exit from a governance structure. He suggested that the ability of parties to exit a governance structure without having to secure approvals indicated an important way in which control would be fragmented.[31]

Examining approval rights suggests a conceptually simple, if not immediately operational, algorithm for identifying independent centers of decision-making within a candidate single entity: For any given proposal that a party might make, identify the cluster of parties that maintains

---

[30]   *HealthAmerica*, p. 428:

An Affiliate must seek approval of Susquehanna Alliance before it acquires, purchases, sells, leases or otherwise transfers any property. No Affiliate may incur any capital indebtedness unless expressly authorized by the Alliance. Absent express authorization, [the constituent parties] NCPHS and PHS may not merge, consolidate, reorganize or enter into any joint venture, management or alliance agreement that would affect autonomy or governance with any entity not a party to the Alliance Agreement. Under the Alliance Agreement, no party may terminate any program or service or initiate any program or service without the prior approval of the Chief Executive Officer or the Board of Directors of Susquehanna Alliance.

[31]   *Chicago Professional Sports*, p. 599, original emphasis:

Whether the [National Basketball Association, NBA] itself is more like a single firm, which would be analyzed only under § 2 of the Sherman Act, or like a joint venture, which would be subject to the Rule of Reason under § 1, is a tough question under *Copperweld*. [The NBA] has characteristics of both. Unlike the colleges and universities that belong to the National Collegiate Athletic Association [NCAA], which the Supreme Court treated as a joint venture in *NCAA*, the NBA has no existence independent of sports. It makes professional basketball; only it can make "NBA Basketball" games; and unlike the NCAA the NBA also "makes" teams. After this case was last here the NBA created new teams in Toronto and Vancouver, stocked with players from the 27 existing teams plus an extra helping of draft choices. All of this makes the league look like a single firm. Yet the 29 clubs [in the NBA], unlike GM's plants, have the right to secede (wouldn't a plant manager relish that!), and rearrange into two or three leagues.

approval rights. (Note that the cluster will always include at least one party, which could be the proposing party itself.) Proceed to identify a cluster for each and every proposal that any party might make. (Any party can even include parties outside of the candidate single entity, because any randomly selected person on the street can propose an action.) The process allows us to identify the universe of clusters. Second, look for clusters of clusters by examining the extent to which clusters overlap or are mutually exclusive. A finding that there exist mutually exclusive clusters of clusters within the candidate single entity suggests that the governance structure features more than one distinct center of decision-making. That, in turn, frustrates the appeal to single-entity status.

We can easily imagine how the business of looking for "clusters of clusters" could get out of hand, and it is not obvious that either the *HealthAmerica* court or the court in *Chicago Professional Sports* explicitly contemplated such a thorough-going examination of approval rights, but the proposition here is that the reasoning both courts advanced is consistent with it – but to a limit. I indicate two limits on the operational significance of appealing to the logic of approval rights:

1. We can operationalize a test of economic unity by limiting analysis to proposals for the wholesale redeployment of assets. Note that the courts did not obsess over each and every proposal that any party might make. "Each and every" spans an infinite, uncountable continuum of possible proposals. One party might, for example, propose expanding production capacity by a marginal amount, but that just leaves open the prospect of expanding capacity by a marginal amount over the marginal amount. The possibilities are infinite. Note, however, that the courts focused on a certain class of discrete proposals – specifically, proposals for the wholesale redeployment of assets by means such as exit, acquisition, merger, sale, purchase, lease or transfer. The focus on redeployment is consistent with a focus on efficient adaptation as the motivation for allocating control rights, including approval rights, in the first place.
2. Even if we ignore certain types of candidate proposals, we still have to decide what types of proposal constitute the most important action. A proposal to spin-off a subsidiary might be important, but what of lesser proposals? A court might give up on the control question and even dispense entirely with the single-entity question, as in *Chicago Professional Sports*.

Both pre- and post-*Copperweld* case law feature examples of single-entity defenses that explicitly failed or satisfied some version of economic unity tests. Single-entity defenses failed such tests in *Freeman* (2003),

New York v. Saint Francis Hospital, Vassar Brothers Hospital and Mid-Hudson Health 94 F.Supp.2d 399 (2000), *Robert M. Bogan v. Northwestern Mutual Life Insurance Company* 953 F.Supp. 532 (1997), *Malcolm Weiss v. York Hospital* 745 F.2d 786 (3rd Circuit 1984) and *National Society of Professional Engineers v. United States* 435 U.S. 679 (1978). The court accepted a single-entity defense on the basis of economic unity in *HealthAmerica* (2003), and *Seagram and Sons v. Hawaiian Oke* (1969) at 83.

Accepting a single-entity defense on the basis of economic unity allows the court to stop analysis of the single-entity issue rather than proceed to other tests, but observe what is and is not going on. Economic unity says nothing about the welfare-enhancing, efficiency-generating features of such agglomerations. Instead, the test provides a safe harbor against the courts marching in and abrogating established control rights. Even so, the law does not restrict single-entity status to agglomerations exhibiting purely top-down, hierarchical control, but it may extend single-entity status to agglomerations that feature less but enough economic unity.

Test 2: The Actual or Potential Competitors Test

The law does not indicate a fine line between enough and not enough economic unity, but "[s]ome decisions have found a single entity even in the absence of economic unity" (*Freeman* at 1148). The law may appeal to a second test in instances in which the degree of economic unity remains in question. Consider, for example, how the law might view a patent licensing agreement. A patent holder and a licensee might each reserve certain control rights, thus deviating from a strict model of top-down, hierarchical control. They might even be members of distinct corporate families. Even so, the law might accept the relationship between the patent holder and licensee as a single entity for the purpose of analyzing competition in certain markets.[32]

There are many ways a licensing agreement may fail a strict economic unity test. A patent holder could not, for example, bar a licensee from liquidating its own assets. A patent license might include important exit provisions that might go some way toward channeling the disposition of parties' assets in the event of liquidation, but it is not obvious that one party could compel the other to remain in business. Even so, for the

---

[32] "Certain markets" is an important qualification. The law might extend single-entity status to parties collaborating in the production of goods or services sold in one market but might deny single-entity status to the same parties were they actual or potential competitors in another market.

purpose of commercializing a patent, a patent holder and licensee might institute a governance structure that features a great deal of economic unity. Specifically, a patent holder might delegate to a licensee all types of functions, which only the patent holder would be in a position to delegate.

Control rights in the patent-licensing example may not be entirely concentrated, but both pre- and post-*Copperweld* single-entity case law make allowances for extending single-entity status to some hybrid arrangements. It does this by extending the analysis to a truncated rule-of-reason analysis. It inquires whether or not parties to the candidate single entity constitute actual or potential competitors. Note that the concept of "actual or potential competition" implies competition in at least one antitrust-cognizable market. For the most part, the case law seems to be occupied with actual or potential competition in the market or markets in which candidate single entity itself competes. By this interpretation, the point of the actual or potential competitors test is to distinguish whether or not the parties to the candidate single entity join, only join, and are only equipped to join, complementary assets, capabilities or other complementary inputs.[33] The alternative is that the parties constitute actual or potential competitors in a certain market, in which case it becomes much less obvious that the candidate single entity is anything but a sham institution.

The *Freeman* court does not use the language of complementarity, but it provides the best statement on this count and picks up on the governance question. The court observed (*Freeman* at 1148–9):

> [I]n the absence of economic unity, the fact that firms are not actual competitors is also usually not enough, by itself, to render them a single entity. Absence of actual competition may simply be a manifestation of the anticompetitive agreement itself, as where firms conspire to divide the market. See *Maricopa County Med. Soc'y*, 457 U.S. at 344 n. 15, 102 S.Ct. 2466 (division of markets is per se illegal). Cases have required instead that the constituent entities be neither actual nor potential competitors, *City of Mt. Pleasant*, 838 F.2d at 276, cf. *Williams*, 794 F.Supp. at 1031.

The appeal to complementarity has enabled courts to fill in one potential pitfall. A court might observe that parties are not "actual competitors", and it would be tempting to then accept a single-entity defense. A problem is that parties could constitute a cartel of "potential competitors". The potential for competition sets up the prospect of conflict, and that motivates a role for the governance of the cartel: to neutralize the prospect

---

[33]   See, for example, *Arizona v. Maricopa County Medical Society* 457 U.S. 332 (1982) at 355–6, the various sports league rulings, and others.

of cartel members actually competing with each other. Thus, absence of actual competition may merely mask the reality of competition that would obtain but for the horizontal restraints instituted in the governance of the cartel. A way to distinguish whether or not parties are potential competitors is to distinguish whether or not they contribute, and only contribute, complementary inputs.

Some of the case law appears to go further than trying to ascertain whether or not parties to a candidate single entity only contribute complementary inputs to some type of joint enterprise. The case law suggests that it is interested in sorting out whether or not "defendants are, or *have been*, actual or potential competitors".[34] Building directly on *Copperweld*, the court in *Mt. Pleasant* opined that "the [plaintiff] must show facts that could lead a reasonable juror to find the coordination between any two defendants to be a 'joining of two independent sources of economic power previously pursuing separate interests'" (p. 276). The *Copperweld* pronouncement that *Mt. Pleasant* and other opinions rely on is ambiguous, however, in that it does not obviously limit the evaluation of "independent sources" and "separate interests" to a particular market. Should jurors limit inquiry to the joining of two independent sources of economic power previously pursuing separate interests in the markets in which the candidate single entity competes, or should jurors extend inquiry to the joining of independent sources of economic power in any market?

The answer provided by most of the single-entity case law involving sports leagues is that defendant entities might secure single-entity status when evaluating competition in one market while failing to secure single-entity status when evaluating competition in another market. For the most part, the sports leagues case law recognizes that one requires more than one team to produce "games" – that is, teams are complements in the production of games.[35] However, teams compete outside the sports arena in labor markets for players and coaches. They are actual or potential competitors in labor markets.[36]

---

[34]   *Mt. Pleasant* at 276, emphasis added.

[35]   The court in *Chicago Professional Sports* actually goes further when it suggests that "the [National Basketball Association] has no existence independent of sports. It makes professional basketball; only it can make 'NBA Basketball' games; and unlike the NCAA the NBA also 'makes' teams" (p. 599). The court is suggesting not merely that one needs more than one team to produce games but that the league itself contributes an input, the NBA brand, to the production of league-branded games.

[36]   In *LA Memorial Coliseum* (1984), the court observed that "the [National Football League] clubs do compete with one another off the field as well as on to acquire players, coaches, and management personnel" (p. 1390). See also *John*

Courts have appealed to complementarity to extend single-entity status to hybrid arrangements such as franchising (*Don Williams v. I.B. Fischer Nevada* 999 F.2d 445 [9th Circuit 1993]), patent licenses (*Levi Case Company, Inc. v. ATS Products, Inc.* 788 F.Supp. 428 [1992]), exclusive contracts (*Calculators Hawaii Inc. v. Brandt Inc.* 724 F.2d 1332 [9th Circuit 1983]; *Superior Models v. Tolkien Enterprises* 1981 WL 40556, 211 U.S.P.Q. 876 [1981]; *Discon Inc. v. NYNEX Corp.* 93 F.3d 1055 [2nd Circuit 1996]), certification authorities (*Jack Russell* 407 F.3d 1027), and networks (*Mt. Pleasant* 838 F.2d 268, *Broadcast Music Inc. v. Columbia Broadcasting System, Inc.* 441 U.S. 1 [1979]). As Lehn and Sykuta (1997) observe, courts have also extended single-entity status on the basis of complementarity in the production of "games" to the National Hockey League (*San Francisco Seals, Ltd. v. National Hockey League* 379 F.Supp. 966 [1974]) but not uniformly to the other leagues, including the National Football League (NFL).[37] In each case parties contributed complementary inputs, although courts were not always explicit about this. In franchising, for example, a franchiser contributes a valuable asset, the brand name. Franchisees contribute labor and other complementary inputs.

Single-entity defenses have failed some version of an actual or potential competitors test in *Rothery Storage & Van Co. v. Atlas Van Lines, Inc.* 792 F.2d 210 (DC Circuit 1986), *Maricopa County* 457 U.S. 332 (medical associations), *Professional Engineers* 435 U.S. 679 (another professional association), and *Citizen Publishing Company v. United States* 394 U.S. 131 (1969) (a joint operating agreement). In *Freeman*, the court had already denied certain governance structures (realtor associations) single-entity status on the basis of a lack of economic unity, but the court proceeded to note that the parties to the candidate single entities were also actual or potential competitors. In *Chicago Professional Sports*, the court observed that the candidate single entity, the NBA maintained attributes of both a single entity and a joint venture. It declined, however, to impose single-entity status for the purpose of analyzing a particular business

---

Mackey v. National Football League 543 F.2d 606 (8th Circuit 1976) or *James McCoy Smith v. Pro Football Inc.* 593 F.2d 1173 (DC Circuit 1979).

[37] The most illuminating example is the experience the NFL had with Al Davis's effort to move the Oakland Raiders to Los Angeles in 1984. In *Los Angeles Memorial Coliseum Commission v. National Football League* (9th Circuit 1984), the court observed that:

It is true that cooperation is necessary to produce a football game. However, as the district court concluded, this does not mean, "that each club can produce football games only as an NFL member." 519 F.Supp. at 584. This is especially evident in light of the emergence of the United States Football League. (p. 1390)

practice of the NBA but rather suggested that the process should move to a rule-of-reason analysis.

CONCLUSION

Like any legal concept, the single-entity concept implies process, and, as with any *per se* concept, it intendedly implies a process of self-enforcement, a process by which prospective plaintiffs never find reason to resort to court ordering, and by which prospective defendant entities never provoke court ordering. Yet, the existence of a corpus of single-entity case law demonstrates the unavoidable reality that there remains some noise in the process.

We might expect noise in the case law to dissipate with time as courts develop experience with different types of governance structures. At first sight, the incidence of single-entity matters suggests little in the way of dissipation, yet, even a casual survey will suggest some degree of convergence in the application of the single-entity concept to specific industries. In the 1970s, for example, the efforts of professional athletes to improve their bargaining position with teams by appealing to free agency and other means induced a wave of litigation involving sports leagues. In the 1980s litigation involving healthcare started to emerge. Since 2000 that litigation has extended to hospital networks. Further examination of the case law will also reveal some global convergence of the single-entity concept.

The main proposition of this chapter is that, if we take a global view of the single-entity case law in antitrust, we can distinguish a few robust ideas in it about what constitutes a single entity. Specifically, we may observe something that looks a lot like Figure 2.1. Figure 2.1 is a roadmap through the tangle of single-entity tests that have been proposed in the case law. The case law may feature an array of single-entity tests, but one can subsume many of these tests in a two-stage sequence of tests. The first stage, labeled here a test of economic unity, inquires whether or not ownership, the control rights ownership implies, and remaining control rights (if any) are concentrated within the candidate single entity. Evidence that control rights are concentrated might allow a court to stop analysis and accept a single-entity defense. In contrast, evidence that control rights are fragmented and are distributed across the parties that constitute the candidate single entity complicates appeals to the single-entity defense. When analyzing governance structures that fail a strict test of economic unity, the law might proceed to a second-stage actual or potential competitors test. The test amounts to a test of complementarity in that it sorts out whether or not the parties that comprise the candidate single entity contribute complementary assets, complementary capabilities or other complementary inputs. Applying the test amounts to a truncated rule-of-reason analysis that starts with the question of whether or not restraints instituted within the governance of the candidate single entity are horizontal or vertical. A finding that restraints are horizontal is tantamount to a finding that parties are not contributing complementary inputs and that the parties are actual or potential competitors. Such a finding frustrates the appeal to the single-entity defense.

The chapter features three other sets of observations. First, we can borrow the concepts of adaptation and control rights from the theory of the firm to begin to operationalize tests of economic unity. The concepts provide an economic rationale for understanding the role of delegation in organizations, and delegation constitutes a way in the case law to characterize how ownership and control are related. Second, the economics provides a rationale for dismissing single-entity tests proposed in the case law that depend on a unity of interests. Some courts have appealed to a unity of interests to suggest that single entities constitute conflict-free enterprises. In contrast, the theory of the firm and other case law are consistent with the proposition that, but for conflict, we would not need to design structures to govern exchange between parties who either constitute a single entity or themselves constitute distinct entities. Short and simply: conflict alone does not inform the single-entity inquiry. Finally, neither economics nor the case law are equipped to definitively dispatch all demands for single-entity inquiries. Courts continue to find themselves obligated to entertain single-entity defenses, and, as in *Chicago Professional Sports*, they sometimes find that they cannot use the single-entity concept to finesse the more traditional process with which they would have otherwise started.

3. Platform competition, the Apple eBooks case and the meaning of agreement to fix prices*

In *United States v. Apple Inc.*, 952 F.Supp.2d 638 (S.D.N.Y. 2013)[1] the district court found that, in early 2010, Apple had "played a central role in facilitating" a conspiracy between five of the "Big Six" publishers "to eliminate retail price competition in order to raise e-book prices".[2] Raising prices involved getting a specific eBook distributor, Amazon, to give up its policy of pricing the eBooks of "New Releases" and "New York Times Bestsellers" at $9.99.[3] Apple had not been in the business of selling eBooks, but it was working up to the April 2010 launch of the iPad, a new platform for selling digital content and services. Apple hoped to complement the launch of the new platform with the launch of new content, and with Amazon having demonstrated that eBooks could be commercialized,[4] why not launch an iBookstore?

The story is that Apple and the Big Six publishers came to commonly

---

*   The views expressed are not purported to reflect those of the U.S. Department of Justice.

[1]   Hereafter, Opinion.

[2]   Opinion, p. 647.

[3]   "Before Apple even met with the first Publisher Defendant in mid-December 2009, it knew that the 'Big Six' of United States publishing . . . wanted to raise e-book prices, in particular above the $9.99 prevailing price charged by Amazon for many ebook versions of *New York Times* bestselling books ('NYT Bestsellers') and other newly released hardcover book ('New Releases')" (Opinion, p. 647).

[4]   "Amazon's Kindle was the first e-reader to gain widespread commercial acceptance. When the Kindle was launched in 2007, Amazon quickly became the market leader in the sale of e-books and e-book readers. Through 2009, Amazon dominated the e-book market, selling nearly 90% of all e-books" (Opinion, pp. 648–9). The declaration of Amazon executive Russ Grandinetti is apposite: "We knew that now that we had established a successful and growing ebooks business, more competition would be coming, and quickly. We didn't know from where, but when something gets that kind of customer excitement and enthusiastic adoption, competitors are sure to follow" (Declaration of Amazon executive Russell C. Grandinetti, paragraph 15, Plaintiff Exhibit [hereafter PX] 0835).

understand that, by committing to participate in the launch of the iBookstore, the publishers would invest each of themselves with more "leverage" (bargaining power) vis-à-vis Amazon.[5] This extra bargaining power might then enable each of them, in what were ostensibly independent, one-on-one negotiations, to force Amazon to give up its $9.99 pricing policy.[6] Five of the Big Six publishers did contract with Apple, and each of those five publishers did manage to get Amazon to give up its $9.99 pricing, although they achieved the result in a roundabout way. Specifically, each publisher induced Amazon to accept the terms of a so-called "agency" contract.[7] The publisher would assume authority to set the retail price for each of its eBooks, and Amazon would be relegated to the role of distribution agent by which it would receive a 30 percent commission for each eBook sold through its Kindle platform. Almost a year later, the sixth and

---

[5]   "With a full appreciation of each other's interests, Apple and the Publisher Defendants agreed to work together to eliminate retail price competition in the e-book market and raise the price of e-books above $9.99" (Opinion, pp. 647–8). "[T]he Publishers were searching for an alternative to Amazon's pricing policies and excited about Apple's entry into the e-book industry and the prospect that that entry would give them leverage in their negotiations with Amazon. Apple appreciated that, in the words of Macmillan's Sargent, the Publishers viewed Apple as 'offer[ing] the single best opportunity [they] would ever have to correct the imbalance in our e-book market'" (Opinion, p. 659). More pointedly:

> Publisher Defendants considered a number of coordinated methods to force Amazon to raise e-book retail prices . . . It was Apple's entry into the e-book business, however, that provided a perfect opportunity collectively to raise e-book prices. In December 2009, Apple approached each Publisher Defendant with news that it intended to sell e-books through its new iBookstore in conjunction with its forthcoming iPad device. Publisher Defendants and Apple soon recognized that they could work together to counter the Amazon-led $9.99 price. (See the Proposed Final Judgment and Competitive Impact Statement with respect to the publishers Hachette, HarperCollins and Simon & Schuster posted on the Federal Register, *77 FR 24518*, April 24, 2012, pp. 24528–9, accessed July 2, 2018 at https://www.gpo.gov/fdsys/pkg/FR-2012-04-24/pdf/2012-9831.pdf)

[6]   The court understood that the publishers' bargaining power obtained from threats by the publishers to withhold eBook content from Amazon. "Amazon customers would cease to have access to many of the most popular e-books, which would hurt Kindle customers and the attractiveness of the Kindle" (Opinion, p. 680).

[7]   "By the end of March 2010, Amazon had completed agency agreements with Macmillan, HarperCollins, Hachette, and S & S. Because of circumstances that were unique to Penguin and its reseller contract, its agency agreement with Amazon was the last to be executed. Penguin signed its agency contract with Amazon on June 2, 2010, but before that date, Penguin had refused to allow Amazon to sell any of Penguin's new e-books" (Opinion, p. 682).

last of the Big Six publishers joined the iBookstore and secured an agency contract with Amazon.

The main proposition of this chapter is that the negotiations between publishers and Amazon were independent in that Amazon would have been unwilling to rebuff any single publisher's demand to move to agency; contracting with Apple invested each publisher with bargaining power that was sufficient to induce Amazon to accept agency. In contrast, the court understood that contracting with Apple was a necessary but insufficient condition for getting Amazon to acquiesce to agency; there had to be more to the conspiracy than merely contracting with Apple. Specifically, the court understood that Amazon perceived it was facing a "united front" of publishers.[8] It further understood that Amazon would have been situated to rebuff demands to move to agency but for the fact that publishers had arrayed themselves in a united front.[9] Amazon argued that, had it been afforded the option of staggering its negotiations with publishers over time, it could have frustrated attempts to assemble a united front and it could then have rebuffed any demands to move to agency.

The main question of the chapter is, were the gambit of contracting to participate in the iBookstore sufficient for inducing Amazon to accept agency, would it nonetheless have been insufficient for establishing a conspiracy? That is, if contract negotiations between publishers and Amazon were independent, then what basis was there for establishing an antitrust-cognizable conspiracy? The main observation of the chapter is that it is not obvious what conduct the court's opinion proscribed. Specifically, it is not obvious that the court's opinion would proscribe the publishers' iBookstore gambit *per se*. The court did motivate how contracting with Apple had invested individual publishers with more bargaining power vis-à-vis Amazon. Among other things, it pointedly explained how a specific provision in the Apple contracts, a most-favored nations clause pertaining to eBook pricing, had made it incumbent upon each, individual publisher to induce Amazon to move to agency.[10] It is not obvious, then, that publish-

---

[8]   "It was clear to Amazon that it was facing a united front" (Opinion, p. 673).

[9]   "Amazon knew that its battle was not just with Macmillan but with five of the Big Six. As [Amazon executive] Grandinetti testified, '[i]f it had been only Macmillan demanding agency, we would not have negotiated an agency contract with them. But having heard the same demand for agency terms coming from all the publishers in such close proximity . . . we really had no choice but to negotiate the best agency contracts we could with these five publishers'" (Opinion, 680).

[10]   "Apple fully understood and intended that the MFN would lead the Publisher Defendants inexorably to demand that Amazon switch to an agency relationship with each of them" (Opinion, p. 692). See, also, the Opinion (pp. 662–3) on "The creation of the MFN clause"; most notably, "as a practical matter,

ers had to organize a united front. It is not even obvious what constituted the united front except the fact that four of the Big Six publishers apprised Amazon of their demands to move to agency within the space of a week.[11] The opinion seems to imply that the gambit might have survived antitrust scrutiny had publishers' demands been staggered over time.

In the next section of the chapter I retrace the evolution of the conspiracy between Apple and the publishers. I then elaborate on the I-know-it-when-I-see-it quality of the opinion. It stems not merely from the problem of inferring agreement – a problem that has been the subject, and remains the subject, of much development in the antitrust case law – but from the problem of inferring agreement to fix prices. The opinion offers an incomplete account of how price fixing actually worked. Also, it offers an incomplete account, because the court does not recognize that "[I]ncentives to cheat are present even in the most homogeneous of cartels" (Hovenkamp 2005, p. 149). Specifically, the opinion is silent on what William Baxter (1977, p. 612) would recognize as the "prisoners' dilemma" problem: the prospect that erstwhile conspirators might cheat on an agreement to fix prices by posting lower-than-agreed-upon prices. Anticipating such cheating, conspirators might agree to set up informal mechanisms for detecting and punishing the posting of low prices all in an effort to discourage parties from cheating in the first place. In contrast – and this is the main point – the absence of such mechanisms suggests that parties did not require an agreement to fix prices. Observed prices may have obtained from non-conspiratorial conduct.

I then take up the court's notion of a united front. It amounts to several negotiations between Amazon and publishers having overlapped with each other. The court understood that Amazon could have rebuffed the demands of any one publisher were negotiations staggered over time but could not resist the demands of publishers clustered "in such close proximity".[12] I then sketch several episodes in which Amazon did acquiesce to agency in isolated contract negotiations. These episodes suggest that either Amazon had, at some point, operated under the illusion that it

---

[the MFN] forc[ed] the publishers to adopt agency across the board" with all eBook retailers.

[11] Opinion, p. 673.

[12] Again, see the Opinion, p. 681 citing Amazon executive Russ Grandinetti. The court also observed that, while Amazon may have acquiesced to agency contracts with the five publishers, "it [had] insisted that each of the five agency agreements have a different termination date" so that Amazon could "avoid being vulnerable in the future to collective pressure during contract negotiations" (Opinion, p. 681).

could have rebuffed publishers in individual negotiations, or Amazon mis-represented its capacity to negotiate with individual publishers knowing full well that it could not have resisted the demands of any one publisher to move to agency.

I close by noting that agency contracting has become dominant. The court did impose restrictions on the types of contracts publishers could con-summate with eBook distributors. The duration of these restrictions varied by publisher, the idea being that varying the duration would amount to staggering the renegotiation of contracts between publishers and Amazon. Amazon would thus only find itself facing a single publisher in a given con-tract renegotiation. That, in turn, would frustrate publishers from assem-bling another united front. However, after those restrictions timed out, publishers again extracted agency contracts from Amazon, one by one, in independent contract negotiations. So it was that the entire case ultimately proved to be no more than a tale, full of sound and fury, signifying nothing.

THE CONSPIRACY

Amazon launched the Kindle platform in 2007, and it wanted readers to know that they could expect to buy the eBook versions of New Releases or New York Times Bestsellers for $9.99.[13] That $9.99 price on any given eBook would not last forever, but a consumer just looking to stuff his or her Kindle-compatible device with new content would know that, at any given time, a portfolio of new or bestselling books priced at $9.99 would be available.

That changed in 2010. The Big Six publishers had been unhappy with Amazon's $9.99 pricing.[14] These were the same publishers that had been best situated to launch books into Bestseller orbit. Between April and June 2010, five of the Big Six publishers induced Amazon to accept new terms of so-called agency contracts.[15] Each publisher would assume authority to

---

[13]   Again, the testimony of Amazon executive Russ Grandinetti is apposite:

From the beginning, publishers complained about our pricing. They repeat-edly complained about our $9.99 pricing for *New York Times* bestsellers and other new releases . . . [B]uilding and maintaining customer trust is critical to Amazon's long term success, and we had made a commitment to customers from the earliest days of the Kindle that most bestsellers would be priced at $9.99. (PX-0835, paras 27–8)

[14]   See section B of the Background of the Opinion, pp. 649–50.
[15]   "[I]n less than two months, Apple had signed agency contracts with five of the six Publishers, and those Publisher Defendants had agreed with each other

set the retail price for each of its eBooks, and Amazon would be relegated to the role of distribution agent by which it would receive a 30 percent commission for each eBook sold through the Kindle platform.[16] In the following January, the sixth and largest of the Big Six publishers, Random House, also secured an agency contract with Amazon.[17] Thus, having ceded retail pricing authority to the publishers, Amazon was no longer able to support its informal commitment to consumers that Bestsellers and new books would be available at $9.99.[18]

Each publisher immediately raised prices from $9.99 to $12.99 or $14.99 on nearly all of its Bestsellers after converting Amazon and other eBook distributors to agency.[19] However, even a few months before the first of Amazon's contracts with publishers converted to agency, Amazon had complained to the Federal Trade Commission.[20] Amazon complained that it had "become increasingly concerned with the parallel steps taken by the major U.S. book publishers". "Parallel steps" implied a conspiracy between publishers – a conspiracy which, Amazon suggested, was "designed to increase the price at which electronic books ('e-books') are sold to consumers".[21]

Before April 2010, Apple had not been in the business of selling eBooks, but the court understood that Apple had facilitated the efforts of five of the publishers to secure agency contracts from Amazon. As the chief executive of Big Six publisher Simon & Schuster observed, Apple's involvement was important in that it had a role in "herding us cats" (the publishers).[22]

Apple had already been working up to the launch of the iPad platform long before it had any interactions with publishers. It was natural, however, for Apple to complement the launch of the iPad with the launch

---

and Apple to solve the 'Amazon issue' and eliminate retail price competition for ebooks. The Publisher Defendants would move as one, first to force Amazon to relinquish control of pricing, and then, when the iBookstore went live, to raise the retail prices for e-book versions of New Releases and NYT Bestsellers to the caps set by Apple" (Opinion, pp. 677–8).

[16] See section N of the Opinion's Background on "The five Amazon agency agreements" (Opinion, pp. 681–2).

[17] "Random House adopted the agency model in early 2011, and promptly raised the prices of its e-books" (Opinion, p. 685). The court understood that Random House succumbed to pressure from Apple to join the iBookstore and shift to agency (Opinion, p. 686).

[18] Again, see PX-0835, paras 27–8.

[19] New Releases were also subject to price increases.

[20] Opinion, p. 681.

[21] Defendant Exhibit (hereafter DX) 282.

[22] Opinion, pp. 678, 693; PX-0782.

of new digital content. Apple had long been in the business of commercializing digital content – most notably digital music on its iTunes platform – but assembling more digital content for the iPad would make the new platform more attractive to users.[23] In late 2009 Apple started talking to publishers about launching an iBookstore for eBooks.

Apple went into individual discussions with publishers with the idea that it might commercialize eBooks much the same way that distributors had traditionally commercialized print books: publishers would establish list prices for new, hardcover books, and they would charge distributors wholesale prices corresponding to roughly half of the list prices.[24] Yet, by the time Apple got around to talking with publishers, the agency meme had already been floating around. The story is that Barnes & Noble had already discussed the idea with some publishers with respect to the impending launch in December 2009 of its own Nook eBook platform.[25] The publisher Hachette subsequently posed the agency concept to Apple. The Apple brain trust let itself contemplate the agency concept over the course of a few days and then proceeded to elaborate on the concept and operationalize it.[26]

Under Apple's proposal, Apple would become a publisher's distribution agent, and it would secure a 30 percent commission on the sale of each eBook. Publishers would assume authority to set retail prices, but, being concerned that publishers might post retail prices that were "sky high",

---

[23]   "Even though the iPad Launch would happen with or without an iBookstore, Apple did hope to announce its new iBookstore at the Launch. This would ensure maximum consumer exposure and provide a dramatic component of the Launch" (Opinion, p. 655). "Apple believed that the iPad would be a transformational e-reader. In contrast to the black-and-white e-reader devices on the market at the time, the iPad would have the capacity to display not only ebook text but also e-book illustrations and photographs in color on a backlit screen. The iPad would also have audio and video capabilities and a touch screen, which Apple believed would be seen by readers as a particularly attractive feature" (Opinion, p. 655).

[24]   "Prior to meeting with the Publishers, Apple assumed that it would purchase e-books from them under the wholesale model and resell them, in line with the arrangement Apple used to obtain movies and TV shows for resale through its iTunes store" (Opinion, p. 656).

[25]   "Hachette and later HarperCollins surprised Apple with their suggestion that, instead of a wholesale model, Apple adopt an agency model for the distribution of ebooks. Hachette told Apple that it had already discussed switching to an agency model with Barnes & Noble and had concluded that it was an attractive business model for selling e-books. During these meetings, [Apple executive Eddy] Cue rejected the idea. Within days, however, he would reconsider their suggestion" (Opinion, p. 657).

[26]   Opinion, p. 659.

Apple proposed a tiered sequence of price caps.[27] Among other things, a publisher could not price a Bestseller in excess of either $12.99 or $14.99. EBooks listed higher than $30 would be capped at $14.99, and those listed at $30 or lower would be capped at $12.99.[28] Finally, Apple proposed a most-favored nations (MFN) clause by which a publisher would commit to posting a retail price in the iBookstore for a given eBook that would be no higher than the retail prices for that same eBook posted at the retail site of any other eBook distributor.[29]

Publishers objected to the price caps,[30] and they offered some resistance to the MFN on retail prices,[31] but Apple perceived that the MFN would make it incumbent upon publishers to turn around and convert other eBook distributors to agency.[32] More generally, Apple understood that imposing the MFN on publishers would enable Apple to effect what Steve Jobs recognized in his biography as an Aikido move:[33] at one stroke the publishers would achieve their principal objective (the end of Amazon's $9.99 pricing policy), Apple could guarantee itself positive gross margins of 30 percent, and Apple would not have to compete with Amazon or any other distributor on price.[34] It would be up to the publishers to compete on price between themselves.

Shifting all distributors to agency may have appeared like something of an over-engineered Rube Goldberg scheme for getting Amazon to give up its $9.99 pricing policy. Why not just impose higher wholesale prices on Amazon and offer other distributors lower prices? One reason is that publishers may have expected that discriminating between distributors would invite an episode of costly antitrust litigation similar to the episodes

---

[27]   "Apple realized . . . that in handing over pricing decisions to the Publishers, it needed to restrain their desire to raise e-book prices sky high. It decided to require retail prices to be restrained by pricing tiers with caps" (Opinion, p. 659).

[28]   See, for example, the Opinion, p. 667. The agency contracts with Apple subjected New Releases to a more elaborate menu of price caps.

[29]   Opinion, p. 666.

[30]   Opinion, p. 669.

[31]   Opinion, p. 666.

[32]   The MFN "literally stiffened the spines of the Publisher Defendants" in their negotiations with Amazon (Opinion, p. 666). Again, see the Opinion, pp. 662–3, 692.

[33]   Opinion, p. 687.

[34]   "In Jobs's own words: . . . [W]e told the publishers, 'We'll go to the agency model, where you set the price, and we get our 30%, and yes, the customer pays a little more, but that's what you want anyway.' But we also asked for a guarantee that if anybody else is selling the books cheaper than we are, then we can sell them at the lower price too. So they went to Amazon and said, 'You're going to sign an agency contract or we're not going to give you the books'" (Opinion, p. 687).

they experienced in the 1980s and through the 1990s with respect to the pricing of print books. Thompson (2010, p. 33) observed that, by the late 1990s, publishers made a point of establishing "a much clearer and more transparent system for discounting and co-op advertising" in order to avoid being drawn into any further litigation. Effectively, publishers may have committed to offering each distributor a *de facto* MFN on wholesale prices. Thompson goes on to suggest that publishers "developed an acute sensitivity to the risks in tampering" with their new MFN policy, a sensitivity that likely informed publishers' views about how to manage the wholesale pricing of eBooks.

Shifting Amazon's status from that of retailer to distribution agent would preclude antitrust concerns about discriminatory wholesale pricing and would, as a matter of course, resolve their basic problem with Amazon's $9.99 pricing policy. However, even before publishers contemplated the agency concept, they had experimented with raising their (non-discriminatory) wholesale prices.[35] Through late 2009 publishers raised prices with the hope that higher prices could induce Amazon to give up its $9.99 pricing. Amazon demonstrated a willingness to absorb losses on eBook sales in order to preserve its $9.99 policy[36] for it, too, was engaged in important platform competition. With Barnes & Noble poised to launch its own Nook platform and then with Apple contemplating the launch of an iBookstore and the launch of the iPad, a race was on to secure the relationship with the customer.[37]

A curious feature of the shift to agency is that it would force Amazon to give up taking losses on Bestsellers and New Releases. Amazon had effectively been subsidizing the publishers' sales, a point that Amazon executive Russ Grandinetti acknowledged, blithely noting that "having some titles as loss leaders is quite common in both book-selling and retailing generally".[38] A bigger puzzle, however, is that, even though retail prices post-agency would generally be higher, publishers would earn lower unit margins. Moreover, higher prices might be expected to yield lower sales volumes, leaving publishers with lower margins across their

---

[35]   Opinion, p. 650.

[36]   The publishers' "tactic" of raising wholesale prices, "failed to convince Amazon to change its pricing policies and it continued to sell many NYT Bestsellers as loss leaders at $9.99.9" (Opinion, p. 650).

[37]   This idea has made it into the economics literature. Beard and Stern (2008, p. 841) are instructive: consumers may "commit" to a particular platform provider when it "offers a sufficiently attractive vector of prices" spanning a broad range of products or services.

[38]   Declaration of Amazon executive Russell C. Grandinetti, para. 25, PX-0835.

entire portfolios of eBooks.[39] Rival distributors might have been under pressure, but should publishers themselves not have been happy to allow Amazon to subsidize their eBook sales? Why was the $9.99 price point "too low"?[40]

The publishers may have perceived short-term advantages to allowing Amazon to maintain its $9.99 pricing (subsidized sales), but they also perceived long-term tradeoffs. Correctly or not, publishers perceived that readers would become accustomed to the idea that books were "worth only" $9.99.[41] Such a development could complicate book pricing in the future, and the $9.99 could "cannibalize" the sales of (potentially higher-margin) print books.[42] Publishers also expressed the concern that Amazon would not be satisfied to subsidize eBook sales indefinitely but would eventually press them for wholesale prices.[43]

Publishers' concerns may or may not have been well founded, but what is clear is that they perceived much uncertainty about the future of book publishing. Barnes & Noble would seem to have been situated to implement its own version of Apple's aikido move, but the publishers ended up anointing Apple as the leader of an effort to impose agency on Amazon.[44] With contracts with the five publishers coming in to place, it

---

[39] The court observed that the defendant publishers appeared to lose sales after shifting to agency whereas the publisher Random House managed to maintain sales volume during the time it remained on wholesale terms with Amazon. (See the Opinion, p. 685 and p. 684, n. 56.) More generally, the court understood that "the Publisher Defendants [had] all acted against their near-term financial interests" (Opinion, p. 693). And specifically the court observed that the chief executive officer (CEO) of the publisher HarperCollins "immediately recognized that '[t]he combination of Apple's proposed pricing tiers and the 30% commission meant that HarperCollins would make less money per book than it was then making on a wholesale model'" (Opinion, p. 667).

[40] Publishers complained of both the $9.99 price and the prices that Apple proposed being "too low". See, for example, the Opinion, pp. 660, 661, 662.

[41] Opinion, p. 652.

[42] Opinion, p. 652; See also Declaration of Macmillan CEO John Sargent (DX-701), para. 14; the Declaration of Hachette Book Group CEO David Young, paras 10–11 (DX-702); DX-047, p. 19433.

[43] Opinion, p. 649.

[44] Quoting Apple executive Eddy Cue, the court observed that "the Publishers had been 'ecstatic' about what Apple's arrival could mean for 'their industry'" (Opinion, p. 657). In a "lengthy response" to James Murdoch of HarperCollins parent NewsCorp, Steve Jobs argued that "If you [the publishers] stick with just Amazon, B[arnes] & N[oble], Sony, etc., you will likely be sitting on the sidelines of the mainstream ebook revolution . . . So far, there are only two companies who have demonstrated online stores with significant transaction volume – Apple and Amazon". Moreover, "We [Apple] will sell more of our new devices [iPads] than

became incumbent upon the publishers to impose contract negotiations on Amazon.[45]

Four of the five publishers had deals with Amazon that enabled them to impose contract renegotiation. Specifically, they each maintained the right to withdraw eBooks from Amazon's portfolio of Kindle eBooks.[46] They were thus situated in early 2010 to shift Amazon to agency in conjunction with the April 2010 launch of the Apple iBookstore. In contrast, the publisher Penguin had a contract with Amazon that obligated it to maintain content it had already contributed to the Kindle store for the duration of the contract. That contract would terminate in the beginning of June 2010, and Amazon was happy to extend contract negotiations with Penguin past the April 3 launch of the iPad and the iBookstore. It ultimately acquiesced to agency as the June termination date approached. Yet, during that two-month interval between the launch of iBookstore and Penguin's move to agency in the Kindle store, Penguin withheld new content from the Kindle store,[47] but once it engaged its new agency contract with Amazon, Penguin synchronized its offerings and prices in the Kindle store with those in the iBookstore.[48]

With the launch of the iBookstore on April 3, 2010, four of the five publishers raised nearly all the prices on the Bestsellers from $9.99 to the price caps of $12.99 and $14.99.[49] Apple maintained the $9.99 on the relevant Penguin books until Amazon's contract with Penguin also shifted to

---

all of the Kindles ever sold during the first few weeks they are on sale" (Opinion, p. 676).

[45]   "[I]n less than two months, Apple had signed agency contracts with five of the six Publishers, and those Publisher Defendants had agreed with each other and Apple to solve the 'Amazon issue' and eliminate retail price competition for e-books. The Publisher Defendants would move as one, first to force Amazon to relinquish control of pricing, and then, when the iBookstore went live, to raise the retail prices for e-book versions of New Releases and NYT Bestsellers to the caps set by Apple" (Opinion, pp. 677–8).

[46]   "In light of their overlapping threats to remove content from Amazon's platform if it did not move to agency in early April, when the iPad became available, Amazon moved quickly to execute agency agreements with the remaining Publisher Defendants [having already secured a contract with the publisher Macmillan]" (Opinion, p. 681).

[47]   "Penguin signed its agency contract with Amazon on June 2, 2010, but before that date, Penguin had refused to allow Amazon to sell any of Penguin's new e-books" (Opinion, p. 682).

[48]   Opinion, pp. 682–3.

[49]   See the discussion on Opinion, p. 682. Among other things, "Just as Apple expected, after the iBookstore opened in April 2010, the price caps in the Agreements became the new retail prices for the Publisher Defendants' ebooks".

agency.[50] Penguin subsequently raised prices. At the end of January 2011, Random House also shifted Amazon to agency, and it raised prices.[51]

THE ECONOMIC THEORY OF COLLUSION AND THE PRACTICE OF COLLUSION

So far the reader might wonder where in this story an antitrust-actionable case might be hiding. Disclosures about "aikido moves" and the "herding of cats" may be colorful and inflammatory, but they may reflect nothing more than the week-to-week drama of hard-nosed bargaining between publishers and distributors. Standing alone, the drama means little absent an effort to do what established case law instructs: to fold it in with other "plus factors" in a larger narrative that would make the conclusion of an antitrust conspiracy "irresistible".[52] That is what the court set out to do. It catalogued a number of plus factors. They included the fact that the move to agency constituted "an abrupt shift from defendants' past behavior", evidence of much communication between the parties when they were deciding whether or not to contract with Apple, and behavior that the court perceived was contrary to each publisher's "individual self-interest".[53] We are invited to conclude that the observed behaviors could not have obtained from purely interdependent decision making but instead could only be explained as the manifestation of an antitrust conspiracy.

Absent further development, a conclusion of antitrust conspiracy leaves

---

[50] Apple executive Eddy Cue reported to Steve Jobs that "Apple was 'changing a bunch of Penguin titles to $9.99 . . . because [Penguin] didn't get [its] Amazon deal done'" (Opinion, p. 682).

[51] "Random House adopted the agency model in early 2011, and promptly raised the prices of its e-books and experienced a concomitant decline in e-book sales" (Opinion, p. 685).

[52] See *C-O-Two Fire Equipment Co. et al. v. United States* 197 F.2d 489 (1952) at 493. The defendants in that matter were accused of fixing prices for fire extinguishers in meetings of the Fire Extinguishers Manufacturers Association. The defendants observed that "there [was] no direct evidence of what transpired at those meetings", the suggestion being that proof of price fixing had eluded the court. The appeals court demurred, noting that:

> the trial court, sitting as the trier of the facts, regarded this evidence as being another one in a series of "plus factors" which, when standing alone and examined separately, could not be said to point directly to the conclusion that the charges of the indictment were true beyond a reasonable doubt, but which, when viewed as a whole, in their proper setting, spelled out that irresistible conclusion.

[53] Opinion, p. 690.

us with the impression that certain strategically interdependent decisions are more equal than other strategically interdependent decisions. We are left, for example, with the impression that the court would sanction Amazon's strategic decision to commit to a loss-leading policy of pricing new books at $9.99. Yet, publishers perceived Amazon's strategic decision to adopt loss-leading pricing as just that: a strategic decision. Specifically, Amazon's decision to commit to its $9.99 pricing policy amounted to a pre-emptive aikido move of its own in that it exploited publishers' own commitments to their *de facto* MFNs on wholesale prices. It was pre-emptive in that rival distributors would either have to match Amazon's retail prices and absorb indefinite streams of losses or post higher retail prices and likely cede sales to Amazon. Publishers understood that Amazon's pricing policy was designed to frustrate the entry or expansion of rival distributors, a point that Barnes & Noble and other parties made plain.[54] Amazon's aikido move imposed indirect pressure on publishers in that rival distributors found themselves looking to publishers for relief. Presumably, publishers could have offered relief by posting wholesale prices lower than $9.99. However, with Amazon having already demonstrated a willingness to absorb losses, Amazon may very well have been content to subsequently post retail prices even lower than $9.99 with the purpose and effect, again, of imposing pressure on rival distributors. Where would the loss-leading pricing stop? More generally, what retail prices and wholesale prices would constitute the right (socially optimal) prices?

The "Wrath of Amazon" and Reputational Effects

We are further left with the impression that the court would sanction or, at least, ignore Amazon's other strategic choices. Specifically, the court made much of the publishers being concerned about attracting the vaunted "wrath of Amazon" were they to contract with Apple under the terms of agency contracts.[55] The "wrath of Amazon", however, was not an exogenous factor. It was a strategic factor that Amazon would have chosen to cultivate. Amazon would have had an incentive to cultivate a reputation for retaliation and for exacting retribution, because fears of retaliation would amplify the strategic uncertainty publishers would have perceived with respect to their decisions, including decisions to participate in Apple's iBookstore.

The purpose of amplifying strategic uncertainty is that it would increase

---

[54] Declaration of HarperCollins CEO Brian Murray, DX-700, paras 6–7; DX-701, para. 11; DX-702, paras 12–13.

[55] Opinion, p. 664.

the likelihood that Apple would fail to secure a critical mass of the major publishers and would therefore decline to launch the iBookstore. Thus, either by its own pre-emptive aikido move (the $9.99 pricing policy) or by cultivating a reputation for retaliation, Amazon could frustrate the entry of prospective competitors. To see the latter point, consider the following game theoretic reasoning. Consider a contracting game featuring an incumbent distributor, a new, prospective distributor and three symmetrically situated publishers. Each publisher distributes content through the incumbent distributor, and each publisher needs to decide whether or not to distribute books through the new distributor. The three publishers commonly understand that contracting with the new distributor would allow each of them to secure payoffs that would exceed the status quo payoffs they can maintain by declining to distribute through the new distributor. Contracting with the new distributor may, for example, enable them to tap into a broader set of buyers and thereby improve on the status quo payoffs. Suppose, further, that the new distributor announces that it will enter distribution only if it can secure the commitments of at least two of the three publishers.

Suppose the publishers perceive long-term payoffs as follows. If all three publishers participate, they perceive payoff A in excess of the status quo. If two publishers participate, they perceive payoffs B, and the third, non-participating publisher perceives payoff C. If the new distributor declines to enter, each publisher perceives payoff D. For now suppose that $A \geq B \geq C \geq D$, and let $D = 0$ given it reflects no change over the status quo. Finally, suppose that the incumbent distributor can implement a menu of rewards for publishers that decline to contract with the new distributor and a menu of punishments for publishers that choose to contract with the new distributor. Punishments amount to attracting the "wrath" of the incumbent whereas rewards amount to receiving favorable treatment (extra promotion, say) or, even, direct payments from the incumbent. Were all three publishers to contract, they each bear punishment x such that the net payoff to contracting with the distributor is $A - x$. If two publishers contract, they each perceive net payoff $B - y$, and if a single publisher contracts, it yields net payoff $D - z$. Yet, if a single publisher declines, it receives reward u, in which case it yields net payoff $C + u$. If two publishers decline, they each yield net payoff $D + v$. If all three decline, they each yield net payoff $D + w$.

Given each of the three publishers can choose to sign a contract or decline, any one of eight outcomes may obtain. These outcomes and corresponding publisher payoffs are indicated in the pair of payoff matrices in Figure 3.1.

So, for example, were publisher 1 to decline and the other two to sign, then publisher 1 would secure a payoff of $C + u$ and the other two would

Publisher 3 chooses 'sign'

Publisher 2

		Sign	Decline
Publisher 1	Sign	$A-x, A-x, A-x$	$B-y, C+u, B-y$
	Decline	$C+u, B-y, B-y$	$D+v, D+v, D-z$

Publisher 3 chooses 'decline'

Publisher 2

		Sign	Decline
Publisher 1	Sign	$B-y, B-y, C+u$	$D-z, D+v, D+v$
	Decline	$D+v, D-z, D+v$	$D+w, D+w, D+w$

Figure 3.1   Three-player contracting game

Publisher 3 chooses '*sign*' Publisher 3 chooses '*decline*'

	Publisher 2			Publisher 2	
	Sign	*Decline*		*Sign*	*Decline*
Sign	2, 2, 2	1, 0, 1	*Sign*	1, 1, 0	0, 0, 0
Decline	0, 1, 1	0, 0, 0	*Decline*	0, 0, 0	0, 0, 0

Publisher 1 (left table), Publisher 1 (right table)

Figure 3.2   Three-player contracting game with a Pareto-superior equilibrium

each secure payoffs of $B - y$. If they were all to sign, they would each secure a payoff of $A - x$.

Suppose, now, that $A > B > C = D = 0$ and that the incumbent distributor is not situated to impose any rewards or punishments such that $u = v = w = x = y = z = 0$. To make matters simpler to grasp, let $A = 2$ and $B = 1$. The payoff matrices then appear as in Figure 3.2.

The strategy profile (sign, sign, sign) would appear to make for a compelling prediction of how publishers would behave in the contracting game. The outcome yields to each publisher higher payoffs than any one of them could secure under an alternative outcome. Further, no single publisher would have a unilateral incentive to deviate from (sign, sign, sign) by declining. Given the other two publishers could be expected to sign, declining to sign a contract would amount to giving up a payoff of 2 for a lower payoff of zero.

The property that no publisher has a unilateral incentive to deviate from (sign, sign, sign) by declining to sign a contract demonstrates that (sign, sign, sign) corresponds to a Nash equilibrium of the game. Less obvious is that (decline, decline, decline) also satisfies the Nash equilibrium property – no party has a unilateral incentive to deviate – albeit only weakly, in that any one publisher is indifferent between signing and declining given the other two publishers are committed to declining. Even so, (sign, sign, sign) dominates (decline, decline, decline) in at least two ways. First, the payoffs secured under (sign, sign, sign) dominate those under (decline, decline, decline) for each of the publishers. Also, it is not the case that a coalition of two publishers can secure higher payoffs by declining. In contrast, a coalition of two publishers (much less the coalition of all three) could profitably deviate from (decline, decline, decline) by signing.[56]

---

[56]   (Sign, sign, sign) corresponds to a strong equilibrium in that no coalition of publishers can do better by deviating.

It is in such obvious ways that the Nash equilibrium corresponding to (sign, sign, sign) would make for a far more compelling prediction of the game than the Nash equilibrium corresponding to (decline, decline, decline). Were we to make some accommodation for the "wrath" of incumbent distributor, however, (sign, sign, sign) can be made to appear far less compelling and far less certain. Indeed, the incumbent distributor can inject strategic uncertainty into the contracting game simply by committing to a policy of punishing publishers that sign a contract with the new distributor. Suppose, for example, the incumbent commits to a policy of imposing punishment $z = 1$ such that menu of punishments $(x, y, z) = (0, 0, 1)$. That is, were a single publisher to defect from (decline, decline, decline) by signing, that publisher would yield a net payoff $D - z = -1$.

Adding a punishment regime would amount to expanding the game into two stages of interaction, an initial stage in which the incumbent commits to a punishment regime followed by a second stage comprised of the contracting game. The punishment policy $(x, y, z) = (0, 0, 1)$ would imply the publisher payoff matrices for the contracting game in Figure 3.3.

The Nash equilibrium corresponding to outcome (sign, sign, sign) still dominates the Nash equilibrium corresponding to (decline, decline, decline) in important ways, but now (decline, decline, decline) is superior to (sign, sign, sign) in one respect. (Decline, decline, decline) is risk dominant in that a publisher can guarantee itself a status quo payoff of 0 by choosing to decline but faces some prospect of bearing the negative payoff of –1 were it to choose to sign.

The incumbent can further aggravate the strategic uncertainty faced by the publishers were it to impose punishments $x = 1$ or $y = 1$. Specifically, were the incumbent to commit to a policy $(x, y, z) = (1, 1, 1)$, then (decline, decline, decline) becomes a far more compelling prediction. Under this punishment regime, any single publisher would be willing to commit to signing or declining on the basis of a coin flip – a 50/50 proposition – given

Publisher 3 chooses '*sign*'				Publisher 3 chooses '*decline*'		
		Publisher 2				**Publisher 2**
		Sign	*Decline*		*Sign*	*Decline*
Publisher 1	*Sign*	2, 2, 2	1, 0, 1	*Sign*	1, 1, 0	–1, 0, 0
	Decline	0, 1, 1	0, 0, –1	*Decline*	0, –1, 0	0, 0, 0

Figure 3.3   Strategic uncertainty: three-player contracting game as a stag hunt game

the other two publishers were committed to deciding on the basis of their own, independent coin flips. Declining would guarantee the status quo payoff of zero, and signing would yield a 25 percent chance of securing a payoff of 1 (given the other two publishers had randomly yet independently selected sign), a 50 percent chance of securing a payoff of zero, and a 25 percent chance of securing a payoff of –1. Altogether, signing would yield an expected payoff of zero which is the same payoff that the publisher could guarantee for itself by choosing decline.[57]

Alternatively, the incumbent can induce the same degree of strategic uncertainty by offering a combination of rewards and punishments. For example, reward and punishment regimes corresponding to $(u, v, w, x, y, z) = (1, 0, 0, 0, 1, 1)$ or $(u, v, w, x, y, z) = (3, 0, 0, 0, 0, 1)$ yields the same result: given the other two publishers were each independently committed to deciding whether or not to sign a contract on the basis of a coin flip, the third publisher would also be willing to make its decision on the basis of a coin flip. In each case, the new distributor fails to line up more than one publisher with probability equal to 1/2, and it only lines up all three publishers with probability 1/8.[58]

It turns out that problems involving strategic uncertainty have a long intellectual history. Fudenberg and Tirole, for example, open their encyclopedic tome *Game Theory* (1992) with a problem involving strategic uncertainty that Jean-Jacques Rousseau had sketched in the second part of his *Discours sur l'Origine et les Fondements de l'Inégalité parmi les Hommes* (1775). A group of hunters endeavor to trap and take down a stag. To do this they must maintain their posts. However, were a hare to wander within the grasp of any single hunter, that hunter might be tempted to leave his post and secure the hare. By securing the hare, the hunter can assure a positive payoff for himself, but, having left his post, the bigger game, the stag, gets away leaving the other hunters to starve. Giving up the post and securing the hare constitutes the risk-dominant course of action.

Economists, political scientists, anthropologists, and biologists have posed stag hunt games as a way of articulating how risk-dominance (and

---

[57] The reader may recognize that the strategy profile by which each publisher determines whether or not to sign or decline on the basis of a coin flip corresponds to a Nash equilibrium in mixed strategies. Specifically, given any two publishers are committed to randomly choosing their actions on the basis of coin flips, the third publisher perceives no disadvantage to randomly choosing its own action. It might as well choose on the basis of its own, independent coin flip.

[58] Lining up all three publishers occurs with probability $(\frac{1}{2})^3 = \frac{1}{8}$. Lining up one or fewer publishers (and choosing to not enter) occurs with probability $(\frac{1}{2})^3 + (\frac{1}{2})^3 + (\frac{1}{2})^3 + (\frac{1}{2})^3 = \frac{1}{2}$.

strategic uncertainty more generally) can make it difficult for parties to a collaborative venture to actually collaborate. Some of these same researchers have used the game to explore how a group (of adults, children, chimpanzees, slime molds, or even bacteria) locked in a stag hunt game can sometimes resolve strategic uncertainty and enable effective collaboration. (See, for example, Skyrms 2004, pp. 45–7; Duguid et al. 2014.)

The contracting game posed here augmented with the reward-and-punishment regime $(u, v, w, x, y, z) = (0, 0, 0, 1, 1, 1)$ or even just $(u, v, w, x, y, z) = (0, 0, 0, 0, 0, 1)$ amounts to a stag hunt game. The games each feature more than one equilibrium in pure strategies – they each feature two such equilibria – a fact that motivates the idea of strategic uncertainty. Meanwhile, the reward-and-punishment regime $(u, v, w, x, y, z) = (3, 0, 0, 0, 0, 1)$ induces a contracting game fraught with no less strategic uncertainty in that it features four equilibria, no one of which corresponds to (sign, sign, sign).[59] It turns out, however, that the incumbent distributor could potentially commit to a more elaborate reward-and-punishment regime that would resolve the strategic uncertainty, albeit not in a way that the publishers would prefer. Specifically, the incumbent might implement a reward-and-punishment regime that would break the equilibrium (sign, sign, sign) and elevate (decline, decline, decline) as the unique equilibrium of the game. For example, a regime $(u, v, w, x, y, z) = (3, 1, 0, 0, 1, 1)$ would render decline a dominant strategy for any one of the publishers. These rewards and punishments imply the publisher payoff matrices in Figure 3.4.

Publisher 3 chooses '*sign*'

		Publisher 2	
		Sign	*Decline*
Sign		2, 2, 2	0, 3, 0
Publisher 1			
Decline		3, 0, 0	1, 1, –1

Publisher 3 chooses '*decline*'

		Publisher 2	
		Sign	*Decline*
Sign		0, 0, 3	–1, 1, 1
Publisher 1			
Decline		1, –1, 1	0, 0, 0

Figure 3.4   Three-player contracting game as a prisoners' dilemma

[59]   The reward $u = 3$ breaks the candidate equilibrium (sign, sign, sign), because any one publisher has a unilateral incentive to defect from (sign, sign, sign). Thus, given two publishers will sign, the third will decline. Yet, given one publisher will sign and a second will decline, the third will sign. These two conditions show that there are three equilibria that feature two publishers signing and one publisher declining. (Decline, decline, decline) also remains an equilibrium of the game.

The incumbent breaks the candidate equilibrium (sign, sign, sign) by offering a reward $u = 3$ to any one single publisher that opts to decline. Thus, given two publishers are committed to signing, the third publisher has a unilateral incentive to decline and thereby secure a higher payoff of 3. More generally, decline renders higher payoffs to a given publisher no matter what other actions the other two publishers choose. So, for example, were one publisher to commit to signing and a second to declining, the third publisher could still do better by declining (and thereby securing a payoff of 1) than signing (which would yield a payoff of zero). Ultimately, (decline, decline, decline) emerges as the only equilibrium of the game. In that equilibrium, the incumbent distributor gets what it wants (no entry) without even having to mete out punishments or pay out rewards.

Readers may recognize this version of the contracting game as a three-player prisoners' dilemma. The publishers' collectively rational outcome would be (sign, sign, sign), but, the fact that each publisher has a unilateral incentive to cheat by declining demonstrates how individual rationality can frustrate collectively rational outcomes. Knowing this, the publishers might endeavor to expand the game by coming up with a reward-and-punishment scheme of their own that would discourage cheating. They might agree, for example, to implement a punishment scheme by which any two publishers that sign would commit to punishing a publisher that declined. With such a scheme in place, any single publisher might be able to credibly commit to not cheating; (sign, sign, sign) would emerge as a compelling equilibrium of the expanded game.

Collective Action: Prisoners' Dilemmas and How to Resolve Them

Prisoners' dilemmas and strategic uncertainty are interesting in that they stand up for the compound proposition that (1) individually rational behavior can yield collectively irrational outcomes, and (2) collective irrationality can motivate demand for collective action to resolve it. Parties engaged in strategic interaction might be able to impose more structure on that interaction and rescue themselves from collectively irrational outcomes. Note, however, that while resolving collective irrationality can be a good thing, it also provides a motivation for conspiracy. Erstwhile conspirators may be engaged in strategic interactions (price competition, say), and these interactions may yield outcomes that they perceive as collectively irrational (prices lower than joint-profit maximizing prices). Conspiracy can thus be identified not so much with the results of conspiratorial conduct (higher pricing) but with the mechanisms conspirators put in place to (encourage higher pricing and thereby) resolve their problem of collective irrationality. However, conspiracy is not what occupied early thinkers about collective action. The early contributors, such as John Locke and Thomas Hobbes, could observe the ravages of civil war on their communities. They were more interested in public policy.

It was not until 1950 that the prisoners' dilemma game assumed the name "prisoners' dilemma", but the idea that prisoners' dilemmas can frustrate collectively rational outcomes already had a history extending back at least 300 years.[60] Peter Ordeshook observes in *Game Theory and Political Theory* (1986, p. 210) that, with Hobbes's *Leviathan* (1651 [2014]) and Locke's *Second Treatise of Government* (1689 [2002]) in mind, "the imperatives of the prisoners' dilemma, if not its mathematical representation, were obvious to political thinkers".[61] Moreover, the prisoners' dilemma had proven to be "central to political science and political theory (and much of economic theory as well)" (Ordeshook 1986, p. 210). Also, ideas about how to resolve prisoners' dilemmas by some means of collective action have nearly as long a history, at least in the public policy sphere, in that "[m]any of the publicly stated justifications for governmental incursions into our lives and for the formulation of specific public policies are arguments for avoiding real or imagined dilemmas" (Ordeshook 1986, p. 210).

By 1950, political thinkers may have had three centuries to puzzle over how collective action could resolve problems involving strategic interdependence and strategic uncertainty, but both economic theory and the antitrust enterprise were stuck on how to think about strategic interdependence in market-mediated exchange. Up to that point economists had concentrated their energies either on (1) understanding the performance of markets in the absence of strategic interdependence or (2) sorting out

---

[60]   In the lore of game theory, the prisoners' dilemma achieved a mathematical representation in the experimental research of Melvin Dresher and Merrill Flood at RAND in 1950. They were interested in non-zero-sum, two-player games, one of which was a game that corresponded to a prisoners' dilemma. The game amounted to an empirical examination of the Nash equilibrium concept that John Nash had also just developed in 1950. In that same year, one of John Nash's professor's at Princeton, Albert Tucker of Kuhn–Tucker Theorem fame, invented the prisoners' dilemma name and fable as a way of making the theory more accessible to non-mathematicians. He was preparing a game theory lecture for the Stanford psychology department. See Goeree and Holt (2001, p. 1403) and Flood (1952, pp. 17–24a).

[61]   These particular political thinkers were motivated by the idea that institutions could be designed in ways that would allow societies to avoid the kind of devastation that they themselves were able to observe during the English Civil Wars. Historians speculate that as much as 4 percent of the combined populations of Scotland and England perished and that a much higher proportion of the Irish population perished after the invasion of Oliver Cromwell's forces.

the performance of oligopolistic markets, the kinds of markets in which strategic interdependence should be abundantly manifest. The former project amounted to identifying conditions (if any) that could motivate the "invisible hand", the intuition that individually rational, self-interested behavior in decentralized, market-mediated exchange could yield socially desirable outcomes. Over many decades the project yielded versions of the First and Second Welfare Theorems, which themselves achieved their first modern formulations in Arrow (1951) and DeBreu (1951). Pure competition could obtain in atomistic markets, and, remarkably, pure competition could enable buyers and suppliers to exhaust gains from trade – a good thing – not only within a given market but across markets spanning the entire economic system.

Such is the magic of markets, at least on paper. Such magic, however, could not be expected to spontaneously obtain in markets served not by atomistic suppliers but by smaller numbers of discrete suppliers. Hence the second project: how to characterize individually rational behavior in oligopolistic markets. (Werden 2004, pp. 725–9, details some of the difficulties. See also Olson 1965, pp. 9-10.) In the context of public policy, parties may want to harness and channel collective action in order to solve problems. In markets, however, collective action among suppliers could amount not to solving problems but to creating problems (cartelization). Yet, theorists debated the hypothesis that, in oligopoly, the individual rationality and the collective rationality of prospective cartel members should spontaneously converge. What made sense for the group should surely make sense for the individual; the individual should perceive no unilateral incentive to deviate. Cartelization should thus obtain without collective action. So, for example, the publishers in the prisoners' dilemma game above should be able to spontaneously converge on (sign, sign, sign) merely by virtue of the collective rationality of that outcome. There would be no need for some more elaborate agreement to compel compliance. Similarly, in the case of oligopoly, suppliers should be able to factor the strategic interdependence of their choices in to their own decisions and spontaneously coordinate on prices or outputs that would collectively yield monopolistic profits. However, there were competing hypotheses: Coordination on collectively rational outcomes, for example, might prove too difficult, and that would create demand for collective action. Yet another, contrasting hypothesis was that potential competition might frustrate cartelization altogether.[62]

---

[62] See, for example, Clark (1912). Compounding the confusion was some perception in policy circles that unrestrained competition could be wasteful, especially

The game theory advances of 1950 and the articulation of the prisoners' dilemma made it possible to articulate three points: (1) purely interdependent decision making could not be expected to yield cartelization. Unilateral incentives to deviate could frustrate cartelization in that any one party would be happy to set slightly lower prices or to expand output given others were raising prices or restricting outputs. Accordingly, (2) there had to be more to cartelization than merely the fact that oligopolists could perceive the collective rationality of achieving cartelization. There would therefore be demand among prospective conspirators for collective action. Collective action might involve agreeing on prices or outputs consistent with monopoly, but the most important action would involve implementing some type of process to enforce compliance with the agreement in the future. (3) Purely interdependent decision making could be expected to yield outcomes situated somewhere between those secured by atomistic competition and cartelization.

As Werden (2004) observes, it took some time (a few decades) for the advances of 1950 to filter into the economics literature. Even so, by the mid-1960s, theorists had started to make some progress with respect to the second point: what would collective action look like? Early contributions such as Stigler (1964) and Orr and MacAvoy (1965) showed that collective action could involve instituting schemes that would enable conspirators to both detect and punish cheating on agreements to raise prices or restrict output. Detection could be problematic in that erstwhile conspirators could secretly cut prices or secretly dump output on markets. There was then the question of how to structure punishments, especially if meting out punishment would itself be punishing to the punishers. Could erstwhile conspirators assemble a credible monitoring and punishment scheme?

---

in the face of economic depression. Writing (unwittingly) on the cusp of the Great Depression, Seager and Gulick (1929, p. 83) further observed that there was some perception that "monopolistic combinations" would be situated to "check a depression before it goes to an extreme". That was not the end of it. Confusion in policy circles was abundantly manifest in the various New Deal initiatives of the first Roosevelt Administration (1933–36). In 1933 the Administration prompted the establishment of the Antitrust Division of the Department of Justice. In that same year, however, it launched various legislative initiatives such as the National Industrial Recovery Act to actively promote cartelization. By late 1937 the second Roosevelt Administration (1937–40) reversed course, having observed that German conglomerates had been actively organizing international cartels in munitions-relevant industries. The Antitrust Division set up a Patent and Cartel Section and started to investigate international cartels (Borkin and Welsh 1943). In 1938 Joseph Borkin assumed leadership of the Patent and Cartel Section.

The principal innovation was to understand cartel enforcement as a matter of monitoring compliance and implementing punishments over time. Erstwhile conspirators could enlist the prospect of cooperation in the future – and the threat of withholding such cooperation – to secure cooperation in the present. In this way punishments would involve the withholding of cooperation. So, for example, erstwhile competitors stuck in repeated play of a prisoners' dilemma game could support cooperation by adopting some version of a tit-for-tat norm: each party commits to cooperating until at least one other party defects in a given iteration of the game. Non-defectors punish defectors by themselves defecting in one or more successive iterations of the game before reverting to cooperation.[63]

The theory of "repeated games" suggests how parties could support cooperation as long as they place sufficient value on future cooperation – and as long as they can implement effective monitoring mechanisms and commit to credible punishment schemes.[64] Yet, even assembling all of that apparatus on paper could make for an ambitious affair, to say nothing of implementing apparati to resolve actual coordination problems and prisoners' dilemmas. The principal weakness of enlisting the prospect of future cooperation to support cooperation in the present is that, absent infinitely repeated interactions, the future eventually runs out and becomes the present. The repeated interaction ultimately converges on the one-shot end game, where unilateral incentives to deviate from cooperation again dominate. It gets worse. Anticipating that cooperation may break down in the last stage of interaction, erstwhile conspirators may defect in the penultimate stage of interaction. Anticipating that, cooperation may break down in the second to last stage of interaction. Cooperation may then unravel at every single stage of interaction.

Theorists have advanced at least three ways of finessing the unraveling problem and showing how parties locked in prisoners' dilemmas could

---

[63] Bergstrom (2002, p. 81, original emphasis) offers a more general observation:

Several game theorists in the 1950s nearly simultaneously discovered a result known as the *folk theorem*, which tells us that in indefinitely repeated games, almost any pattern of individual behavior can be sustained as a Nash equilibria by a stable, self-policing norm. Such a norm prescribes a course of action to each player and includes instructions to punish anyone who violates his prescribed course of action.

[64] Green and Porter (1984) inspired research on imperfect monitoring. Effective policing might yet obtain even if monitoring were imperfect. Cooperation might even appear to break down periodically as conspirators would punish each other for apparent (if not actual) deviations. Cooperation over the long term would thus not appear perfect and seamless.

yet support cooperation over some portion of a finite sequence of repeated interactions.[65] Practitioners, meanwhile, who have been unencumbered with theoretical concerns about the unraveling of cooperative schemes, have sometimes demonstrated ability to sustain cooperation in interactions that extend over a finite (albeit uncertain) horizon. Indeed, practitioners have sometimes managed to sustain cooperation in environments that would appear to have been savagely hostile to cooperation. Social scientists of a certain age, for example, will know the account in Robert Axelrod's classic book *The Evolution of Cooperation* (1984) of the often successful collusion between opposing troops in the trenches of the Western Front in World War I to subvert the murderous plans of French, British and German High Command.

Axelrod's account was much inspired by the careful study of Tony Ashworth (1980), which bore the unrevealing title *Trench Warfare 1914–1918*. It also bore the illuminating sub-title *The Live and Let Live System*. The point was that different norms developed along the Western Front of World War I. A norm of "kill or be killed" prevailed in the killing fields of Ypres, Verdun and the Somme. In "cushy" sectors, a norm of "live and let live" developed by which combatants on both sides of the line tacitly agreed to shirk their duties. Shirking entailed making a great show to High Command of bombarding or shooting at their adversaries while making a point, however, of aiming high or attempting to drop barrages of artillery shells harmlessly in No Man's Land.

The central research question was, how is it that opposing forces managed to collude against their High Commands at some times and in some sectors while kill or be killed prevailed at other times and in other sectors? At first sight it might appear surprising that a norm of live and let live

---

[65] In *Competition, Collusion and Game Theory* (1972, pp. 142–3), Lester Telser observes that we can interpret the rate at which parties discount future payoffs as the likelihood that interaction will continue for one more period. As long as parties are expected-utility maximizers, we end up with a mathematically isomorphic problem. In place of an infinite sequence of interactions, we end up with a sequence of finite expected duration. Radner (1980) substitutes the Nash solution concept with an approximate Nash concept and shows that players adopting this satisficing (rather than strictly optimizing) behavior may be able to sustain cooperation for all but the final stages of interaction. Kreps and Wilson (1982) finesse the problem by posing a two-player prisoners' dilemma in which at least one player assigns a (possibly very small) probability to the prospect that the other player is committed to an irrational tit-for-tat strategy. Relatedly, a large body of research in evolutionary game theory exploits the idea that some players may be irrational, conditional cooperators who would adopt strategies such as tit-for-tat. See, for example, Ostrom (2000) or Bowles and Gintis (2011, pp. 59–61).

emerged anywhere at all given opposing forces started the conflict committed to killing each other, but further reflection suggests the alternative. It may be surprising that such accommodating norms did not diffuse up and down the entire Western Front, for British Field Marshall Douglas Haig had made plain to King George V what duty entailed: "to go forward as an organised unit in the face of almost certain death".[66] Figuring out ways to shirk duty would thus offer obvious advantages. At the beginning of the war, however, the prospect of "going over the top" and having to face almost certain death seemed more remote. "In 1914 the authoritative view was that future wars would be both mobile and short" (Ashworth 1980, p. 1). The guns of August 1914 erupted. The Germans planned to sweep around Paris behind the opposing armies, and bring the fighting to an end before the close of the year. By early September German armies were already on the outskirts of Paris. Yet, the French counterattack on the German flank along the Marne pushed the Germans back. The antagonists then attempted to outflank each other in what amounted to a race to the North Sea with each side feverishly digging trenches along the way. The front bisected Belgium with a locus of trenches that ran just east of Ypres. The fighting then degenerated into a war of attrition in the trenches.

Thus the war was not going to be over by Christmas, and it was not obvious which side would ultimately prevail. Troops on each side of the line, clustered in their cold, wet trenches, had time for introspection. With victory no longer in view, the problem of merely surviving the war assumed more prominence. Troops on each side settled down to daily routines. They also came to appreciate that troops on the other side of the line settled down to similar routines. These included being less occupied with the daily discourtesies of war (such as sniping at neighbors at mealtimes). So it was that unwittingly parallel conduct made grindingly witting over the course of a long sequence of cold, waterlogged mornings became the basis for tacit understandings. Ashworth, for example, recounts the observation of Ian Hay of the Ninth Division of the British Expeditionary Force:

> It would be child's play to shell the road behind the enemy's trenches, crowded as it must be with the ration wagons and water carts, into a bloodstained

---

[66]   The larger context is that Haig was trying to impress on King George V that troops had to be prepared for the experience of war. Yet even the first engagement outside Ypres, about which Haig was speaking, was exceptional in Haig's own long military experience in that he could observe retreating troops "having thrown everything they could, including their rifles and packs, in order to escape, with a look of absolute terror on their faces, such as I have never before seen on any human being's face" (Blake 1952, p. 79).

wilderness ... but on the whole there is silence. After all, if you prevent your enemy from drawing his rations, his remedy is simple: he will prevent you from drawing yours. (Ashworth 1980, p. 26)

In such ways it seems natural that conscious parallelism would evolve in that parties on both sides of the line might choose to refrain from interfering with each other's mealtime routines and might even choose to draw rations at about the same times. "But on an active front," Ashworth (1980, p. 26) observes, "each side considered the other's rations as a prime target." How, then, might antagonists be induced to forbear? Ian Hay's observation provides a clue: the antagonists were not engaged in a one-shot interaction. They were engaged in a stream of interactions that would unfold over an interval of indefinite duration. There would be opportunities for one side to punish the other were it to defect from an agreement to exercise forbearance.

A norm of tit-for-tat retaliation could thus discourage defection and sustain collusion. Opposing forces could then concentrate on developing norms of ritualized aggression and perfunctory performance in order to mask their shirking from High Command. Shells could be expected to fall at certain places at certain times of the day. It was possible to anticipate "the evening gun" of the British, observed one German soldier, that came so regularly that "you could set your watch by it ... it always had the same objective, its range was accurate, it never varied laterally or went beyond or fell short of its mark" (Ashworth 1980, p. 127). Similarly, machine gunners could be expected to make ostentatious but predictable demonstrations of raking the other side of the line. "One ingenious machine gunner could 'loose off' to the time of the well known line in [the popular tune] 'Policeman's Holiday' and a dozen machine guns, on both sides, would answer with [the] two shots – 'Bang-Bang'" (Ashworth 1980, p. 116). Parties on each side of the line might even stage-manage irregular events that could have destabilized their relationships. A unit of German soldiers from Saxony situated a stone's throw from a British trench did, in fact, send a message tied to a stone: "We are going to send a 40lb. bomb. We have got to do it, but don't want to. I[t] will come this evening, and we will whistle first to warn you" (Ashworth 1980, p. 35; Hills 1919, pp. 46–7).

One of the potentially easiest ways of breaking collusion between opposing forces would be to shuffle them around. Shuffling troops around might deny them the opportunity to develop relationships with opposing troops that extend over time. Relationships would degenerate into something closer to one-shot interactions, a condition under which unilateral incentives to deviate may frustrate collusion. However, collusive norms proliferated so widely on the Western Front that troops coming in to the line to relieve other troops merely had to inquire what the local norms were. Even so, some local norms were contrary to collusion. Active fronts were active for a reason: High Command had chosen to press offensive operations in selected sectors. German Army Chief of Staff Erich von Falkenhayn perceived, for example, that the failure to end the fighting by December 1914 had thrust the opposing armies into a war of attrition – a war he surmised (correctly) that Germany would be less well situated than the allies to sustain (Falkenhayn 1919, p. 23). Hence the motivation to pursue a war of attrition under physical conditions more favorable to the Germans. German armies invested what had been a quiet sector along the Meuse River and launched their initiative to take Verdun. "Within our reach . . . are objectives for the retention of which the French General Staff would be compelled to throw in every man they have. If they do so the forces of France will bleed to death" (Falkenhayn 1919, p. 217). The French might then be compelled to sue for peace, and the war could be drawn to a close in 1916.

Alas, Verdun ended up putting as much strain on the Germans as it did on the French, and the war did not end in 1916. Neither, however, did collusion cease in "quiet" sectors. What definitively brought collusion to an end, however, was the allies' successful effort to break the German lines in 1918 and compel Germany to sue for peace. The great mass of American troops had finally streamed into France by the middle of 1918, and they were impatient with the ritualized aggression that prevailed over many parts of the front. The 129th Field Artillery regiment, for example, settled into the line in the Vosges Mountains where, as Ferrell (1998, p. 269) observes, "neither side had disturbed the line in more than ritual ways for nearly four years". A unit of the 129th endeavored to exploit and undermine the live-and-let-live agreement by inducing the end game. Specifically, a battery of 129th, captained by Harry S. Truman, planned on launching a massive bombardment and then organizing its defection from the agreement in a way that would diminish the effects of the expected retaliatory strike. The battery called up horses to the front so that it might strike the Germans with a barrage of 500 gas shells and take away its field guns before the Germans could respond.[67]

---

[67] Horses were reportedly drawn up too late to avoid the retaliatory German shelling. Some men scattered while others persisted in rigging up their guns to teams of horses. In an oral history Private Vere Leigh recalled:

[W]e were firing away and having a hell of a good time doing it until they began to fire back. We tried to hitch up the horses and get out of there but we couldn't move the guns . . . If I remember right, we were firing some gas that night, and woke somebody up over there.

The practice of collusion on the Western Front of World War I anticipated the development of a monitoring-and-punishment paradigm in the
economic theory of collusion by more than half a century. Collusion could
not be expected to spontaneously obtain, and it could not be expected to
spontaneously persist. Erstwhile antagonists had to come up with agreements about what conduct would constitute cooperation. Further, these
agreements had to be tacit so that conspirators could frustrate detection
by the authorities (High Command or the antitrust authorities) against
whom they endeavored to collude. More importantly, they had to come
up with tacit agreements about how to enforce compliance. Enforcement
would involve the monitoring of behaviors over time as well as the punishment of deviations from cooperation. As Hovenkamp (2005, p. 153) put it,
"Detecting cheating by cartel members is one thing. Punishing it is quite
another. Most importantly, cartels are illegal, and the members of a cartel
cannot take cheaters to court. They must devise ways to punish cheaters
that simultaneously (a) make cheating unprofitable without (b) causing
public discovery of the cartel".[68]
The antitrust enterprise has come to recognize the monitoring-and-
enforcement paradigm in the case law,[69] and we can find references to it

---

In a letter to his wife, the unit commander, Captain Harry S. Truman, observed
that he "had one high old time getting out" of the engagement – an engagement
that "the boys" came to know as the "Battle of Who Run".

[68]   Even when cartels were legal, both the detection and punishment of cheating
could be imperfect. See, for example, Porter (1983) with respect to operation of the
"Joint Executive Committee", a cartel scheme that preceded the Sherman Act by
a decade.

[69]   See, for example, *Blomkest Fertilizer v. Potash of Saskatchewan* 203 F.3d 1028
(8th Circuit 2000) at 1042–3. The court observed that "a cartel can only succeed for
any period of time if it has the ability to detect cheating and punish it effectively".
In re Baby Food Antitrust Litigation 166 F.3d 112 (3rd Circuit 1999) at 137, the
court observed that "There is no evidence that . . . there was any mechanism in
place to detect conspirator cheating. Without such a mechanism, no conspiracy,
if it existed, could long endure". In *Petruzzi's IGA v. Darling-Delaware Company*
998 F.2d 1224 (3rd Circuit 1993) at 1233 the court observed that conspirators
endeavored to raise prices by allocating customers, compliance would be secured
by threats to bid aggressively for the accounts of a noncomplying party. The court
further explained, "Game theory teaches us that a cartel cannot survive absent
some enforcement mechanism because otherwise the incentives to cheat are too
great". In *Fleischman v. Albany Medical Center* 728 F.Supp.2d 130 (2010) at 153–4,
166, the court admitted an economic expert's testimony that an "information
exchange" could help parties monitor and police compliance with a price-fixing
agreement; In *CostCo Wholesale Corporation v. Maleng* 522 F.3d 874 (9th Circuit
2008) at 896 the court observed that alcohol distributors in the state of Washington
exploited regulations in ways that would enable them to monitor and police a

in every iteration of the *Horizontal Merger Guidelines* of the Antitrust Division since 1982.[70] It has also made it into various Division enforcement actions resolved by consent decree.[71] In contrast, the court in the Apple eBooks matter does not recognize that publishers may have perceived incentives to cheat on an agreement to fix prices. The court understood that publishers would fix prices at the price caps indicated in the Apple

---

price-fixing agreement. In *Federal Trade Commission v. University Health, Inc.* 938 F.2d 1206 (11th Circuit 1991) at 938, conspirators endeavored to raise price by suppressing investments in new capacity, regulatory requirements enabled them to credibly commit to forgo investing in new capacity, and regulatory reporting requirements enabled costless monitoring of planned investments in new capacity, and that same regulation enabled conspirators to block any other party's planned investments. In *Federal Trade Commission v. Owens-Illinois, Inc.* 681 F.Supp. 27 (1988) at 51–2, the court recognized the erstwhile conspirators would require some means of "policing" an agreement to fix prices but that incentives to "cheat" were so strong that it was not obvious that any agreement could be sustained. In *Hospital Corporation of America v. Federal Trade Commission* 807 F.2d 1381 (7th Circuit 1986) at 1387, 1391, the court observed that erstwhile competitors could raise prices by restricting investments in new capacity, and the regulatory structure would enable conspirators to costlessly detect planned investments in new capacity and to take "countermeasures".

[70] The relevant passages in the 2010 incarnation of the *Horizontal Merger Guidelines* pertain to how a merger could make a market more susceptible to coordinated interaction between firms. "Coordinated interaction" includes behaviors that may obtain from a "common understanding that is not explicitly negotiated but would be enforced by the detection and punishment of deviations that would undermine the coordinated interaction" (accessed November 7, 2018 at https://www.justice.gov/atr/horizontal-merger-guidelines-08192010).

[71] In 2001 the Antitrust Division filed suit to block the proposed acquisition of Masonite Corporation, a subsidiary of the International Paper Company, by Premdor, Inc. The matter was resolved by the divestiture of a doorskin manufacturing plant. The Division argued that, absent the divestiture, the merged firm would have both greater incentives and ability to collude. Specifically, erstwhile competitors would become better situated to "monitor and punish deviations from attempted coordination on the terms of sale of interior molded doorskins" (see the Competitive Impact Statement filed August 3, 2001, accessed November 7, 2018 at https://www.justice.gov/atr/case-document/competitive-impact-statement-174). In 1992 the Antitrust Division filed a complaint against the Airline Tariff Publishing Company (ATP) and participating airlines alleging that the airlines used the ATP to facilitate price-fixing agreements. The Division noted, among other things, that the airlines used the ATP to identify "particular discounts offered by one of a few competitors and solicited agreements to eliminate these fares. In these cases, the soliciting airline would punish the disruptive airline by filing similar discounts in the city pairs where the disruptive airline preferred higher fares" (see the Competitive Impact Statement filed on March 17, 1994, accessed November 7, 2018 at https://www.justice.gov/atr/case-document/competitive-impact-statement-3).

contracts.[72] Yet, if these price caps had exceeded the prices that would have obtained under publishers' purely interdependent decision making, then conspirators would have needed to institute some type of scheme to compel each other to post higher, cap-consistent prices. Affirmatively characterizing incentives to cheat as well as characterizing the informal mechanisms the publishers had used to discourage that same cheating could have gone far toward establishing an agreement to fix prices.[73] Nonetheless, the court was silent about how publishers would police a price-fixing agreement. Alternatively, were the price caps to prove to be lower than the prices that would have obtained under purely interdependent decision making, then publishers' purely interdependent but cap-constrained decisions would have yielded prices consistent with the price caps. No agreement to fix prices at the price caps would have been necessary.[74]

In the eBooks matter we are left to wonder that publishers declined to implement any enforcement mechanisms, because they perceived no incentives to cheat; and they perceived no incentives to cheat, because the pricing that obtained after the implementation of agency was consistent with their purely interdependent decision making. The court, meanwhile, appears to have accepted the kind of proposition that Mancur Olson (1965) had set out to dispel in *The Logic of Collective Action*, that upon recognizing a collectively rational outcome – in this case, prices higher than those that would obtain under purely interdependent decision making – publishers should have been able to spontaneously converge on it. The court does not acknowledge the possibility that a prisoners' dilemma may have obtained in that individually rational behaviors might have deviated from collectively rational behaviors. Instead, we are invited to conclude that, upon observing spontaneous convergence on an outcome, the outcome corresponds to collusion. However, this amounts to circular logic in that it ends up equating purely interdependent decision making with collusion.

---

[72]   "Through Apple's adoption of price caps in its Agreements, it took on the role of setting the prices for the Publisher Defendants' e-books and eventually for much of the e-book industry" (Opinion, p. 670).

[73]   Shulman (2006, p. 502) advances much the same proposition from the perspective of expert testimony:

> [A]n expert economist can often persuasively rebut a claim that conduct has been contrary to independent self-interest by showing that the paradigm of the Prisoners' Dilemma does not apply to the fact of the case, and therefore the conduct cannot be assumed to be the result of agreement in the legal sense.

[74]   Shulman (2006, p. 502) again advances a parallel proposition: "[T]here may be instances where an economist may be able to say that conduct does fit the Prisoners' Dilemma and is therefore consistent with agreement."

THE UNITED FRONT

The court was occupied with two types of collective action. The first involved collective action on the part of publishers and Apple to deal with the "wrath of Amazon". This involved a single episode of interaction between the publishers, Apple and Amazon and resulted in five of the Big Six publishers signing agency contracts with Apple. The five publishers then turned around and secured agency contracts from Amazon. The second type of collective action involved the actual fixing of prices. Price fixing is not the kind of conduct that unfolds within the space of a single episode of strategic interactions, but is the kind of conduct that unfolds indefinitely over time.

The court made much of price fixing, but it did so without characterizing how conspirators would police pricing behaviors. The court thus demonstrated that it was unencumbered with both theoretical and practical developments in the social sciences and in the intersection of law and economics since the Age of Reason about how parties who would otherwise be engaged in fierce competition can sometimes neutralize incentives to cheat and thereby sustain collusion. We are invited to conclude that the Age of Reason was just something that happened to other people. However, price-fixing aside, the more important aspect of the Apple matter pertains to the proposition that publishers had to present Amazon with a united front in order it to induce it to accept the terms of agency contracts. The court understood that, absent a united front, Amazon could have rebuffed any single publisher's demand to move to agency.

The basis for the court's understanding is a passage from the direct testimony of Amazon executive, Russ Grandinetti. Macmillan, the smallest of the five publishers, had been the first to apprise Amazon of its desire to move to an agency contract. However, the court observed:

> Amazon knew that its battle was not just with Macmillan but with five of the Big Six. As Grandinetti testified, "If it had been only Macmillan demanding agency, we would not have negotiated an agency contract with them. But having heard the same demand for agency terms coming from all the publishers in such close proximity . . . we really had no choice but to negotiate the best agency contracts we could with these five publishers".[75]

Amazon proceeded to acquiesce to Macmillan's demand to move to agency, and it subsequently negotiated agency contracts with four of the other five publishers.

---

[75] Opinion, p. 680.

Note that, were Amazon unwilling to rebuff the demands of any one publisher, the same result would have obtained: Amazon would have negotiated an agency contract with each of the five publishers. What is it, then, about negotiations with publishers being compressed in close proximity that could enable any one publisher to secure an agency contract that otherwise would have been out of its reach? An answer developed here is that proximity had little or no effect on the bargaining once Amazon came to appreciate what the publishers' move to agency with Apple and likely with all other distributors in the future would mean: under agency other platforms would be viable in the future. Barnes & Noble and other distributors would be relieved of the prospect of either matching Amazon's loss-leading pricing on Bestsellers and New Releases – an unsustainable program – or ceding all of the sales of such eBooks to Amazon. Absent agency, a publisher could only hope to support its eBook business through other distributors were it willing to exclude Amazon. (Would the matter of excluding Amazon also have been subject to antitrust scrutiny?) Post-agency, a publisher could expect to support its eBook business in the future with or without Amazon. Anticipating this, Amazon would have had to decide between acquiescing to agency or losing equal access to a publisher's catalogue.[76] The court itself observed that, "Unless it moved to an agency distribution model for e-books, Amazon customers would cease to have access to many of the most popular e-books, which would hurt Kindle customers and the attractiveness of the Kindle".[77] Amazon chose to avoid losing access – which likely would have conformed to all parties' least preferred outcome – and accepted agency.

To see this, consider the following simple bargaining game between a publisher and Amazon. Bargaining will yield one of three outcomes. The two parties may continue to maintain their wholesale contract (Wholesale). Alternatively, the two parties will shift to agency (Agency). Third and last, the publisher may leave the Kindle platform (Leaving Amazon). Remaining on wholesale terms implies a certain value of the relationship to the publisher, and it implies a certain value to Amazon. Shifting to agency implies different values of the relationship in the future to both the publisher and to Amazon. Leaving Amazon, with, perhaps, some prospect of restoring the relationship in the future, implies yet other values in the future. What is important is how each party ranks each out-

[76]   Macmillan offered Amazon two options: accept agency or be willing to accept Bestsellers and New Releases after a delay of several months. See the declaration of Macmillan CEO, John Sargent (DX-701, para. 46).

[77]   Opinion, p. 680.

come. Specifically, suppose in the pre-agency environment that the publisher prefers Agency to Wholesale and Wholesale to Leaving Amazon. Suppose also that Amazon prefers Wholesale to Agency and Agency to Leaving Amazon. To make matters easier to see, suppose that both parties assign the value zero to Wholesale, reflecting the fact that remaining on wholesale terms amounts to no change from the status quo. Suppose the publisher assigns value 2 to Agency and –1 to Leaving Amazon. Suppose Amazon assigns value –1 to Agency and –2 to Leaving Amazon.

These payoffs can be indicated in the game tree in Figure 3.5. Each bracket indicates the payoff to a given outcome secured by the publisher (the number at the top of each bracket) as well as the payoff secured by Amazon (the lower number in each bracket).

The game tree indicates a sequence of as many as three moves with the publisher moving first. At the first node of the game, the publisher may choose to make no demand for an agency contract, in which case the game ends and the two parties collect their status quo payoffs of zero. Amazon may never even know that the publisher contemplated making a demand for agency. Alternatively, the publisher may choose to apprise

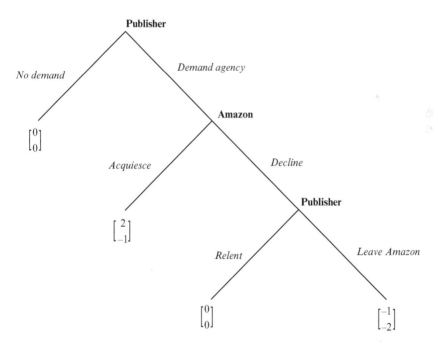

Figure 3.5   *Amazon/publisher bargaining game in which the threat to leave Amazon is non-credible*

Amazon of its demand for agency, in which case the game moves to the next decision node. That node is occupied by Amazon, where it may choose to acquiesce, in which case the game ends and both parties realize their payoffs from agency. Alternatively, Amazon may choose to decline the demand to move to agency. The game then moves to the third and last node of the game. The last node reflects the moment of truth in that the publisher must decide whether to relent (and revert to wholesale terms) or to actually leave Amazon.

One of the publisher's strategies would be to demand agency and then leave Amazon were Amazon to decline to accept agency. Given Amazon expects the publisher to leave were it to decline, it would make sense for Amazon to acquiesce to agency. Also, given the publisher expects Amazon to acquiesce, it makes sense to demand agency and to threaten to leave. Thus, the sequence of actions to demand agency and acquiesce, combined with the threat to leave, corresponds to a Nash equilibrium of the game. However, note that the threat to leave is more of a bluff than a credible threat, because Amazon can call publisher's bluff by declining and forcing the publisher to choose between relenting (and earning a payoff of zero) or following through on its threat to leave (and securing a lower payoff of -1).[78] Following through is not credible; the publisher can be expected to relent, in which case no change from the status quo obtains.

In this version of the game, Amazon effectively commands all of the bargaining power and virtually dictates the outcome of the game. The key assumption is that the publisher prefers the status quo to actually leaving Amazon. Why this would be so is not immediately obvious, and making one seemingly small change to the game has the effect of shifting the bargaining power from Amazon to the publisher. Specifically, were the publisher to prefer leaving to relenting, then the publisher's threat to leave becomes credible. So, for example, if the value of leaving were 1 instead of -1, the publisher could credibly commit to leaving. Anticipating this, Amazon would acquiesce to agency.

This version of the game has a unique Nash equilibrium by which the publisher demands agency and credibly commits to leaving, and Amazon acquiesces. The two parties end up moving from wholesale terms of contract to an agency contract no matter how other publishers contract with Amazon. The question is, however, what did contracting with Apple

---

[78]   There are four Nash equilibria in this game, two of which involve the non-credible threat to leave. The two most compelling equilibria, however, involve the publisher relenting at the last decision node, in Figure 3.5, if and when it comes time to decide between relenting and leaving.

have to do with this? Even before Apple advanced plans to open an iBookstore, should not each individual publisher have preferred to leave Amazon and pursue their fortunes with other eBook distributors either on wholesale or agency terms? Even in a wholesale environment, leaving Amazon would have relieved other distributors from having to meet Amazon's $9.99 pricing. Even so, publishers' behaviors seem to reveal that they did not perceive other platforms as robust alternatives to the Kindle platform. Their behaviors also reveal, however, that they perceived the launch of the iBookstore and iPad platform as a credible alternative. The expectation maintained by all parties that Apple's iBookstore would be successful made the prospect of leaving Amazon more credible.[79] Thus, the gambit alone of contracting with Apple may well have invested each publisher individually with bargaining power sufficient to induce Amazon to acquiesce to agency.

In the bargaining game just described, the notion of a united front is superfluous. What was important was collectively sponsoring the launch of a credible platform. Once the launch of the new platform was virtually secured, publishers did not need to coordinate the timing of their contract negotiations in order to secure agency contracts from Amazon. Even so, the fact that Amazon and four of the five publishers negotiated agency contracts in close proximity makes the notion of a united front appear at least superficially plausible. What makes the notion of a united front less compelling, however, is that Amazon acquiesced to agency contracts under bargaining conditions that Amazon argued would have enabled it to rebuff any single publisher's demands. Specifically, the record is replete with examples of contracting episodes between Amazon and a single publisher that did not overlap with negotiations between Amazon and other publishers and yet resulted in agency contracts.

The first example is the set of contract negotiations between Amazon and Penguin after the launch of the iPad and the iBookstore. Penguin already had an agency contract with Apple by the time the iBookstore went live on April 3, 2010, and the four other publishers engaged their agency contracts with Amazon at that same time. Penguin's existing wholesale contract with Amazon, however, had a fixed term that would expire at the end May 2010. Amazon was thus able to force Penguin to remain on wholesale terms with it for nearly two months after the launch

---

[79]   The court observed that, for its part, "Apple expected that its entry into the market with an iBookstore on this device [the iPad] would help make books 'cool' for the iTunes generation and quickly make Apple the vehicle through which a significant percentage of e-books were sold" (Opinion, p. 656).

of iBookstore. During that time, Amazon continued to negotiate with Penguin. Amazon's negotiations with Penguin were thus isolated from its contract negotiations with other publishers. Yet Amazon ultimately gave in and acquiesced to agency with Penguin. Amazon and Penguin shifted to agency at the beginning of June 2010.

Random House was the next publisher to induce Amazon to accept an agency contract. Random House had not participated in the launch of the iBookstore, but in January 2011 it contracted with both Apple and Amazon under agency terms. Its contract negotiations with Amazon were isolated from the contract negotiations that Amazon had already consummated with the five other publishers in 2010, but Amazon still acquiesced to agency. Random House subsequently raised prices on its Bestsellers and New Releases.

One thing Amazon did manage to do was stagger the termination dates of the agency contracts with the five publishers. It did this, the court observed, "to avoid being vulnerable in the future to collective pressure during contract negotiations . . . The final five contracts ranged in length from terms of eighteen months to three years".[80] Amazon did this so that it would not again have to face a united front of publishers. But two questions remain unexplored. If publishers could anticipate the need to reconstitute their united front, why would they not have insisted on contracts of similar duration? Further, why might they not have forestalled the matter of reconstituting a united front by insisting on contracts of even longer duration? One answer is that they did not perceive advantages to coordinating the duration of their contracts, and they may have perceived no advantage, because a united front offered no extra bargaining power that the gambit of contracting with Apple alone afforded.

As it turned out, Amazon did not have to renegotiate with publishers under the terms it had secured for itself. The five publishers eventually settled with the plaintiffs and committed to negotiating new contracts with Amazon, Apple, and all other distributors. The terms of the settlements did not preclude the publishers from negotiating new agency agreements, but they did provide a distributor with what amounted to a limited budget for discounting eBooks even under an agency agreement. Further, the settlements made some provision for staggering the termination of the obligations imposed on the publishers. There was some variation in the duration of the restrictions on contracting, and distributors (such as Amazon) were afforded the capacity to terminate a given agreement with

---

[80]   Opinion, p. 681.

30 days' notice.[81] Any single distributor, including Amazon, was thus afforded more scope to "stagger the termination dates of its contracts to ensure that it [would end up] negotiating with only one Settling Defendant at a time to avoid joint conduct that could lead to a return to the collusively established previous outcome".[82] The settlements did restrict publishers from imposing MFNs in their contracts for five years, but the constraints with respect to discounting that had been imposed on Macmillan would terminate on December 18, 2014. The constraints on the other four publishers with respect to discounting would terminate two years after either the prevailing agency contract or notice from the publisher to a distributor that the publisher would cease to demand compliance with the terms of the agency contract. Such constraints were imposed on three of the publishers in September 2012, and they were imposed on Penguin in December 2012.

All of the publishers reverted to agency with Amazon, albeit without MFNs but with the provision for limited retailer discounting in place. Since then, all of the defendant publishers have been relieved of the court-imposed constraints on discounting, and four of the publishers reverted to agency contracts with Amazon. (The fifth defendant publisher, Penguin, merged with the largest of the Big Six publishers, Random House, in 2013. Random House was not a defendant in the eBooks matter.) The four publishers secured agency contracts even though the restrictions on MFNs had remained in place. On December 18, 2014, the day the constraints on Macmillan with respect to discounting were lifted, the *Wall Street Journal* reported that Macmillan had "struck a new multiyear agreement" with Amazon.[83] The new agreement indicated that "Macmillan will set the consumer prices of its digital prices". The publisher Hachette achieved much

[81]   See the Final Judgment filed September 6, 2012 with respect to the publishers Hachette, Simon & Schuster and HarperCollins at https://www.justice.gov/atr/case-document/final-judgment-defendants-hachette-harpercollins-and-simon-schuster; the Final Judgment filed on August 12, 2013 with respect to Macmillan at https://www.justice.gov/atr/case-document/final-judgment-defendants-verlags gruppe-georg-von-holtzbrinck-gmbh-holtzbrinck; and the Final Judgment filed May 17, 2013 with respect to Penguin at https://www.justice.gov/atr/case-document/final-judgment-defendants-penguin-group-division-pearson-plc-and-penguin-group-usa (all three websites accessed March 30, 2015).
[82]   Again, see the Proposed Final Judgment and Competitive Impact Statement with respect to the publishers Hachette, HarperCollins and Simon & Schuster posted on the Federal Register, 77 FR 24518, April 24, 2012, p. 24530, accessed March 30, 2015 at https://www.gpo.gov/fdsys/pkg/FR-2012-04-24/pdf/2012-9831.pdf.
[83]   "Macmillan, Amazon reach new deal," *Wall Street Journal*, December 18, 2014.

the same thing by November 13, 2014: "Under the new pact, Hachette will set the prices of its digital books."[84] By October 20, 2014, Simon & Schuster also secured a contract by which it would "set the consumer prices of its digital books".[85] By April 13, 2015 HarperCollins also secured an agency contract with Amazon.[86]

CONCLUSION

With or without MFNs, Amazon has acquiesced to agency contracts in all negotiations between it and each of the Big Six publishers even when negotiations were insulated from the influences of a united front. Amazon had argued that it could have rebuffed any single publisher's demands for agency had any one set of contract negotiations been insulated from a united front. The more obvious explanation, however, is that the united front was a fiction, and the "wrath of Amazon" it was supposed to defeat was a bluff. Publishers did not need to concentrate contract negotiations in close proximity in order to induce Amazon to acquiesce to agency. Rather, the gambit of contracting with Apple and sponsoring the launch of the iBookstore was sufficient to individually invest each publisher with bargaining power sufficient to induce Amazon to acquiesce to agency.

After engaging agency contracts, publishers raised prices on Bestsellers and New Releases. They raised prices to benchmarks (price caps) indicated in their contracts with Apple. The court determined that raising prices to the price caps constituted price fixing. It is not obvious, however, that pricing post-agency did not derive from publishers' purely interdependent decision making. No evidence was presented that publishers would have had to institute some type of scheme to compel compliance with pricing consistent with the price caps in the future. Evidence of such a scheme could have gone far toward proving an agreement to fix prices.

---

[84] "Amazon, Hachette end publishing dispute," *Wall Street Journal*, November 13, 2014.

[85] "Amazon, Simon & Schuster reach book contract," *Wall Street Journal*, October 20, 2014. The contract reportedly gave Amazon some capacity to discount titles in certain situations.

[86] "Amazon, HarperCollins reach multiyear publishing deal," *Wall Street Journal*, April 13, 2015: "Under the so-called agency pricing model, publishers keep roughly 70% of the revenue from each individual sale, with retailers receiving an estimated 30% as their fee. Discounting is done only with approval of the publisher."

That leaves the publishers' gambit of contracting with Apple in early 2010. The publishers and Apple may have plainly appreciated the strategic interdependence of their decisions about whether or not to participate in the iBookstore, and they may have appreciated what contracting with Apple would achieve – more bargaining power in individual contract negotiations vis-à-vis Amazon – but, could the gambit alone constitute an antitrust conspiracy?

4. Adaptation in long-term exchange relations: evidence of the complementarity and ancillarity of dimensions of electricity marketing contracts

This chapter takes up an old, enduring question about what contracting parties can achieve in a long-term contract that they cannot achieve by a sequence of short-term contracts. In the environment examined here, the action depends on the role of both programmed renegotiation and unprogrammable demands for renegotiation in enabling contracting parties to adapt terms of exchange over time to changing conditions. As a matter of course, short-term contracts enable parties to renegotiate and adapt terms of exchange after a short term (Williamson 1971, p.116; Myers 1977, p.158). Thus, if adaptation over the long term is important, why would parties ever commit to long terms? One part of the answer advanced here is that long-term contracts allow parties to program fewer, rather than more, costly instances of renegotiation. A familiar tradeoff obtains between enabling flexibility in contractual relations and the costs of supporting that flexibility: a sequence of short-term contracts may afford greater flexibility, but programming a sequence of short-term contracts also entails programming a sequence of costly renegotiations (Masten and Crocker 1985; Crocker and Masten 1988). Longer terms may not neutralize the prospect of unprogrammable demands for renegotiation, but they diminish the frequency of programmed renegotiations.

Managing tradeoffs between flexibility and renegotiation suggests that efficient adaptation can be an interesting economic problem (Crocker and Masten 1991), but that is just one consideration in a much larger contracting problem. The first-order action pertains to investment incentives (Williamson 1971, p.116). In the environment examined here, adaptation may involve expanding, withdrawing, or tuning up production capacity over the course of (possibly) long-term exchange. A difficulty is that one party's decision to expand, withdraw, or tune up capacity can diminish the payoffs of counterparties joined in long-term contracts. Thus, the prospect of changing production capacity might induce demands by counterparties to either adjust other terms of contract in response to changes in capacity, or to circumscribe any one party's plans to change capacity. Specifically, counterparties might demand safeguards in long-term contracts in the form of provisions that enable them to impose renegotiation in response to other parties' proposals to expand, withdraw, or tune up capacity. Alternatively, they might demand shorter-term contracts. We thus come full circle. Contract duration is one instrument parties can use for containing the frequency of costly renegotiations, but renegotiation itself constitutes an instrument parties may use for adapting terms of contract as well as production capacity over the course of long-term exchange – which in turn may affect the duration of contracts and the incentives of parties to invest in production capacity in the first place.

In this chapter I examine an environment in which contract duration constitutes but one of four instruments parties use for managing adaptation over the course of long-term exchange. I examine an environment in which parties tailor (1) contract duration, (2) veto provisions, (3) risk-sharing schemes, and (4) financial structure (debt or equity) to support investment in production capacity. Similar to Crocker and Masten (1988), this chapter accommodates the prospect that there can be important interactions between contract duration and the contractual mechanisms parties use to enable adaptation. I elaborate on the hypothesis of Williamson (1988) that debt financing requires fewer costly monitoring mechanisms than does equity financing.[1] With this hypothesis, we can craft an organic explanation of the role of both programmed and unprogrammed renegotiation in enabling parties to adapt terms of contract over the course of long-term exchange and the prevalence of debt over equity in the financing of highly redeployable assets.

The environment I examine is not specific to electricity generation, but is inspired by problems parties encounter in mobilizing investment in electricity-generation capacity. Firms that develop generation facilities (hereafter, generators) tell a compelling but incomplete story about how they organize the financing of specific generation capacity. They line up long-term contracts with electricity marketers. Marketers trade electricity on wholesale electricity markets, and they often secure dispatch rights from generators – rights to make real-time demands for electricity generation as well as demands to cease generation. In return, marketers compensate generators according to two-part schemes. The variable

---

[1] The discussion of Hansmann and Kraakman (2000, pp. 399–401) on monitoring and "asset-partitioning" is apposite. See, also, Chapter 5 in this volume.

part of the scheme compensates generators for their operating costs, and generators extract profits through the fixed part of the scheme. Marketers end up bearing risk for generators, and generators turn around and appeal to prospective creditors (the bank) for loans to finance the construction or acquisition of electricity-generation capacity. Indeed, generators report that they need to line up two-part compensation in order to motivate creditors to finance investment in generation capacity that can support timely dispatch demands.[2]

After parties have committed to a contract, the prospect of adding, withdrawing or tuning up capacity can pose an interesting problem. Changing capacity can affect the vertical rent that the parties share, but note the incentives of the generator. If the generator has already secured its share of the rent by means of a two-part compensation scheme, it may perceive private benefits to expanding capacity. A problem is that bringing new capacity online can complicate the efforts of the marketer to commercialize capacity that is already under contract.[3] At the very least, a marketer might be compelled to demand adjustment of the fixed part of the two-part compensation scheme. Anticipating this, the parties might craft contracts that enable them to jointly internalize the effects of changing capacity. One way to do this would be to allow each party to veto proposals by the other to expand capacity. The point is not that a party would veto a proposal but that veto provisions enable parties to impose renegotiation when and if the counterparty proposes a change in capacity.

---

[2]   For example, Black Hills Corporation reported that:

We aim to secure long-term power sales contracts in conjunction with project financing. This enables us to minimize our liability and to design a debt repayment schedule to closely match the term of the power sales contracts so that at the end of the contract term, the debt has largely been repaid. (Black Hills Power, Inc. 2002, SEC Form 10-K for the year ending December 31, 2001, p. 10)

Similarly, AES Ironwood, LLC reported that:

Each monthly payment by [our marketer] Williams Energy will consist of a total fixed payment, a fuel conversion payment and a start-up payment. The total fixed payment, which is payable regardless of facility dispatch by Williams . . . is anticipated to be sufficient to cover our debt service and fixed operating and maintenance costs and to provide us a return on equity. (AES Ironwood, LLC 2002, SEC Form 10-K for the year ending December 31, 2001, p. 6)

[3]   For example, output from new capacity can induce congestion on transmission networks thus complicating transmission of electricity from capacity under contract. Output from new capacity may also depress prices in wholesale markets or make existing capacity "out of the money" (unprofitable).

One hazard that veto provisions pose is that the antitrust authorities might take an interest in what is going on; indeed, it was this kind of interest that motivated this study. However, the bigger issue is that the generators pose an incomplete rationale for contracts that involve the combination of (1) long terms, (2) two-part compensation, (3) debt financing, and (4) veto provisions. If adapting terms of contract is so important, why not commit to a short-term, because, as a matter of course, a short-term contract enables renegotiation (and, thus, adaptation) after a short term? Alternatively, if two-part compensation induces the generator to over-invest in production capacity, why not dispense with two-part compensation, as contracting parties sometimes do, and impose something like linear pricing, that is, a price per kilowatt-hour? Finally, what is so special about fobbing off all of the market risk onto marketers to support debt financing, because fobbing off risks onto another party does not make risks disappear?

We might be tempted to suggest that electricity-generation firms are risk-averse and that marketing firms are better equipped to deal with risk. Risk aversion is, however, too facile a hypothesis to appeal to, and it becomes interesting to pose the alternative hypothesis that these multi-billion dollar firms are risk-neutral. I put risk aversion aside and characterize an environment in which it can nonetheless be efficient for parties to impose all market risk on the marketer. I present a simple model that features tradeoffs between the four instruments. The general model yields hypotheses about patterns of complementarity and substitution between the four instruments. These hypotheses are interesting, because they lend themselves to a simple narrative about how electricity marketing contracts work: veto provisions and contract duration complement each other in that long terms increase the prospect of unprogrammed demands for adaptation, and veto provisions allow parties to impose renegotiation as a way of addressing unprogrammed demands. At the same time, short-term contracts tend not to feature veto provisions, because short terms afford parties the option of renegotiating after a short term. Meanwhile, imposing the residual claim on marketers allows investors to concentrate costly monitoring on marketers and to relieve themselves of having to monitor generators' fixed streams of payoffs. Lower monitoring costs increase the vertical rent that marketers and generators extract. Nonetheless, there is an advantage to imposing some risk on generators. Imposing this risk would induce them to internalize at least some of the rent-diminishing effects (if any) of expanding capacity, but parties can address generators' distorted investment incentives by imposing shorter terms. Shorter terms, however, give rise to a greater frequency of programmed renegotiations. The upshot is that different combinations of contract duration, veto provisions and risk-sharing feature different advantages and disadvantages.

A restricted version of the model also yields hypotheses about patterns of complementarity and substitution, but it also yields hypotheses of the ancillarity of certain dimensions of contract. That is, contracting parties may not determine all dimensions of contract simultaneously. They may determine dimensions in a multi-stage process. Specifically, they may determine contract duration and the structure of profit sharing in order to support their choice of financing. They may then determine whether or not to insert a veto provision in the contract if the contract were to feature a long term and a two-part compensation. In such an arrangement, veto provisions appear not so much as a complement to long terms and two-part compensation but rather as an ancillary dimension of contract in that they support long-term contracts and debt financing.

Having hypothesized patterns complementarity, substitutability, and ancillarity, I then examine a dataset of 101 electricity marketing contracts. The empirical results are consistent with efficient adaptation being an important economic problem. More to the point, they illuminate a triangular, multi-stage structure of contract design. Veto provisions show up in a supportive role. They are not simultaneously determined with other dimensions of contract.

The results are also interesting, because they are relevant to antitrust analysis. The results suggest that veto provisions enable contracting parties to maximize the private benefits (the vertical rent) that they collectively perceive. In instances in which a single marketer contracts with more than one competing generator, we can easily suggest that generators themselves use veto provisions as a way of committing to restrict investment in production capacity in the future. Restricting capacity constitutes a robust means of committing to restrain output and raise wholesale electricity prices. Now consider the case of a marketer contracting with a single generator. Again, veto provisions enable the parties to maximize the vertical rent, but it would be difficult to suggest how maximizing the vertical rent is anticompetitive. Rather, veto provisions enable the parties to induce no less investment in the future than the generator would pursue were it responsible for marketing its own output. Were the antitrust authorities to bar parties from imposing veto provisions in their contracts, generators might have more difficulty mobilizing investment in which they end up underinvesting in capacity or even forgoing investment entirely.

Finally, the results are interesting as a matter of theory and in how they inform empirical analysis. Substitution may preclude appeal to monotone comparative statics, and that complicates the effort to yield policy-relevant conclusions. The theoretical model is not supermodular, and supermodularity could not rationalize a triangular, multi-stage design process anyway. Accordingly, all of the analytical shortcuts that super-modularity might otherwise imply are not available. We have to do more work. In addition, much of the traditional comparative static analysis is not immediately available. In the environment explored here, the economics include discrete choices – decisions to include or exclude certain contractual provisions – as well as continuous choices, such as contract duration. Discrete choices preclude appeal to traditional comparative statics based on the envelope theorem. Even so, I explore an environment that is simple enough so that we can extract results from examination of something of a discrete-continuous envelope of contracts.

The remainder of the chapter proceeds in three sections. The first lays out a simple model of a contracting problem in which contract duration, veto provisions, risk-sharing and financial structure are endogenous. The model is not specific to electricity marketing, but subsumes the generator's and marketer's contracting problem in a more general framework. The advantage of the generalized framework is that it can accommodate analysis in environments that feature either highly redeployable assets or assets that are highly relationship-specific. The results demonstrate patterns of complementarity and substitution between contract duration, veto provisions, risk-sharing, and financial structure. The second section of the chapter describes the structure of electricity marketing contracts and presents empirical results. The final section concludes.

MODELS AND HYPOTHESES

Even though the model is not specific to electricity marketing, I refer to the two contracting parties as the generator and the marketer. The two risk-neutral parties craft a contract that extends over an interval of duration $T \geq 0$. Parties contribute assets that may or may not be highly redeployable outside their specific relationship. The generator contributes production assets that involve significant sunk costs. The marketer contributes complementary assets or capabilities, and the parties produce in as many as two states. In the initial state, the parties anticipate a continuous and stationary stream of payoffs $z(t)$ with $E[z(t)] = z$. The state may change in that at any time $t^* \in [0, T]$ the stream of payoffs may change. I am agnostic on how the payoffs change, but I characterize the change by a continuation value $S(t^*) = S$. We can, for example, understand the continuation value as the expected salvage value. Realizing the continuation value entails either redeploying assets or adding, withdrawing, or tuning up capacity, as well as adapting the terms of contract. I am agnostic on how parties respond to the change in states, but I do suggest that implementing a cost-effective response may involve some dissipation of surplus. The extent of rent dissipation will depend partly on how parties design their contract.

Terms of contract include contract duration T and three binary choices. First, parties decide whether or not to impose the residual claim on the marketer, in which case the generator receives a fixed payoff at every $t < t^*$. I pose the alternative as sharing risk, although the alternative could entail imposing the residual claim on the generator. Second, the parties decide whether or not to impose a veto provision in the contract. Specifically, they decide whether or not to impose a provision according to which either party might veto the proposal of the other to add, withdraw or tune up the generator's production capacity. Hence, a contract is a quadruple (s, v, d, T) with:

T = Contract duration

$$s = \begin{cases} 1 & \text{marketer bears all risk} \\ 0 & \text{generator bears some risk} \end{cases}$$

$$v = \begin{cases} 1 & \text{Veto provision included} \\ 0 & \text{No veto provision} \end{cases}$$

$$d = \begin{cases} 1 & \text{Debt financing} \\ 0 & \text{Equity financing} \end{cases}$$

Parameters

Parties can use the veto provision to impose renegotiation over the terms of contract and over the prospect of adding, withdrawing or tuning up production capacity. The interpretation is that renegotiation forces the parties to realize adjustments in capacity, including the prospect of liquidation, which maximize the vertical rent. The adjustments the parties have to make may be unprogrammable which renders them noncontractible. Thus, renegotiation may serve the purpose of enabling the parties to realize rent-maximizing adjustments. The key issue is that renegotiation may itself entail some dissipation of rent, which I indicate by the parameter R. Failure to realize the vertical rent invites some dissipation of rents, which I indicate as a tax of proportion δ of the continuation value S. Meanwhile, imposing a risky stream of payoffs on the generator raises the (instantaneous) auditing/monitoring costs of outside investors by increment m.

The Monitoring Hypothesis

I justify this characterization of monitoring costs as follows: the marketer may be involved in a broad portfolio of projects with any number of generators. Pooling streams from different projects amounts to pooling risks, but pooling risks may make it more difficult for outside investors to disentangle and monitor streams thus creating demands for costly auditing schemes. The generator, however, may separately incorporate each of its production projects.[4] In the language of Hansmann and Kraakman (2000), the generator may be able to partition assets across separately incorporated entities so that outside investors may forgo the costs of disentangling any single project's streams from those of other projects. However, risky streams still require monitoring, because generators might cheat investors by misrepresenting their payoffs. Also, relieving the generator of project-specific risk relieves outside investors of having to bear incremental monitoring and auditing costs. Thus, imposing the residual claims on the marketer still enables risk pooling, but it also enables parties to economize on auditing and monitoring costs; investors need only concentrate the lens of costly auditing and monitoring on the marketer.

I indicate K as the sunk costs of instituting a mechanism to monitor the generator's payoffs,[5] and I indicate c as the instantaneous marginal cost of producing instantaneous output z. I indicate ρ as a discount rate and λ as a hazard rate reflecting the instantaneous likelihood of the state reverting to the continuation state. Next, I indicate γ as the instantaneous rate at which the cost of producing output increases.[6]

Finally, I indicate $\alpha \in [0, 1]$ as the proportion of the vertical rent that is relationship-specific – that is, α indicates asset-specificity, the degree to which assets committed to the relationship cannot be redeployed without dissipating value. The appeal to asset-specificity will provide a way to characterize tradeoffs between debt and equity financing of the sort anticipated in Williamson (1988).

---

[4] In the electricity-generation context, generators uniformly incorporate generating projects in distinct production limited liability companies (LLCs).

[5] The sunk costs are important, and the appeal to them is consistent with the framework of Williamson (1988).

[6] Imposing $\gamma > 0$ may seem artificial, but it constitutes a simple way of securing the second-order conditions for an interior solution of the optimal contract duration. The key issue, however, is that there are any number of isomorphic ways to secure an interior solution. For example, the term γ constitutes an indirect way of modeling depreciation of production capacity. I suggest that imposing γ constitutes little loss of generality and does not otherwise constitute an interesting, instructive assumption.

To recap, the parameters of the system are:

z = Instantaneous income at time $t \in [0,T]$
c = Instantaneous cost of producing z
m = Instantaneous monitoring costs
K = Cost of instituting monitoring mechanism
R = Dissipation due to renegotiation
S = Continuation value
δ = Dissipation, proportional to the continuation value S, that results from distorted investment incentives
ρ = Discount rate
α = Degree of asset-specificity
γ = Rate of cost appreciation
λ = Hazard rate

Given a contingency occurs at time t^*, the parties at time $t = 0$ perceive a discounted vertical rent V:

$$V(t^*;T) = \int_0^{t^*} (z - ce^{\gamma t} - (1-sd)\alpha^d m)e^{-\rho t}dt + [S - vR]e^{-\rho t^*} -$$
$$[d\alpha + (1-v)s\delta]S(e^{\rho(T-t^*)} - 1)$$

While this expression appears to be complex, its interpretation is straightforward. Contracting parties would realize an (expected) vertical rent,

$$V(t^*;T) = \int_0^{t^*} (z - ce^{\gamma t})e^{-\rho t}dt + Se^{-\rho t^*},$$

but for a series of negative deviations from the vertical rent that depend on how parties structure their financing and design their contract. The interpretation is that imposing veto provisions ($v = 1$) allows the parties to avoid the (discounted) rent dissipation δS that occurs at time t^*, but setting $v = 1$ forces them to bear the (discounted) renegotiation tax R.[7] Parties secure the (discounted) continuation value S, and they secure the expected stream of payments z through time t^* less the costs of producing that stream. Finally, imposing risk on the generator ($s = 0$) forces the parties to bear incremental monitoring costs m, but imposing risk forces the generator to internalize the effects of inefficient investment at time t^*,

---

[7]   Note that the rent dissipation that attends distorted investment at time t^* is diminishing with time. This is not an important assumption.

thus enabling the parties to avoid the tax δS. In contrast, relieving the generator of risk and imposing the residual claim on the marketer enables the parties to avoid incremental monitoring costs but introduces the prospect of distorted investment at time t^*. Note that either imposing the veto or imposing risk on the generator allows the parties to avoid the tax δS.

Asset-specificity enters V in two places. First, parties perceive monitoring costs $\alpha^d m$. Thus, in the absence of other remedies, parties perceive monitoring costs m under equity financing $(d = 0)$ but perceive lower monitoring costs αm under debt financing $(d = 1)$. The difficulty with debt, however, is that it frustrates efforts to work things out (Williamson 1988) and salvage relationship-specific value in the event the stream of payoffs revert to the continuation payoffs. Specifically, parties perceive a tax $d\alpha S$ proportional to the continuation value S.[8] The advantage of equity – indeed, the entire purpose of equity in this environment – is to allow parties to avoid the rent dissipation αS that attends ventures featuring some degree of relationship-specific value.

If we let $F(t^*; \cdot)$ indicate the probability of an unprogrammable contingency occurring by time t^* – with corresponding probability mass function $f(t^*; \cdot)$, and if we lets EV indicate the expectation of V, then we can characterize the parties expected payoff at time $t = 0$ as

$$E\pi = EV - (1 - sd)\alpha^d K = \int_0^T V(t^*; T) f(t^*; \cdot) \, dt^* + (1 - F(T; \cdot)) V(T; T) - (1 - sd)\alpha^d K$$

Note that imposing $s = 1$ (the marketer bears all risk) and $d = 1$ also allows the parties to avoid the upfront sunk costs K of instituting a monitoring mechanism.

Now, if we let λ indicate the hazard rate, then the density function corresponds to the exponential density $f(t; \lambda) = \lambda e^{-\lambda t}$ and $(1 - F(t; \lambda)) = e^{-\lambda t}$. Economic modelers often use the Poisson distribution to model the number of unprogrammed events that may occur within a given interval of time, but the exponential distribution constitutes the reverse side of the coin; it constitutes a way of modeling the time that lapses until the next contingency occurs. In the environment explored here, we are interested in the time it takes for a single event, the realization of the continuation value, to occur.

With exponential hazards in hand, we have

---

[8]   The rent dissipation that attends failure to work things out is also diminishing with time.

$$E\pi(s,v,d,T) = \left[\frac{z-(1-sd)\alpha^d m}{\rho+\lambda}\right](1-e^{-(\rho+\lambda)T}) + \left[\frac{c}{\gamma-\rho-\lambda}\right](1-e^{(\gamma-\rho-\lambda)T}) - (1-sd)\alpha^d K$$

$$+\left[\frac{S-vR}{\rho+\lambda}\right](\lambda+\rho e^{-(\rho+\lambda)T}) - \left[\frac{d\alpha+(1-v)s\delta}{\rho+\lambda}\right]S[\rho(e^{-\lambda T}-1)+\lambda(e^{\rho T}-1)]$$

This last expression for the expected vertical rent $E\pi(s, v, d, T)$ yields complementarity and substitutability results.

Proposition 1:   Given α, δ, ρ, K, R, S each greater than zero, then

1. v and T are strict complements,
2. v and s are strict complements,
3. v and d are weakly substitutes and complements,
4. s and d are strict complements,
5. s and T are neither generally complements nor substitutes, but given $m = 0$, s and T are weakly substitutes, and
6. d and T may be neither complements nor substitutes, but for low degrees of asset-specificity (low α) and $m > 0$, d and T may be complements.

Proof: We can prove each item by characterizing whether or not the function $E\pi(s, v, d, T)$ has increasing or decreasing differences in each of the six possible pairs of inputs (Topkis 1998, p.42). I demonstrate the results for items 1, 4 and 5:

We can conclude that v and T are complements if the function $E\pi(s, v, d, T)$ exhibits increasing differences in v and T. The function $E\pi(s, v, d, T)$ exhibits increasing differences if, for all $T_1 > T_0$,

$$E\pi(s, 1, d, T_1) - E\pi(s, 0, d, T_1) \geq E\pi(s, 1, d, T_0) - E\pi(s, 0, d, T_0),$$

It is sufficient to show that $E\pi(s, 1, d, T) - E\pi(s, 0, d, T)$ is increasing in T or, the same thing, that

$$\frac{\partial}{\partial T}\{E\pi(s, 1, d, T) - E\pi(s, 0, d, T)\} \geq 0.$$

This last expression yields

$$R\rho e^{-(\rho+\lambda)T} + \left(\frac{\lambda\rho}{\rho+\lambda}\right)s\delta S(e^{\rho T} - e^{-\lambda T}) \geq 0,$$

which holds for any R and ρ both greater than zero.

By similar calculations, we can show that s and T are neither generally complements nor substitutes. We can conclude that s and T are weakly complements if the function $E\pi(s, v, d, T)$ exhibits increasing differences in s and T – that is, if

$$\frac{\partial}{\partial T}\{E\pi(1, v, d, T) - E\pi(0, v, d, T)\} \geq 0.$$

This last condition yields

$$d\alpha^d m e^{-(\rho+\lambda)T} - \left(\frac{\lambda\rho}{\rho+\lambda}\right)(1-v)\delta S(e^{\rho T} - e^{-\lambda T}) \geq 0,$$

which is satisfied if $d = 1$, $m > 0$ and $\delta S = 0$.

We can establish the complementarity of s and d by showing that

$$E\pi(1, v, 1, T) - E\pi(1, v, 0, T) \geq E\pi(0, v, 1, T) - E\pi(0, v, 0, T) \geq 0.$$

This expression yields

$$K + \left(\frac{\alpha m}{\rho+\lambda}\right)(1 - e^{-(\rho+\lambda)T}) \geq 0.$$

Counterfactual Policy Experiment

Item 1 in proposition 1 indicates that v and T are complementary, and it would be tempting to pose a counterfactual policy experiment suggestive of an appeal to the LeChatelier Principle and conclude that barring parties from including veto provisions in their contracts – that is, imposing $v = 0$ on the contracting parties – would induce them to craft shorter-term contracts. Such a conclusion would be appropriate were the function $E\pi(s, v, d, T)$ supermodular in (s, v, d, T) – that is, were each of the four inputs complements to each other. (See Topkis 1998, pp. 80–81, 92–3.) Items 5 and 6 in proposition 1 imply that the function $E\pi(s, v, d, T)$ is not supermodular, in which case imposing $v = 0$ may induce parties to adopt a bundle of adaptations (s', d', T') that features T' greater than the contract term featured in the original contract. Accordingly, I have to develop more results in order to motivate a counterfactual policy experiment.

Note that we can partition contracts into $2^3 = 8$ types $(s, v, d) \in \{(0,1) \times (0,1) \times (0,1)\}$. I motivate a counterfactual policy experiment by characterizing the envelope of contract duration $T(s, v, d) = \arg\max E\pi(s, v, d, \hat{T})$ and by evaluating $T(s, v, d)$ along the envelope of undominated triples (s, v, d). I will be able to show that barring parties from using veto provisions does induce a reduction in contract duration. In the next proposition I characterize $T(s, v, d)$ for a given triple (s, v, d), and then I characterize the envelope of undominated triples. I close the section by graphically demonstrating the proposition in Williamson (1988) that equity lines up with higher degrees of asset-specificity and debt lines up with lower degrees of asset-specificity.

In the first lemma I show that contract duration $T(s, v, d)$ is greater than zero and finite under plausible parameterizations. I then show that four of the eight types of contracts can never be efficient, but I will need $T(s, v, d) > 0$ for all s, v, and d to demonstrate that the remaining four types can be efficient.

Lemma 1:   Given $z - c - m - \rho S > 0$ and γ, ρ and c each greater than zero, then contract duration $T(s, v, d)$ achieves a unique optimum conforming to the identity

$$T(s, v, d) = \frac{1}{\gamma} \ln \left\{ \frac{[z - (1-sd)\alpha^d m] - \rho [S - vR]}{c} \right.$$
$$\left. - \left(\frac{\lambda \rho}{\rho + \lambda}\right)[d\alpha + (1-v)s\delta] \left(\frac{Se^{\rho T(s,v,d)}}{c}\right)[e^{(\rho+\lambda)T(s,v,d)} - 1]\right\}$$

with

$$0 < T(s, v, d) < \frac{1}{\gamma} \ln \left[\frac{z + \rho R}{c}\right].$$

Moreover, inspection yields:

$T(1,1,0) = T(0,1,0) \geq T(0,0,0) \geq T(1,0,0) > 0$
$T(1,1,1) \geq T(1,0,1) > 0$
$T(1,1,1) \geq T(0,1,1) \geq T(0,0,1) > 0$

Proof: Differentiating $E\pi$ with respect to T yields

$$\frac{\partial E\pi}{\partial T} = V(T;T)f(T;\cdot) - f(T;\cdot)V(T;T) + \int_0^T V_2(t^*;T) f(t^*;\cdot)dt^*$$
$$- (1 - F(T;\cdot))(V_1(T;T) + V_2(T;T))$$
$$= \int_0^T V_2(t^*;T)f(t^*;\cdot)dt^* - (1 - F(T;\cdot))(V_1(T;T) + V_2(T;T))$$

or

$$\frac{\partial E\pi}{\partial T} = [z - (1-sd)\alpha^d m]e^{-(\rho+\lambda)T} - \rho[S - vR]e^{-(\rho+\lambda)T} - ce^{(\gamma-\rho-\lambda)T}$$
$$- \left(\frac{\lambda \rho}{\rho + \lambda}\right)[d\alpha + (1-v)s\delta] S(e^{\rho T} - e^{-\lambda T})$$

The first-order condition $\dfrac{\partial E\pi}{\partial T} = 0$ can be rearranged as

$$e^{\gamma T} = k_0(s, v, d) - k_1(s, v, d)e^{\rho T}[e^{(\rho + \lambda)T} - 1]$$

where

$$k_0(s, v, d) = \frac{[z - (1 - sd)\alpha^d m] - \rho[S - vR]}{c}$$

and

$$k_1(s, v, d) = \left(\frac{\lambda\rho}{\rho + \lambda}\right)[d\alpha + (1 - v)s\delta]\left(\frac{S}{c}\right).$$

The premises $z - c - m - \rho S > 0$ and $c > 0$ imply $k_0 > 1$ which amounts to saying that the stream z outweighs the cost of producing that stream $(c + m)$ and the opportunity cost of forgoing the salvage value S (ρS). The premises $\rho > 0$ and $c > 0$ imply that $k_1 \geq 0$ is well defined. The second-order condition is

$$\frac{\partial^2 E\pi}{\partial T^2} = -\gamma c e^{(\gamma - \rho - \lambda)T} - \lambda\rho[d\alpha + (1 - v)s\delta]S\left\{e^{\rho T} + r\left(\frac{e^{\rho T} - e^{-\lambda T}}{\lambda + \rho}\right)\right\}$$

Thus imposing $\gamma > 0$ implies that the second-order condition for a unique solution

$$\frac{\partial^2 E\pi}{\partial T^2} < 0$$

strictly holds. In turn, implicit differentiation yields

$$\frac{\partial T}{\partial k_0} = \frac{1}{\gamma e^{\gamma T} + k_1 e^{\rho T}[(2\rho + \lambda)e^{(\rho + \lambda)T} - \rho]} > 0.$$

Note that the first-order condition implies $T = 0$ given $k_0 = 1$. Thus, imposing $k_0 > 1$ yields optimal contract duration $T > 0$. Inspection of the first-order conditions over the eight types of contracts $(s, v, d) \in \{(0, 1) \times (0, 1) \times (0, 1)\}$ yields the sequence of inequalities and the upper bound

$$T(s, v, d) < \frac{1}{\gamma}\ln\left[\frac{z + \rho R}{c}\right].$$

See Appendix 4A.2.

Lemma 2 and lemma 3 demonstrate that four types of contracts are never efficient under certain plausible parameterizations. Lemma 2 indicates that contracts featuring both risk-sharing and veto provisions are dominated by other types of contracts and therefore should not be observed in the contract data. Lemma 2 yields a "no belts and braces" result. It shows that, given renegotiation is costly, any contract featuring the combination of risk-sharing ($s = 0$) and a veto provision ($v = 1$) is dominated. Contracting parties do not have to impose both risk-sharing on the generator and a veto provision in order to avoid big distortions in the generator's investment decisions in the future. Thus, contracts may feature one or the other provision, but not both. We will use this result in the empirical analysis.

Lemma 2: Given R greater than zero, contracts conforming to $(s, v, d) = (0, 1, d)$ are never efficient.

Proof: There exist contracts conforming to $(s, v, d) = (0, 0, d)$ that strictly dominate any one contract conforming to $(s, v, d) = (0, 1, d)$. See Appendix 4A.3.

Lemma 3 indicates that contracts that support equity financing and impose all of the risk on marketers should not be observed in the data. Assigning all the marketing risk to the marketer may support debt financing, but there is no need to do that to support equity financing.

Lemma 3: Given R and ρ each greater than zero, contracts conforming to $(s, v, d) = (1, 0, 0)$ and $(1, 1, 0)$ are never efficient.

Proof: There exist contracts conforming to $(s, v, d) = (0, 0, 0)$ that strictly dominate any one contract conforming to $(s, v, d) = (1, 0, 0)$ or $(1, 1, 0)$. See Appendix 4A.3.

I now show that the remaining four types of contracts can be efficient.

Proposition 2: Assume that at least one type of contract other than the null contract is efficient. Any one contract conforming to $(s, v, d) \in \{(0, 0, 0), (0, 0, 1), (1, 0, 1), (1, 1, 1)\}$ may dominate.

Proof: Let

$$T_{svd} = T(s, v, d) = \arg\max_{\hat{T}} E\pi(s, v, d, \hat{T})$$

indicate the envelope of contract duration.

Lemma 2 and 3 imply that we have only four out of the eight types of contracts to consider. The object is to find parameterizations under which any one of the four remaining types of contracts would be efficient.

Thus, for each of these four contracts we must characterize a particular parameterization and make three pair-wise comparisons.

1. First I show that there exists a parameterization under which $(0,0,1)$ is efficient. Let $\alpha = 0$, $\gamma > 0$, $\delta > 0$, $\rho > 0$, $\lambda > 0$, $c > 0$, $R > 0$, $S > 0$, $K > 0$, and $z - c - m - \rho S > 0$. Then $E\pi\,(0,0,1,T) - E\pi\,(0,0,0,T) \geq K > 0$. Further, optimization implies that $E\pi\,(s, v, d, T_{svd}) \geq E\pi\,(s, v, d, T_{s'v'd'})$ for all (s,v,d) and $(s',v',d') \in \{(0,1)\times(0,1)\times(0,1)\}$, so, all along the contract duration envelope we have $E\pi\,(0,0,1,T_{001}) \geq E\pi\,(0,0,1,T_{000}) > E\pi\,(0,0,0,T_{000}) \geq E\pi(0,0,0,T_{001})$. Thus the contract $(0,0,1)$ dominates the one equity contract conforming to $(0,0,0)$.
    Next, observe that

    $$E\pi\,(0,0,1,T) - E\pi\,(1,0,1,T) = \left(\frac{\delta S}{\rho + \lambda}\right)[\lambda(e^{\rho T} - 1) + \rho(e^{-\lambda T} - 1)] > 0$$

    for any $T > 0$. Under the premises of Lemma 1 we know that $T_{101} > 0$ which in turn implies $E\pi\,(0,0,1,T_{101}) - E\pi\,(1,0,1,T_{101}) > 0$. This inequality and optimization imply that along the contract duration envelope

    $$E\pi\,(0,0,1,T_{001}) \geq E\pi\,(0,0,1,T_{101}) > E\pi\,(1,0,1,T_{101}) \geq E\pi\,(1,0,1,T_{001})$$

    Thus $(0,0,1)$ dominates $(1,0,1)$.
    Finally we must show that $(0,0,1)$ dominates $(1,1,1)$. Observe that

    $$E\pi\,(0,0,1,T) - E\pi\,(1,1,1,T) = \left(\frac{R}{\rho + \lambda}\right)(\lambda + \rho e^{-(\rho + \lambda)T}) > 0.$$

    This inequality and optimization imply that along the contract duration envelope

    $$E\pi\,(0,0,1,T_{001}) \geq E\pi\,(0,0,1,T_{111}) > E\pi\,(1,1,1,T_{111}) \geq E\pi\,(1,1,1,T_{001})$$

    Thus $(0,0,1)$ dominates $(1,1,1)$, and one can conclude that $(0,0,1)$ is efficient. Similar calculations along the contract duration envelope yield the following results:

2. Under the premises of lemma 1 one can show that $T_{000} > 0$. In turn, one can show that

    $$\delta = 0, \lambda > 0, R > 0, S > 0, K > 0 \text{ and } 0 < \alpha < \frac{m(1 - e^{-(\rho + \lambda)T_{000}}) + K(\rho + \lambda)}{S[\rho(e^{-\lambda T_{000}} - 1) + \lambda(e^{\rho T_{000}} - 1)]}$$

    implies $(s, v, d) = (1,0,1)$ is efficient.

3. Again, under the premises of Lemma 1 one can show that $T_{001} > 0$ and $T_{101} > 0$. We can then judiciously choose $\alpha > 0$, $\delta > 0$, $\lambda > 0$, $m \geq 0$, $R \geq 0$, $S > 0$ and $K > 0$ so that

$$0 \leq R < \delta S \left[\frac{\rho(e^{-\lambda T_{101}} - 1) + \lambda(e^{\rho T_{101}} - 1)}{\rho e^{-(\rho + \lambda)T_{101}} + \lambda} \right], \ 0 \leq R < \alpha \left[\frac{m(1 - e^{-(\rho + \lambda)T_{001}}) + K}{\rho e^{-(\rho + \lambda)T_{001}} + \lambda} \right],$$

and

$$0 \leq R < \left[\frac{m(1 - e^{-(\rho + \lambda)T_{000}}) + K(\rho + \lambda) - \alpha S[\rho(e^{-\lambda T_{000}} - 1) + \lambda(e^{\rho T_{000}} - 1)]}{\rho e^{-(\rho + \lambda)T_{000}} + \lambda} \right].$$

   All of these inequalities imply $(s, v, d) = (1, 1, 1)$ is efficient.
4. Finally, $m = K = 0$, $\rho > 0$, $\lambda > 0$, $\alpha > 0$, and imply $(s, v, d) = (0, 0, 0)$ is efficient.

The next proposition amounts to restricting the results of lemma 1 to the undominated contracts identified in proposition 2.

Proposition 3: Given $z - c - m - \rho S > 0$ and $\alpha, \delta, \lambda, \rho, m, c, R, S$ each greater than zero, then $T(1, 1, 1) > T(1, 0, 1) > 0$ and $T(1, 1, 1) > T(0, 0, 1) > 0$.

In general, it is not possible to rank $T(0, 0, 0)$ and $T(1, 1, 1)$. However, if we impose α sufficiently small – take $\alpha = 0$, for example – then one can rank the pair $T(0, 0, 1)$ and $T(1, 0, 1)$ and the pair $T(0, 0, 1)$ and $T(0, 0, 0)$. Specifically, we get our next proposition.

Proposition 4: Given $z - c - m - \rho S > 0$, $\delta, \lambda, \rho, m, c, R, S$, each greater than zero, and α small enough and monitoring costs m large enough such that

$$(1 - \alpha)m > \alpha S \left(\frac{\lambda \rho}{\lambda + \rho} \right) \left(\frac{z - \alpha m - \rho S}{c} \right)^{\frac{\rho}{\gamma}} \left\{ \left(\frac{z - \alpha m - \rho S}{c} \right)^{\frac{\rho + \lambda}{\gamma}} - 1 \right\},$$

then

$$T(1, 1, 1) > T(0, 0, 1) > \begin{cases} T(1, 0, 1) \\ T(0, 0, 0) \end{cases}$$

See Appendix 4A.4.

Remark: For α sufficiently small, contract duration T and s appear as substitutes among undominated contracts in that $T(0, 0, 1) > T(1, 0, 1)$. The key point, however, is that, other things equal, the duration of contracts featuring veto provisions exceeds that of all other undominated contracts.

Taken together, propositions 2 and 4 yield a counterfactual policy experiment. According to proposition 2, one can pose the hypothesis that $(s, v, d) = (1, 1, 1)$ is optimal. Suppose, now, that the antitrust authorities block $v = 1$. The contract parties then deviate to either $(s, v, d) = (0, 0, 1)$, $(s, v, d) = (1, 0, 1), (s, v, d) = (0, 0, 0)$, or the null contract. If the parties continue to contract, then proposition 4 implies that the new contract features a shorter term than that of the blocked contract. Thus parties end up underinvesting or, in expectation, dissipating too much surplus through more frequent contract renegotiations.

Remark on the Role of Relationship-specific Investment

We might be tempted to suggest that long terms of contract reflect the efforts of contracting parties to remedy under-investment in relationship-specific assets (the hold-up problem). However, note that the complementarity and substitution results are functions of the index asset-specificity but are not principally driven by asset-specificity. Rather, they are driven by the various sources of friction and investment distortions, and asset-specificity interacts with these sources of friction and distortions. Similarly, we could also go ahead and show that contract duration is principally determined by the problem of minimizing friction and distortions rather than on the degree to which investments are relationship-specific. Differentiating the vertical rent $E\pi$ with respect to T (given s, v, d) does not yield a closed-form solution for the optimal contract duration

$$T(s, v, d) = arg \max_{\hat{T}} E\pi(s, v, d, \hat{T}),$$

but we can show that, given $z - c - m - \rho S > 0$, and $\gamma, \rho,$ and c each greater than zero, then contract duration $T(s, v, d)$ achieves a unique optimum conforming to the identity

$$T(s, v, d) = \frac{1}{\gamma} \ln \left\{ \frac{[z - (1 - sd)\alpha^d m] - \rho[S - vR]}{c} \right.$$
$$\left. - \left(\frac{\lambda\rho}{\rho + \lambda}\right)[d\alpha + (1 - v)s\delta] \left(\frac{Se^{\rho T(s, v, d)}}{c}\right)[e^{(\rho + \lambda)T(s, v, d)} - 1] \right\}$$

with

$$0 < T(s, v, d) < \frac{1}{\gamma} \ln \left[\frac{z + \rho R}{c}\right].$$

Inspection allows us to see that there is more to contract duration in the environment explored here than resolving hold-up problems of the sort examined in such classic studies as Joskow (1987).

Financial Structure and Asset-specificity

Thus far the propositions make nothing more than passing contact with the choice of financial structure, yet some simple results are immediately available. Inspection of the expected vertical rents indicated in Appendix 4A.2 shows that the contract (0, 0, 1) dominates when assets are completely redeployable. That is, given $\alpha = 0$,

$$E\pi\,(0,0,1,T_{001};\alpha=0) > \begin{cases} E\pi\,(0,0,0,T_{000};\alpha=0) \\ E\pi\,(1,0,1,T_{101};\alpha=0) \\ E\pi\,(1,1,1,T_{111};\alpha=0) \end{cases}$$

Furthermore, given $\alpha=1$ $E\pi\,(0,0,0,T_{000};\alpha=1) > E\pi\,(0,0,1,T_{001};\alpha=1)$, although it is not the case that the equity contract $(0,0,0,T_{000};\alpha=1)$ necessarily dominates $(1,0,1,T_{101};\alpha=1)$ and $(1,1,1,T_{111};\alpha=1)$. That is, even when all value is relationship-specific ($\alpha=1$), the results suggest that debt financing might still prevail, although the prevailing contract would impose the residual claim on the marketer ($s=1$).

We can graphically characterize the choice of financial structure by mapping the vertical rent $E\pi$ against the index of asset-specificity α. First note that $E\pi$ is linear in α so that the loci of points in $E\pi - \alpha$ space is linear for each type of contracts (s,v,d). Differentiating $E\pi$ with respect to α yields

$$\frac{\partial E\pi\,(s,v,1,T_{sv1})}{\partial\alpha} = -\left[\frac{(1-s)m}{\rho+\lambda}\right](1-e^{-(\rho+\lambda)T_{sv1}})-(1-s)K$$
$$-\left[\frac{S}{\rho+\lambda}\right][\rho(e^{-\lambda T_{sv1}}-1)+\lambda(e^{\rho T_{sv1}}-1)]\leq 0$$

and

$$\frac{\partial E\pi\,(s,v,0,T_{sv0})}{\partial\alpha}=0.$$

Evaluating the derivatives for each of the four undominated modes of contracting yields

$$\frac{\partial E\pi\,(1,1,1,T_{111})}{\partial\alpha} < \frac{\partial E\pi\,(1,0,1,T_{101})}{\partial\alpha} < 0 = \frac{\partial E\pi\,(0,0,0,T_{000})}{\partial\alpha}$$

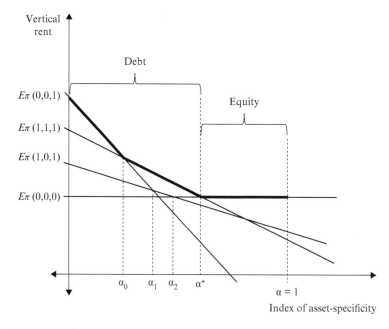

Figure 4.1   The envelope of contract selection

and for K large enough

$$\frac{\partial E\pi(0,0,1,T_{001})}{\partial \alpha} < \frac{\partial E\pi(1,1,1,T_{111})}{\partial \alpha} < \frac{\partial E\pi(1,0,1,T_{101})}{\partial \alpha} < 0 = \frac{\partial E\pi(0,0,0,T_{000})}{\partial \alpha}$$

Thus the locus of points corresponding to $(s,v,d) = (0,0,0)$ in $E\pi - \alpha$ space is a horizontal line. The loci corresponding to $(1,0,1)$, $(1,1,1)$ and $(0,0,1)$ are lines with increasingly negative slopes.

Figure 4.1 features a possible configuration of contracts. The contract $(0, 0, 1)$ is efficient at $\alpha = 0$, and $(0,0,0)$ dominates it at $\alpha = 1$. As drawn here, the contracts, $(0,0,1),(1,1,1)$ and $(0,0,0)$ collectively dominate $(1,0,1)$ over the entire interval $\alpha \in [0,1]$ and collectively constitute the contract envelope.

Now, let α^* indicate the cutoff point between debt and equity. Thus, if α^* exists, it solves $E\pi(0,0,0) = E\pi(s,v,1)$. Let $\bar{\pi}$ indicate the value of the parties' outside option. $E\pi(0,0,0,T) > \bar{\pi}$ implies $E\pi(0,0,1,T) > E\pi(0,0,0,T) > \bar{\pi}$ – that is, $(s,v,d) = (0,0,1)$ is on the contract envelope. $E\pi(0,0,1) < \bar{\pi}$ implies that only the null contract is on the contract envelope. More generally, if $\alpha \leq \alpha^*$ and $E\pi(0,0,0) \geq \bar{\pi}$, then $d = 1$ is efficient. If $\alpha < \alpha^*$, then $d = 0$ is never efficient.

Multi-stage Contract Design

Proposition 1 characterizes patterns of complementarity and substitutability between four dimensions of contract in an environment in which contracting parties simultaneously determine all four dimensions. Industry practice, meanwhile, suggests that contracting parties may determine these factors not in a single, comprehensive stage of contract design but in a process that unfolds over at least two stages. Firms organizing the financing of generation projects indicate that they align the schedule of payments in electricity marketing contracts with the schedule of debt payments. Contract duration and, possibly, two-part compensation may thus obtain as predetermined factors in decisions to institute veto provisions. Specifically, industry practice suggests a two-stage process for determining contract duration (T), risk-bearing (s), veto provisions (v), and financial structure (d): contracting parties determine optimal T, s, and d under the constraint $\delta = 0$ (the absence of distorted investment incentives). Under this constraint, parties determine contract duration as if there were no prospect of the generator's investment incentives to be distorted in the future. Contracting parties never adopt a veto provision, because no party would have a reason to demand renegotiation. In the second stage, after parties have determined T, s, and d, they relieve the constraints (they factor in distortions) and determine whether or not to implement a veto provision.

The patterns of complementarity and substitutability that derive from such a two-stage process deviate from those obtained in the comprehensive process in at least two important respects. The first is that risk-bearing and contract duration may now appear as complements, a result we will examine in the empirical analysis. Second, veto provisions emerge not as pair-wise complements to contract duration but as ancillary provisions supporting long-term contracts that assign all risk to marketers. Thus, for example, contracting parties may commit to a long-term contract and to assigning all of the marketing risk to marketer all in order to support debt financing. But they may then adopt a veto provision if contract duration exceeds a threshold beyond which expected demands to renegotiate outweigh the costs of renegotiation. Veto provisions thus attend longer-term contracts but not short-term contracts. Further, contracting parties consider implementing veto provisions if they agree to impose all of the marketing risk on the generator.

I develop these two results below.

Proposition 5:   Given α, ρ, K, R each greater than zero and $\delta = 0$, then s and T are weak complements.

Proof: Recall from above that

$$\frac{\partial}{\partial T}\{E\pi(1,v,d,T)-E\pi(0,v,d,T)\}=d\alpha^d me^{-(\rho+\lambda)T}-\left(\frac{\lambda\rho}{\rho+\lambda}\right)(1-v)\delta S(e^{\rho T}-e^{-\lambda T}).$$

Given $\delta = 0$, we have

$$\frac{\partial}{\partial T}\{E\pi(1,v,d,T)-E\pi(0,v,d,T)\}=d\alpha^d me^{-(\rho+\lambda)T}\geq 0.\ E\pi(s,v,d,T)$$

exhibits (weakly) increasing difference in s and T given $\delta = 0$.

Note that, given a contract is supported by debt financing and $m > 0$, s and T are strictly complementary. We will appeal to this result when we examine the contract data, because all of the contracts in the dataset are supported by debt. Meanwhile, s and d remain strict complements, and, again, d and T may be complements but for low degrees of asset-specificity (low α) and $m > 0$.

Now consider the decision in the second stage to adopt a veto provision. Inspection of the expected vertical rent $E\pi(s,v,d,T)$ shows that adopting a veto provision amounts to bearing the expected cost

$$\left(\frac{R}{\rho+\lambda}\right)(\lambda+\rho e^{-(\rho+\lambda)T})$$

and forgoing expected cost

$$\left(\frac{s\delta}{\rho+\lambda}\right)S[\rho(e^{-\lambda T}-1)+\lambda(e^{\rho T}-1)].$$

Both expressions are differentiable in T, but, given renegotiation costs are positive ($R > 0$), the first expression is strictly positive and decreasing in T. It approaches the asymptotic value of

$$\left(\frac{R}{\rho+\lambda}\right)\lambda$$

as T increases. The second expression is zero at $T = 0$ but, given $s\delta S>0$, it is increasing and unbounded. Thus, if contracting parties have committed to share risks ($s = 0$), the second expression is zero, indicating that there are no costs to leaving out a veto provision. In contrast, if parties impose all of the risk on the marketer ($s = 1$), then there is some finite threshold $\hat{T}>0$ such that the parties will adopt a veto for contracts featuring duration in excess of $\hat{T}$ and will leave out a veto for contracts featuring duration less than $\hat{T}$. Specifically, $\hat{T}$ solves

$$\left(\frac{R}{\rho+\lambda}\right)(\lambda+\rho e^{-(\rho+\lambda)\hat{T}})=\left(\frac{s\delta}{\rho+\lambda}\right)S[\rho(e^{-\lambda\hat{T}}-1)+\lambda(e^{\rho\hat{T}}-1)].$$

Hypotheses

The propositions and discussion suggest a number of qualitative patterns we might observe in contract data, including electricity marketing contract data. Some of these patterns, insofar as they exist at all, can be exhibited in simple cross-tabulations. Others can be teased out using regression analysis.

The formal model itself does not immediately lend itself to hypothesis testing, but it does suggest that we can interpret the optimal choice of contract duration (T), risk-bearing (s), veto provisions (v), and financial structure (d) as functions of each other. I next pose the hypothesis that we can approximate the joint selection of T, s, v, and d by a system of linear equations:

$$T = \alpha_T + \beta_{Ts}s + \beta_{Tv}v + \beta_{Td}d + \gamma_T W_T + \varepsilon_T$$
$$s = \alpha_s + \beta_{sT}T + \beta_{sv}v + \beta_{sd}d + \gamma_s W_s + \varepsilon_s$$
$$v = \alpha_v + \beta_{vT}T + \beta_{vs}s + \beta_{vd}d + \gamma_v W_v + \varepsilon_v$$
$$d = \alpha_d + \beta_{dT}T + \beta_{ds}s + \beta_{dv}v + \gamma_d W_d + \varepsilon_d$$

where W_T, W_s, W_v and W_d indicate vectors of predetermined variables with corresponding vectors of coefficients $\gamma_T, \gamma_s, \gamma_v$ and γ_d, and $\varepsilon_T, \varepsilon_s, \varepsilon_v$ and ε_d indicate (possibly non-normal) error processes. This system of equations can be understood as the first-order conditions for maximizing the vertical rent of a very specific functional form. See Appendix 4A.5 for details.

Let $E\pi = \max_{s,\, v,\, d,\, T} E\pi(s, v, d, T; \cdot)$ indicate the value function. The inputs T and v are Edgeworth complements if

$$\frac{\partial^2 E\pi}{\partial T \partial v} > 0$$

which implies

$$\frac{\partial T}{\partial v} > 0 \text{ and } \frac{\partial v}{\partial T} > 0.$$

In this linear version of the model featured in Appendix 4A.5, the hypothesis that contract duration T and veto provisions v are complements amounts to

$$\frac{\partial^2 E\pi}{\partial T \partial v} = B^{Tv} = \rho_T \beta^{Tv} > 0$$

where ρ_T is a constant of proportionality. While it is not possible to estimate ρ_T, the test of complementarity amounts to a test of the hypothesis

$$\frac{\partial T}{\partial v} = -\left(\frac{\partial^2 E\pi}{\partial T \partial v} \bigg/ \frac{\partial^2 E\pi}{\partial T^2}\right) = \beta_{Tv} > 0.$$

Similarly,

$$\frac{\partial v}{\partial T} = -\left(\frac{\partial^2 E\pi}{\partial T \partial v} \bigg/ \frac{\partial^2 E\pi}{\partial v^2}\right) > 0$$

implies $\beta_{vT} > 0$.

Similar calculations, which I state without proof, yield the following: The complementarity of two-part risk-sharing s and veto provisions v implies $\beta_{sv} > 0$ and $\beta_{vs} > 0$; the complementarity of two-part risk-sharing s and debt d implies $\beta_{sd} > 0$ and $\beta_{ds} > 0$.

Note that appealing to multi-stage contract design amounts to deviating from the strict optimization of contract design. Within the context of the model, it amounts to ignoring some of the potential interactions between choice variables. It also amounts to substituting the concept of Edgeworth complementarity with a concept of the ancillarity of certain dimensions of contract. Within the context of the linearized version of the model, posing the hypothesis that veto provisions support longer-term contracts in which parties relieve the generator of marketing risk yields $\beta_{vT} > 0$ and $\beta_{vs} > 0$ under the constraints $\beta_{Tv} = \beta_{sv} = 0$.

In all that follows, I limit estimation to a system of three equations that excludes a fourth debt equation, because the data indicate little evidence of variation in the financial structure of electricity generating projects.[9] Some contracts make explicit reference to underlying credit agreements. Others indicate lenders in the background, and yet others indicate both underlying credit agreements and lenders. No contracts make reference to equity financing, although some generating projects are organized by joint ventures – clusters of investors who make nominal equity infusions. These joint ventures organize the financing, construction and operation of generation of merchant plants, from which such joint ventures may

---

[9] Some contracts make explicit reference to underlying credit agreements. Others indicate lenders in the background, and yet others indicate both underlying credit agreements and lenders. No contracts make explicit reference to equity financing, although some generating projects are organized by clusters of investors who make nominal equity infusions in joint ventures that are designed to organize the financing, construction and operation of merchant plants. Yet even these investors explicitly line up debt financing. Finally, I note that even generators that are affiliated with their marketers depend on debt financing. Duke Energy, for example, maintains both a marketing subsidiary and generating subsidiaries. Duke sets up each generating project as an LLC responsible for organizing its own financing.

assume some of the marketing risk themselves. Yet even these merchant investors explicitly line up debt financing.

We are almost situated to operationalize hypotheses that we can bring to contract data. I introduce one more piece of apparatus. I explore the validity of the multi-stage contracting hypothesis by appealing to the method of two-stage conditional maximum likelihood (2SCML) proposed by Rivers and Vuong (1988). Two-stage conditional maximum likelihood affords a method of dealing with categorical (binary) explanatory variables that are potentially endogenous, and it affords a two-stage, Hausman-like test of endogeneity. The first stage involves securing residuals from regressions of contract duration (T) and risk-sharing (s) against a set of instrumental variables. The second stage involves including the residuals in a probit analysis of the selection of veto provisions. Evidence that coefficients assigned to the residuals are indistinguishable from zero would be consistent with contract duration and risk-sharing being determined before the determination of veto provisions. See Wooldridge (2002, pp. 472–4) for further details.

I now organize hypotheses in three sets. The first set pertains to patterns of dominance. The general model and even the model of multi-stage contract design imply that certain types of contracts should never appear. The second indicates patterns of complementarity implied by the linearized, three-equation version of the model. The third indicates patterns of ancillarity implied by the model of multi-stage contract design. I also pose hypotheses about the exogeneity of contract duration and risk-sharing with respect to the determination of veto provisions.

Hypothesis 1:   Contracts corresponding to $(s, v) = (0, 1)$ should never appear.

This is the "No 'belts and braces'" result. Contracts that relieve generators of marketing risk should not feature veto provisions.

Hypothesis 2.1:   Contract duration T and veto provisions v are complements. Within the context of the linear model, this amounts to $\beta_{Tv} > 0$ and $\beta_{vT} > 0$.

That is, allowing parties to impose unprogrammed renegotiation allows them to reduce the frequency of programmed renegotiation. Also, imposing the residual claim on marketers increases the prospect of distorted investment; neutralizing the prospect of unprogrammed renegotiation induces parties to increase the frequency of programmed renegotiation by imposing a shorter term.

Hypothesis 2.2: Two-part risk-sharing s and veto provisions v are complements. Within the context of the linear model, this amounts to $\beta_{sv} > 0$ and $\beta_{vs} > 0$.

Hypothesis 2.3: Two-part risk-sharing s and debt d are complements. Within the context of the linear model, this amounts to $\beta_{sd} > 0$ and $\beta_{ds} > 0$.

I include this hypothesis for completeness, but the data will not afford a test of it.

Hypothesis 3.1: Tests of exogeneity inspired by Rivers and Vuong (1988) are consistent with contract duration and risk-sharing being determined before veto provisions.

Hypothesis 3.2: Veto provisions attend longer-term contracts. Within the context of the multi-stage contracting model, $\beta_{vT} > 0$ given $\beta_{Tv} = 0$.

Hypothesis 3.3: Relieving the generator of marketing risk (imposing $s = 1$) increases the likelihood of imposing a veto provision. Within the context of the multi-stage contracting model, $\beta_{vs} > 0$ given $\beta_{sv} = 0$.

The linearized, multi-stage contracting model admits a weaker version of the "No 'belts and braces'" result:

Hypothesis 3.4: Within the context of the multi-stage contracting model, contract duration and risk-sharing are weakly complementary. Specifically, $\beta_{sT} \geq 0$ and $\beta_{Ts} \geq 0$.

DATA AND ESTIMATION

I work out of a dataset of 101 electricity marketing contracts that contracting parties recognize either as power sales agreements, tolling agreements, or power purchase agreements. These contracts join an entity that owns and operates generating assets and an energy marketer who acquires rights to dispatch electricity from the generating assets. Sixty-nine of the contracts were acquired from the filings parties made to the Federal Energy Regulatory Commission (FERC).[10] I extracted one contract from

---

[10] See Appendix 4A.6. The FERC stopped requiring marketers to file contracts in 2002. The dataset features every contract I could identify in all available filings.

one generator's filing to the Securities and Exchange Commission. The remaining 31 contracts derive from filings parties made to the Justice Department in connection with antitrust investigations.

Electricity marketing contracts often pertain to transactions between corporate affiliates or to transactions that are not specific to generating units. So, for example, one energy marketer might commit to deliver some volume of electricity to another marketer at some node in the electricity transmission grid, but such a transaction may not specify a source of the generation. In contrast, all of the contracts in the dataset involve specific generating assets. Corporate subsidiaries such as Duke Energy Marketing may market electricity for other Duke subsidiaries that manage generation assets.[11] A few such contracts are featured in the dataset.

In Table 4.1 I distinguish the duration of contracts (in years) and the generation capacity placed under contracts (in megawatts, MW) by type of generation. I distinguish generation by six types of fuel: gas-fired generation (Gas in Table 4.1), nuclear, coal-fired generation (Coal), oil, wind-driven generation (Wind), and all other (Other). "Other" includes projects that burn waste from fiber products mills. A great deal of gas-fired generation constitutes capacity that responds to marginal demands, whereas nuclear and coal-fired generation is suited to serve baseload demands.[12] Baseload capacity generates electricity at the lowest marginal costs (lowest cost per MW). It is therefore well suited to serving the baseload demand. The optimal program for baseload capacity is to fire it up and let it run indefinitely. In contrast, marginal capacity operates at higher marginal costs. Baseload capacity would seem to dominate marginal capacity, but marginal capacity is better suited to economically

---

[11]   Duke Energy Corporation owns or leases generation in California through four wholly owned subsidiaries. These four subsidiaries maintain marketing contracts with Duke Energy Marketing. See the Duke Energy filing with the FERC dated June 25, 1998 at docket # ER98-2680-002, the FERC filing dated December 31, 1998 at docket # ER99-1199, and the Duke Energy Corporation SEC filing 10-K for the year 1999.

[12]   The contract data pre-date the "fracking" phenomenon in the United States. Fracking has induced a decline in natural gas prices and a subsequent displacement of coal-fired generation capacity. Low gas prices have even jeopardized the economics underlying nuclear generation. Yet, as of the time of the data collection (before the fracking revolution), not all gas-fired generation capacity had operated at the margin. Jet engine-type generators constitute capacity that is suited to serving peaking demands, because they are amenable to serving dispatch demands at short notice. Combined cycle gas-fired generators may be less amenable to dispatch demands but are more efficient than peaking generators, because they include systems to recover the heat that jet engines dissipate.

Table 4.1 Contract duration and generation capacity by fuel type

	Gas*	Nuclear	Coal*	Oil*	Other fuel	Wind	All capacity
Observations	79	4	11	7	5	6	101
Contract duration (years)							
Mean	12.39	9.18	5.69	4.07	5.04	14.87	11.59
Std deviation	7.98	4.49	2.74	1.22	3.01	8.19	1.79
Minimum	0.22	30.40	2.92	2.50	2.18	2.45	0.22
Maximum	28.19	13.00	11.81	5.17	10.00	26.08	28.19
Generation Capacity (MW)							
Mean	635.62	909.30	1592.60	2350.71	27.50	81.75	599.61
Std deviation	961.51	559.55	2012.08	2177.80	16.93	109.89	909.57
Minimum	27.00	500.00	20.00	292.00	6.50	5.00	5.00
Maximum	5645.00	1730.00	5645.00	5645.00	52.00	300.00	5645.00

Note: * The columns do not partition the dataset. Instead, some contracts feature distinct generating units fired by natural gas, coal, or oil. Such contracts are double or triple counted in the columns Gas, Coal, and Oil.

141

ramping up and responding to fluctuations in demand. Generators reserve it to serve peaks in demand that might, for example, attend the hottest hours of a hot day during which everyone turns on their air conditioning. Wind-driven generation is hybrid in that it does not easily fit into a marginal/baseload dichotomy. To begin with, it is less well suited to responding to peak demands, because the wind is not subject to generators' control.

Table 4.1 indicates the 101 contracts feature an average duration of 11.59 years, although the shortest ran about two weeks, and the longest ran 28.19 years. Contracts that included baseload capacity (nuclear and coal) tended to feature short terms whereas those that included gas-fired generation averaged 12.39 years in duration, and those pertaining to wind-driven generation averaged 14.87 years. On average, each contract covered 599.61 MW of generation capacity. Contracts pertaining to wind-driven generation or other generation covered, on average, 81.75 MW and 71.58 MW respectively. Contracts that included gas-fired generation averaged 635.62 MW per contract.

Seventy-nine of the 101 contracts included gas-fired generation. Twenty-one of these eighty contracts featured provisions that allow at least one party, the marketer, to impose renegotiation. (See Table 4.2.) I count all 21 provisions as *de facto* veto provisions, but, strictly speaking, only eight of these 21 provisions are *de jure* veto provisions. The 15 other provisions are composed of rights-of-first-refusal or first-offer. A generator may, for example, propose an expansion of generation capacity. A right-of-first-refusal gives the incumbent marketer an opportunity to evaluate the proposal and, more importantly, to hold up the prospect of the generator contracting with a different marketer. For example, the marketer Williams Marketing Energy & Trading maintains rights of first-offer, but no

Table 4.2   The assignment of risk by fuel type

		Gas*	Nuclear	Coal*	Oil*	Other fuel	Wind	All capacity
Marketer bears risk	($s = 1$)	62	1	6	5	1	–	66
Veto provision	($v = 1$)	21	–	–	–	–	–	21
Parties share risk	($s = 0$)	17	3	5	2	4	6	35
Veto provision	($v = 1$)	–	–	–	–	–	2	2
Total contracts		79	4	11	7	5	6	

Note: * The columns do not partition the dataset. Instead, some contracts feature distinct generating units fired by natural gas, coal, or oil. Such contracts are double or triple counted in the columns Gas, Coal, and Oil.

veto rights, in its relationship with the generator Cleco Evangeline.[13] In another contract, the marketer Coral Power LLC maintains the right to veto upgrades of generating units that the generator Baconton Power LLC might propose. The parties agree to make "equitable adjustments" to the two-part compensation scheme in the event they proceed with such upgrades.[14] A contract between Williams and the generator AES Southland features an explicit veto in that both parties reserve the right to veto proposals by the other to expand or withdraw capacity.[15]

Only two other contracts, both pertaining to wind, featured veto provisions. The two wind contracts both feature explicit veto provision, probably because wind-driven generation tends to rely on subsidies to be economical. Parties may not be too keen to invest heavily in long-lived assets only to find subsidies taken away in the future.

Overall, 66 of the 101 contracts imposed the residual claim on marketers ($s = 1$). Sixty-two of the 66 contracts pertained to gas-fired generation. Of the 21 non-gas contracts, only four imposed the residual claim on marketers. This is not surprising. Sometimes marketers share risk with generators ($s = 0$) by compensating them according to linear schemes; they pay fixed fees per unit output, usually a kilowatt-hour. Meanwhile, marginal generation, by virtue of being marginal, is more subject to variation in dispatch demands. A combination of variation in dispatch and linear compensation yields variation in compensation whereas schemes that impose the residual claim on marketers yield fixed streams to generators. In contrast, baseload capacity generally features little variation in dispatch, thus the combination of baseload capacity and linear compensation tends to yield streams that are subject to little or no variation. Wind is a little different in that generators do not control all dimensions of the technology; they cannot ramp up if the wind is inadequate. Wind tends to feature linear compensation which, in turn, implies some variation in the stream of payments marketers yield to generators.

I constructed nine variables that I apply to estimation of a system of three equations.

Dependent Variables

1. *Contract duration:* the duration in years of terms of the contract, excluding options to extend.

---

[13] See the FERC filing dated June 30, 2000 at docket # ER00-3058-001.
[14] See page 46 of the Baconton filing dated July 10, 2000 at docket # ER00-3096.
[15] See page 2 of the Williams/AES agreement filed May 7, 2001 at docket # ER98-2184-006.

2. *Two-part compensation:* a binary indication that the risk-bearing scheme assigns the residual claim to the marketer ($s = 1$) by means of a two-part scheme. Two-part schemes usually render a fixed fee to the generator and a set of payments that cover its marginal costs. Almost all other sharing rules are linear ($s = 0$).
3. *Veto provision:* a binary indication that the contract features a veto provision ($v = 1$).

Explanatory Variables

4. *New capacity:* a binary indication that the contract covers new generation capacity.
5. *Yield ten-year bonds:* the yield on ten-year treasury bills at the time of contracting.
6. *Gas-fired generation:* a binary indication of whether the generation project included gas-fired generators.
7. *Joint venture:* a binary indicator identifying merchant plants organized by a group of investors.
8. *Gas and oil extraction gross state product (GSP):* the GSP in the $billions by year generated by gas and oil extraction.
9. *Time trend:* a time trend enumerated in days.

I indicate descriptive statistics in Table 4.3.

The first three variables indicate the dependent variables in the system of three equations. These variables indicate how generators and marketers organize the supply of electricity to wholesale markets. Meanwhile, the explanatory variables reflect both supply-side and demand-side considerations. Some variables reflect marginal dispatch demands, and others reflect the feasibility of responding to marginal demands. Other variables

Table 4.3   Descriptive statistics

	Mean	Median	Std dev.	Min.	Max.
Veto provision	0.228	0	0.421	0	1
Contract duration (years)	11.59	11.42	7.79	0.22	28.19
Two-part compensation	0.653	1	0.478	0	1
Gas-fired generation	0.782	1	0.415	0	1
Joint venture	0.267	0	0.445	0	1
New construction	0.604	1	0.492	0	1
Yield ten-year bonds	0.0554	0.0542	0.0056	0.0431	0.0666
Time trend (days)	1380	1453	405	0	2091
Oil and gas extraction GSP ($billions)	$2.319	$0.091	$6.461	$0.000	$42.975

indicate demands for both programmable and unprogrammable demands for adapting contracts.

I use the variables *new capacity* and *gas-fired generation* to reflect different types of demand for adaptation. Insofar as "new" reflects the expected economic life of generating units, then it reflects programmable opportunities to salvage assets. The gas variable constitutes a means for distinguishing marginal generation capacity, capacity that intendedly serves marginal demands, from inframarginal generation capacity (baseload capacity) that is subject to more regular demands (the baseload).[16]

I include these variables to control for the prospect that marginal capacity may be more susceptible to three types of hazards and may, in turn, be subject to unprogrammable demands for adaptation. The hazards are (1) the unprogrammable prospect of being crowded out by new capacity and knocked out of the money, (2) transmission congestion that may attend peaking demands for electricity, and (3) higher monitoring costs that can attend generation capacity that is more subject to variable dispatch demands. I illustrate the crowding-out hazard in Figure 4.2. Consider a market institution under which the marginal cost of marginal capacity imposes a uniform wholesale price. Adding inframarginal capacity may shift the supply curve from S_0 to S_1. Capacity located at B_0 gets displaced to B_1. In demand state D a price of P_0 would have prevailed, and capacity at B_0 would have been "in the money" – the marketer would have been able to realize a positive price-cost margin were it to exercise its option to dispatch electricity. After the addition of new capacity, a lower price of P_1 obtains, in which case the capacity at B_1 get knocked out of the money. (The parties lose marginal revenue at a rate equal to the cross-hatched rectangle above B_1.) Meanwhile, the capacity at A remains in the money, but the marginal review diminishes by $P_0 - P_1 > 0$. (The parties lose marginal revenue at a rate equal to the cross-hatched rectangle above A.) The margin still gives the contracting parties some capacity to service

---

[16]   I had also crafted a variable "capacity factor" as an alternative means of distinguishing marginal capacity from capacity subject to more regular dispatch. I gathered from the Energy Information Agency (EIA) of the Department of Energy annual indications of the proportion of time capacity under contract was dispatched. Capacity factor is a forward-looking variable in that it depends on data generated after contracting. Specifically, I took the average of time dispatched over the years 1996 through to 2002 for each generating site. I do not feature this variable in the regression analyses presented here, however, because it is highly correlated with gas-fired generation. Including capacity factor did substantially increase the R-squares of the linear two-part compensation regressions, but inclusion did not otherwise inform the results pertaining to the complementarity, substitutability or ancillarity of the dimensions of contract.

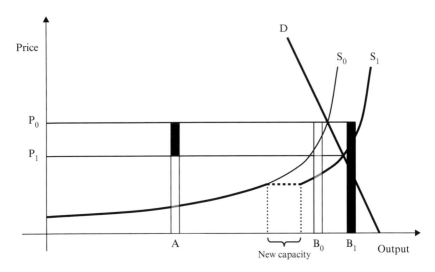

Figure 4.2   An electricity dispatch schedule

underlying debt obligations in demand state D, but the parties responsible for managing capacity displaced to B_1 lose all capacity to service debt in demand states like D.

I use the variable *gas-fired generation* to control for the feasibility of time-sensitive dispatch. *Gas-fired generation* provides a way of distinguishing capacity that can technically accommodate dispatch demands from capacity that is less amenable to timely dispatch. Again, the important idea is that marginal generation can involve greater monitoring costs. Absent remedies such as two-part compensation, parties might have to engage more efforts to monitor and audit the streams of revenues that derive from the irregular dispatch of marginal units. It is reasonable, then, to expect that generating units that can accommodate dispatch demands, such as gas turbine units, will tend to align with two-part compensation.

I use the variable *joint venture* to control for the prospect that parties to a generation project may have already established structures to govern their relationships that they could use to monitor and police performance within their generation projects. Relationships already invested with important structure might require less such structure in electricity marketing contracts. Joint ventures, for example, might invest themselves with monitoring schemes that could be extended to the monitoring and accounting of the distribution of payoffs from marketing activity.

Methods of Estimation

I examine a system of three equations, an equation characterizing contract duration, another characterizing the selection or exclusion of veto provisions, and a third equation characterizing the selection or inclusion of two-part compensation. I apply both single-equation methods (ordinary least squares, OLS, and two-stage least squares, 2SLS) and a full-information estimation method (three part least squares, 3SLS) to linearized system. I also apply probit analyses to the selection of veto provisions and two-part compensation. I then appeal to 2SCML to explore the exogeneity of contract duration and two-part compensation with respect to the selection of veto provisions. I also appeal to 2SCML to explore the exogeneity of contract duration and two-part compensation with respect to each other.[17] I do all of this by applying 2SCML to both probit estimation and to estimation of linear equations.

I apply bootstrapped standard errors to the linear probability models for veto provisions and two-part compensation estimated by OLS, 2SLS, and 3SLS. Imposing linear probability may induce heteroskedastistic residuals. Bootstrap methods can be applied to 3SLS estimation (Freedman and Peters 1984; MacKinnon 2002) as well as to OLS and 2SLS. Further, bootstrapping data directly (pairs bootstrap), in contrast to bootstrapping residuals from the original estimations, constitutes a method of generating standard errors and confidence intervals that are robust to heteroskedasticity (Johnston and Dinardo 1997, p. 369; MacKinnon 2006, p. 9).[18] It also constitutes a method of accommodating error processes that may be non-normal.

Results

I enumerate the results in one-to-one correspondence with the hypotheses listed above.

---

[17] Applying 2SCML to the (linear) duration equation yields the same coefficient estimates that we would obtain from 2SLS and yields virtually the same standard errors (Davidson and MacKinnon 1993, p. 240). As Petrin and Train (2003) observe, 2SCML constitutes an application of the "control function" approach to probit models. It is a single equation method that accommodates continuous endogenous explanatory variables and provides simple Hausman-like endogeneity tests (Hausman 1978) of both continuous and discrete explanatory variables (Rivers and Vuong 1988, p. 358; Wooldridge 2002, p. 474).

[18] More generally, as Nevitt and Hancock (2001) observe, the bootstrap provides an alternative and often superior means of generating standard errors with small datasets featuring data that may be non-normal.

Table 4.4   All contracts

	Risk-sharing	Two-part compensation	Row total
No veto provision	33	45	78
Veto provision	2	21	23
Column total	35	66	101

Result 1:   "No 'belts and braces'": contracts that feature the combination of veto provisions and risk-sharing do not appear among the 95 contracts that exclude wind-driven generation capacity.

Table 4.4 is a cross-tabulation of veto provisions and two-part compensation across all 101 contracts. Thirty-five contracts feature linear pricing between the generator and marketer. In these contracts, the marketer pays the generator a fixed price per unit (kilowatt-hour) of electricity it elects to dispatch from the generating units. The other 66 contracts feature two-part compensation: the generator pays a fixed fee for the right to make dispatch demands, and it pays a fee per unit that is designed to cover the generator's incremental costs of generating those units of electricity.

Twenty-three veto provisions show up in these 101 contracts, and 21 of those veto provisions show up in contracts that feature two-part compensation. The other two veto provisions do show up in contracts that feature risk-sharing. It turns out, however, that those two contracts pertain to wind-driven generation. (Again, see Table 4.2.) Of the 101 contracts, 95 do not involve wind-driven generation, and it is in these 95 contracts that the "no belts and braces" result obtains. (See Table 4.5.) Of 21 contracts featuring veto provisions, none feature two-part compensation.

Certain aspects of wind projects lie outside the scope of the model. The model contemplates generation capacity that, in principle, could be subject to dispatch demands. In contrast, wind-driven generation can only be dispatched when the wind blows. More importantly, the economics of wind-driven generation depend on subsidies to remain economically viable. The prospect of the loss of subsidies could jeopardize investments.

Table 4.5   Contracts excluding wind-driven generation

	Risk-sharing	Two-part compensation	Row total
No veto provision	29	45	74
Veto provision	0	21	21
Column total	29	66	95

Contracting parties would thus be more careful about controlling investment over the course of long-term exchange, for they would not want to sink expand capacity only to have subsidies subsequently withdrawn. They might therefore be more likely to include veto provisions in their contracts.

The result supports hypothesis 1.

Result 2: The determination of contract duration, two-part compensation and veto provisions is inconsistent with a symmetric, simultaneous contract design process.

Evidence includes results from Hausman-like tests of endogeneity afforded by application of 2SCML to probit analyses as well as actual Hausman tests derived from the application of OLS to the determination of *veto provision, contract duration,* and *two-part compensation.* (See Alvarez and Glasgow 1999 for a discussion of 2SCML and an illustrative application.) The tests involve including residuals from reduced-form equations in the explanatory variables of a given probit analysis or OLS estimation. Specifically, the residuals derive from regressing the variables *veto provision, contract duration,* and *two-part compensation* on the six explanatory variables (*gas-fired generation, joint venture, yield ten-year bonds, time trend,* and *oil and gas extraction GSP*).

Tables 4.6, 4.7 and 4.8 report estimation results pertaining, respectively, to the determination of *veto provision, contract duration,* and *two-part compensation.* These tables report coefficient estimates and corresponding *t*-statistics.

The first specification in both Tables 4.6 and 4.8 indicates estimation results from the application of 2SCML to the determination of veto provisions and two-part compensation, respectively. The results in Table 4.6 are consistent with *contract duration* and *two-part compensation* being predetermined as regards the variable *veto provision* in that the coefficient estimates are statistically indistinguishable from zero. (The standard errors on the coefficients yield small *t*-statistics of 0.21 and 0.22.) The suggestion is that *contract duration* and *two-part compensation* could be included as explanatory variables in a probit analysis of veto provisions without distorting the estimation of standard errors. (Again, see Wooldridge 2002, pp. 472–8 on the application of 2SCML to accommodate both real-valued and binary regressors that may be endogenous.)

Meanwhile, the result in Specification 1 of Table 4.7 is consistent with *contract duration* not being predetermined with respect to *two-part compensation.* The coefficient estimate on reduced form residuals of *contract duration* are statistically significant. The suggestion is that either (1) some accommodation must be made for the apparent endogeneity of *contract duration*

Table 4.6 *Veto provisions*

Specification	1 2SCML	2 Probit	3 OLS	4 OLS	5 3SLS
Contract duration	0.122*** 2.63	0.127*** 4.93	3.02%*** 2.78	2.91%*** 5.57	2.98%*** 3.07
Two-part compensation	1.190 1.35	1.309*** 2.61	19.49% 1.59	20.58%*** 3.67	19.65% 1.55
Joint venture	−1.224** −2.35	−1.199*** −2.63	−26.50%*** −2.88	−25.88%*** −2.98	−26.04%*** −2.85
Constant	−3.078*** −4.22	−3.219*** −5.14	−17.93%** −2.05	−17.53%*** −3.06	−17.61%** −2.11
Contract duration (reduced form residuals)	0.012 0.21		−0.14% −0.12		
Two-part compensation (reduced form residuals)	0.236 0.22		1.12% 0.08		
R-squared			0.3754	0.3752	0.3750
Log likelihood	−31.74	−31.80			

Notes:
The notations ***, **, and * respectively indicate 1 percent, 5 percent, and 10 percent levels of significance.
The linear specifications feature bootstrapped standard errors.

150

Table 4.7   Contract duration

Specification	1 OLS	2 OLS	3 3SLS
Two-part compensation	−1.91	−2.21	−1.98
	−0.71	−1.61	−0.95
New construction	7.27***	7.37***	7.41***
	4.73	5.81	5.66
Yield ten-year bonds	−417.25***	−416.50***	−415.13***
	−3.38	−3.41	−3.20
Time trend	−0.0053***	−0.0053***	−0.0053***
	−3.00	−3.02	−2.77
Oil and gas extraction GSP	0.2933***	0.2953***	0.2939*
($billions)	3.78	3.85	1.77
Constant	38.19***	38.28***	38.01***
	4.65	4.67	4.46
Two-part compensation	−0.41		
(reduced form residuals)	−0.14		
R-squared	0.3633	0.3632	0.3629

Notes:
The notations ***, **, and * respectively indicate 1 percent, 5 percent, and 10 percent levels of significance.
The specification estimated by 3SLS features bootstrapped standard errors.

in an analysis of *two-part compensation*, or (2) *two-part compensation* might actually be predetermined relative to *contract duration*. The results from the estimation of specification 1 in Table 4.7 support the latter interpretation. That specification operationalizes a Hausman test of the endogeneity of *two-part compensation* relative to *contract duration*. The coefficient estimate on the residuals from the *two-part compensation* reduced form is statistically indistinguishable from zero. (The *t*-statistic is −0.14.)

The results from estimation of specifications 1 in Tables 4.6, 4.7 and 4.8 are consistent with (1) *two-part compensation* being determined before *contract duration*, and (2) both *contract duration* and *two-part compensation* being determined before the determination of *veto provisions*. Specifications 3 in Tables 4.6 and 4.8 yield consistent results. These specifications are linear counterparts (OLS estimation with bootstrapped standard errors) to the probit analyses, and they support Hausman tests. These specifications yield estimates of similar magnitude. *Two-part compensation* and *contract duration* appear predetermined relative to *veto provision*, and *two-part compensation* appears predetermined relative to *contract duration*.

Other evidence is consistent with these results of endogeneity

Table 4.8 Two-part compensation

Specification	1 2SCML	2 Probit	3 OLS	4 OLS	5 3SLS
Contract duration	0.104**		1.93%**		
	2.48		2.11		
Gas-fired generation	1.822***	1.912***	58.24%***	64.10%***	64.27%***
	4.58	5.14	5.43	6.85	7.62
Joint venture	-1.346***	-0.776**	-30.27%***	-22.70%**	-22.36%**
	-3.42	-2.40	-3.01	-2.34	-2.18
Constant	-1.755***	-0.841***	5.50%	21.28%**	21.05%***
	-3.21	-2.65	0.46	2.47	2.76
Contract duration (reduced form residuals)	-0.143***		-2.80%**		
	-2.88		-2.49		
R-squared			0.357	0.3170	0.3170
Log Likelihood	-44.75	-48.64			

Notes:
The notations ***, **, and * respectively indicate 1 percent, 5 percent, and 10 percent levels of significance.
The linear specifications feature bootstrapped standard errors.

tests. Specifically, the hypothesis that the dimensions of contract are simultaneously determined implies that, in a linearized system of equations in which *veto provision, contract duration,* and *two-part compensation* are functions of each other, then the signs of the coefficient estimates should exhibit symmetry. The estimated coefficients on the two dimensions of contract that are complements should be positive. The coefficients on substitutes should both be negative. It turns out, however, that estimates (not reported here) in a model that fully accommodates pair-wise endogeneity are not symmetric. The point estimates of coefficients relating to *contract duration* and *veto provision* have opposite signs, and the estimates of coefficients relating to *contract duration* and *two-part compensation* have opposite signs.

The results are inconsistent with hypotheses 2.1 and 2.2 but are consistent with hypotheses 3.1, 3.2, and 3.3.

Result 3: The determination of contract duration, two-part compensation and veto provisions is consistent with a triangular, three-stage contract design process.

The foregoing discussion substantiates the triangularity of the system of three equations.

Result 4: Veto provisions and contract duration do not manifest themselves as pair-wise complements, but, rather, veto provisions are ancillary with respect to contract duration.

All five specifications indicated in Table 4.6 yield estimates that are consistent with veto provisions being ancillary with respect to contract duration. The first and second specifications yield probit coefficients of 0.122 and 0.127 respectively. These coefficients are statistically significant, and both imply marginal effects in excess of 2.4 percent. (These marginal effects are calculated by the delta method, and are evaluated at the mean value of contract duration.) A marginal effect of 2.4 percent implies that a contract of 20 years duration would be 24 percent more likely to be supported by a veto provision than a contract of 10 years duration.

The marginal effects estimated by linear methods (OLS and 3SLS) in specifications 3, 4, and 5 are also statistically significant, and they all exceed 2.9 percent. A marginal effect in excess of 2.9 percent implies that a contract of 20 years duration would be more than 29 percent more likely to be supported by a veto provision than a contract of 10 years duration.

These results are consistent with hypothesis 3.2.

Result 5: There is weaker evidence that veto provisions are ancillary with respect to two-part compensation.

The coefficient estimates on *two-part compensation* in Table 4.6 are all positive, but not all of them are statistically significant. Nonetheless, the results are weakly consistent with hypothesis 3.2.

Result 6:   Contract terms of short duration weakly appear as ancillary to two-part compensation.

The coefficient estimates on *two-part compensation* in the *contract duration* specifications indicated in Table 4.7 are all negative, but none of them are statistically significant.

The results are consistent with contract duration and two-part compensation exerting no effect on each other. Such a result is not inconsistent with hypothesis 3.4 *per se*, but the apparent triangularity of the system is not strictly consistent with the theoretical motivation for that hypothesis.

Other Empirical Regularities

The formal model illuminates important patterns of complementarity and ancillarity between dimensions of contract, but it does not explicitly identify a set of explanatory variables. Firm narratives, however, do offer insights into how electricity marketing contracts are designed. These insights themselves suggested some variables that could influence contract design. Specifically, firm narratives illuminate (1) a correlation between gas-fired generation and two-part compensation, and (2) a relationship between the financing of merchant plants and the joint ventures that govern them. No less importantly, firm narratives imply that contract duration should be influenced by the financing of generation assets. These implications motivated the inclusion of the variables *new generation, gas-fired generation, joint venture* and *yield ten-year bonds* in the estimation of the equations for two-part compensation and contract duration. Specifically, these narratives implied some number of informal hypotheses:

Informal hypothesis 1:   Contract duration should increase in the expected life of underlying generation assets. Specifically, *contract duration* should be increasing in the term *new generation*.

Informal hypothesis 2:   Given joint venture partners finance the construction or acquisition of "merchant plants" in order to participate in risk-sharing, then joint venture investors should be less willing to commit to two-part compensation.

Informal hypothesis 3:   Given gas-fired generation is more amenable to serving peaking demands and had been less well situated to serve baseload demands, dispatch demands on gas-fired generation should be more variable, and that variability should create demands for two-part compensation.

Each of these informal hypotheses bears out robustly in the data. Table 4.7 shows that contracts involving the financing of new generation tend to feature contract terms that are more than seven years longer than the terms of other contracts. Meanwhile, each specification in Table 4.8 shows that contracts featuring gas-fired generation tend to be about 60 percent more likely to feature two-part compensation. At the same time, the results of the estimation of each specification in Table 4.8 imply that contracts supporting merchant plants are at least 21 percent less likely to feature two-part compensation.

Other regularities obtain. A single point increase in underlying borrowing rates (as proxied by the yield on ten-year government bonds) corresponds to more than a four-year decrease in contract duration. As interest rates go up, investors select projects that they can pay off sooner. Contracting parties tend to commit to longer terms for projects involving generation capacity constructed in areas with readier access to gas infrastructure (as proxied by *oil and gas extraction GSP*). Each $10 billion of state GSP in oil and gas extraction amounts to almost a three-year increase in contract duration.

CONCLUSION

Why would one party (the generator, say) yield to a second party (the marketer) the right to veto decisions as important as investment decisions that the generator might make at any point over a long interval of time? It might seem natural to suggest that the two parties together have committed to a scheme to restrain investment in production capacity, all in a larger effort to restrain competition. The hypothesis is incomplete, however, insofar as the two parties themselves are not competitors in some market. Alternatively, the hypothesis would be much more compelling were we to find that the marketer maintains contractual relations with more than one competing generator. In such a context, veto provisions in long-term contracts may enable competing generators to commit to restraining investment in production capacity, all in a larger effort to restrain competition between each other.

In this chapter I develop an alternative efficient adaptation hypothesis much in the spirit of the early work of Masten and Crocker. In some contexts we might understand veto provisions as mechanisms parties use to facilitate contract adjustment over the course of long-term exchange. To understand this hypothesis and to operationalize tests of the hypothesis, we cannot focus on veto provisions in isolation but must characterize interactions with other dimensions of contract. I examine an environment in which there exist important interactions between four dimensions of contract: veto provisions, financial structure, contract duration, and risk-sharing. Efficient adaptation suggests patterns of substitution and complementarity between these four instruments. Efficient adaptation also suggests the ancillarity of certain dimensions of contract: contracting parties may first sort out the fundamental economics of their relationship, but they may subsequently add on safeguards to accommodate eventualities to which it is hard to assign any value or likelihood at the time of contracting.

The patterns of complementarity, substitutability and ancillarity are consistent with friction and investment incentives being the principal factors motivating the design of contracts. Asset-specificity (relationship-specific investment) can also distort investment incentives (the hold-up problem), but asset-specificity is not the only driver of distortions. Asset-specificity interacts with friction and other sources of distortions.

Ancillarity is interesting, because it suggests at least two ways in which contracting parties deviate from hyper-rationality in designing contracts. First, hyper-rationality implies that contracting parties should factor feedback from the selection of any one dimension of contract into the selection of any one other dimension of contract. Instead, parties appear to design contracts in multi-stage processes. In the first stage they determine the dimensions of contract that enable them to organize exchange under prevailing circumstances. In one or more successive stages, they may include dimensions that provide some degree of flexibility. Such dimensions could include veto provisions pertaining to investment proposals. Contracting parties use veto provisions not to frustrate investment, but to enable parties to require joint evaluation of the changes in vertical rents that new investment would induce. Veto provisions thus emerge as safeguards against inefficient investment over the course of long-term exchange.

Second, hyper-rationality implies that, absent costs of writing contracts, contracting parties should be able to specify all payoff-relevant contingencies and to program adaptations for each such contingency. Contracting parties could then dispense with veto provisions; but they do not. Instead, they dispense with complete programming. They find themselves with the prospect of having to deal with unprogrammable demands to renegotiate the terms of exchange. Provisions such as vetoes afford them the flexibility to adapt to unprogrammable contingencies as needs arise.

APPENDIX 4A.1

We can conclude that v and T are complements if the function $E\pi\,(s, v, d, T)$ exhibits increasing differences in v and T. The function $E\pi\,(s, v, d, T)$ exhibits increasing differences if, for all $T_1 > T_0$,

$$E\pi\,(s, 1, d, T_1) - E\pi\,(s, 0, d, T_1) \geq E\pi\,(s, 1, d, T_0) - E\pi\,(s, 0, d, T_0),$$

It is sufficient to show that $E\pi\,(s, 1, d, T) - E\pi\,(s, 0, d, T)$ is increasing in T or, the same thing, that

$$\frac{\partial}{\partial T}\{E\pi(s, 1, d, T) - E\pi\,(s, 0, d, T)\} \geq 0.$$

This last expression yields

$$R\rho e^{-(\rho + \lambda)T} + \left(\frac{\lambda\rho}{\rho + \lambda}\right)s\delta S(e^{\rho T} - e^{-\lambda T}) \geq 0,$$

which holds for any R and ρ both greater than zero.

By similar calculations, we can show that s and T are not complements and may be substitutes. One can conclude that s and T are substitutes if the function $E\pi\,(s, v, d, T)$ exhibits decreasing differences in s and T – that is, if

$$\frac{\partial}{\partial T}\{E\pi\,(1, v, d, T) - E\pi\,(0, v, d, T)\} \leq 0.$$

This last condition yields

$$d\alpha^d m e^{-(\rho + \lambda)T} - \left(\frac{\lambda\rho}{\rho + \lambda}\right)(1 - v)\delta S(e^{\rho T} - e^{-\lambda T}) \leq 0,$$

which fails if $d = v = 1$ and $m > 0$. This condition is satisfied if $\alpha m = 0$.

APPENDIX 4A.2

First-order Conditions

Equity ($d = 0$):

$$T(0,0,0) = \frac{1}{\gamma}\ln\left[\frac{(z - m) - \rho S}{c}\right]$$

$$T(0,1,0) = \frac{1}{\gamma}\ln\left[\frac{(z - m) - \rho(S - R)}{c}\right]$$

$$T(1,0,0) = \frac{1}{\gamma} \ln \left[\frac{(z-m)-\rho S}{c} - \left(\frac{\lambda\rho}{\rho+\lambda}\right)\left(\frac{\delta Se^{\rho T}}{c}\right)(e^{(\rho+\lambda)T}-1) \right]$$

$$\leq \frac{1}{\gamma} \ln \left[\frac{(z-m)-\rho S}{c} \right]$$

$$T(1,1,0) = \frac{1}{\gamma} \ln \left[\frac{(z-m)-\rho(S-R)}{c} \right]$$

Debt ($d = 1$):

$$T(0,0,1) = \frac{1}{\gamma} \ln \left[\frac{(z-\alpha m)-\rho S}{c} - \left(\frac{\lambda\rho}{\rho+\lambda}\right)\left(\frac{\alpha Se^{\rho T}}{c}\right)(e^{(\rho+\lambda)T}-1) \right]$$

$$\leq \frac{1}{\gamma} \ln \left[\frac{(z-\alpha m)-\rho S}{c} \right]$$

$$T(0,1,1) = \frac{1}{\gamma} \ln \left[\frac{(z-\alpha m)-\rho(S-R)}{c} - \left(\frac{\lambda\rho}{\rho+\lambda}\right)\left(\frac{\alpha Se^{\rho T}}{c}\right)(e^{(\rho+\lambda)T}-1) \right]$$

$$\leq \frac{1}{\gamma} \ln \left[\frac{(z-\alpha m)-\rho(S-R)}{c} \right]$$

$$T(1,0,1) = \frac{1}{\gamma} \ln \left[\frac{z-\rho S}{c} - \left(\frac{\lambda\rho}{\rho+\lambda}\right)\left(\frac{[\alpha+\delta]Se^{\rho T}}{c}\right)(e^{(\rho+\lambda)T}-1) \right]$$

$$\leq \frac{1}{\gamma} \ln \left[\frac{z-\rho S}{c} \right]$$

$$T(1,1,1) = \frac{1}{\gamma} \ln \left[\frac{z-\rho(S-R)}{c} - \left(\frac{\lambda\rho}{\rho+\lambda}\right)\left(\frac{\alpha Se^{\rho T}}{c}\right)(e^{(\rho+\lambda)T}-1) \right]$$

$$\leq \frac{1}{\gamma} \ln \left[\frac{z-\rho(S-R)}{c} \right]$$

APPENDIX 4A.3

I list here the vertical rents that obtain under each of the eight types of contracts for any one given parameterization.

Equity ($d = 0$):

$$E\pi(0,0,0,T) = \left[\frac{z-m}{\rho+\lambda}\right](1-e^{-(\rho+\lambda)T}) + \left[\frac{c}{\gamma-\rho-\lambda}\right](1-e^{(\gamma-\rho-\lambda)T}) +$$

$$\left[\frac{S}{\rho+\lambda}\right](\lambda+\rho e^{-(\rho+\lambda)T}) - K$$

$$E\pi(0,1,0,T) = \left[\frac{z-m}{\rho+\lambda}\right](1-e^{-(\rho+\lambda)T}) + \left[\frac{c}{\gamma-\rho-\lambda}\right](1-e^{(\gamma-\rho-\lambda)T}) +$$

$$\left[\frac{S-R}{\rho+\lambda}\right](\lambda + \rho e^{-(\rho+\lambda)T}) - K$$

$$E\pi(1,0,0,T) = \left[\frac{z-m}{\rho+\lambda}\right](1-e^{-(\rho+\lambda)T}) + \left[\frac{c}{\gamma-\rho-\lambda}\right](1-e^{(\gamma-\rho-\lambda)T}) +$$

$$\left[\frac{S}{\rho+\lambda}\right](\lambda + \rho e^{-(\rho+\lambda)T}) - K - \left[\frac{\delta}{\rho+\lambda}\right]S[\rho(e^{-\lambda T}-1) + \lambda(e^{\rho T}-1)]$$

$$E\pi(1,1,0,T) = \left[\frac{z-m}{\rho+\lambda}\right](1-e^{-(\rho+\lambda)T}) + \left[\frac{c}{\gamma-\rho-\lambda}\right](1-e^{(\gamma-\rho-\lambda)T}) +$$

$$\left[\frac{S-R}{\rho+\lambda}\right](\lambda + \rho e^{-(\rho+\lambda)T}) - K$$

Debt ($d = 1$):

$$E\pi(0,0,1,T) = \left[\frac{z-\alpha m}{\rho+\lambda}\right](1-e^{-(\rho+\lambda)T}) + \left[\frac{c}{\gamma-\rho-\lambda}\right](1-e^{(\gamma-\rho-\lambda)T}) +$$

$$\left[\frac{S}{\rho+\lambda}\right](\lambda + \rho e^{-(\rho+\lambda)T}) - \alpha K - \left[\frac{\alpha}{\rho+\lambda}\right]S[\rho(e^{-\lambda T}-1) + \lambda(e^{\rho T}-1)]$$

$$E\pi(0,1,1,T) = \left[\frac{z-\alpha m}{\rho+\lambda}\right](1-e^{-(\rho+\lambda)T}) + \left[\frac{c}{\gamma-\rho-\lambda}\right](1-e^{(\gamma-\rho-\lambda)T}) +$$

$$\left[\frac{S-R}{\rho+\lambda}\right](\lambda + \rho e^{-(\rho+\lambda)T}) - \alpha K - \left[\frac{\alpha}{\rho+\lambda}\right]S[\rho(e^{-\lambda T}-1) + \lambda(e^{\rho T}-1)]$$

$$E\pi(1,0,1,T) = \left[\frac{z}{\rho+\lambda}\right](1-e^{-(\rho+\lambda)T}) + \left[\frac{c}{\gamma-\rho-\lambda}\right](1-e^{(\gamma-\rho-\lambda)T}) +$$

$$\left[\frac{S}{\rho+\lambda}\right](\lambda + \rho e^{-(\rho+\lambda)T}) - \left[\frac{\alpha+\delta}{\rho+\lambda}\right]S[\rho(e^{-\lambda T}-1) + \lambda(e^{\rho T}-1)]$$

$$E\pi(1,1,1,T) = \left[\frac{z}{\rho+\lambda}\right](1-e^{-(\rho+\lambda)T}) + \left[\frac{c}{\gamma-\rho-\lambda}\right](1-e^{(\gamma-\rho-\lambda)T}) +$$

$$\left[\frac{S-R}{\rho+\lambda}\right](\lambda + \rho e^{-(\rho+\lambda)T}) - \left[\frac{\alpha}{\rho+\lambda}\right]S[\rho(e^{-\lambda T}-1) + \lambda(e^{\rho T}-1)]$$

Let $T(s,v,d) = \arg \max_{\hat{T}} E\pi(s,v,d,\hat{T})$ indicate the envelope of contract duration. Inspection immediately yields for any given T: $E\pi(0,0,0,T) \geq E\pi(0,1,0,T) = E\pi(1,1,0,T)$.

Given any $R > 0$, the inequality is strict. Thus, it is even the case that $E\pi(0,0,0,T(0,1,0)) \geq E\pi(0,1,0,T(0,1,0))$ with strict inequality given $R > 0$. That is, deviating from $(0,1,0,T)$ to $(0,0,0,T)$ given any T, including $T(0,1,0)$ is profitable. Accordingly, contracts conforming to $(s,v,d) = (0,1,0)$ can never dominate other contracts.

Further inspection yields $E\pi(0,0,1,T) \geq E\pi(0,1,1,T)$ with strict inequality given $R > 0$. We also have $E\pi(1,1,1,T) \geq E\pi(0,1,1,T)$ with strict inequality given $\alpha m > 0$.

Similar reasoning indicates that $(0,1,1)$ can never dominate other contracts. This establishes lemma 1.

Finally, similar reasoning indicates that $(1,0,0)$ and $(1,1,0)$ never dominate. We already have $E\pi(0,0,0,T) \geq E\pi(0,1,0,T) = E\pi(1,1,0,T)$ with strict inequality given $R > 0$.

Further inspection yields $E\pi(0,0,0,T) \geq E\pi(1,0,0,T)$ with strict inequality given $\delta > 0$.

APPENDIX 4A.4

The inequality

$$(1-\alpha)m > \alpha S\left(\frac{\lambda\rho}{\lambda+\rho}\right)\left(\frac{z-\alpha m-\rho S}{c}\right)^{\frac{\rho}{\gamma}}\left\{\left(\frac{z-\alpha m-\rho S}{c}\right)^{\frac{\rho+\lambda}{\gamma}}-1\right\}$$

implies $T(0,0,1) > T(0,0,0)$. To see this, note that

$$T(0,0,1) \leq T^* = \frac{1}{\gamma}\ln\left[\frac{z-\alpha m-\rho S}{c}\right].$$

Note also that

$$e^{\gamma T(0,0,1)} = \frac{(z-\alpha m)-\rho S}{c} - \left(\frac{\lambda\rho}{\rho+\lambda}\right)\left(\frac{\alpha S e^{\rho T(0,0,1)}}{c}\right)(e^{(\rho+\lambda)T(0,0,1)}-1)$$

$$\geq \frac{(z-\alpha m)-\rho S}{c} - \left(\frac{\lambda\rho}{\rho+\lambda}\right)\left(\frac{\alpha S e^{\rho T^*}}{c}\right)(e^{(\rho+\lambda)T^*}-1) = e^{\gamma T^*}$$

Thus, imposing $e^{\gamma T(0,0,0)} < e^{\gamma T^*} \leq e^{\gamma T(0,0,1)}$ yields $T(0,0,1) > T(0,0,0)$. Evaluating $e^{\gamma T(0,0,0)} < e^{\gamma T^*}$ yields the inequality in the premise of proposition 3.

APPENDIX 4A.5

I interpret s, v, and d as continuous variables, and I pose the joint payoff (the vertical rent) of representative contracting parties as

$$E\pi = k + \rho_T T\left(\alpha_T - \frac{T}{2}\right) + \rho_s s\left(\alpha_s - \frac{s}{2}\right) + \rho_v v\left(\alpha_v - \frac{v}{2}\right) + \rho_d d\left(\alpha_d - \frac{d}{2}\right)$$
$$+ \rho_T T\gamma_T W_T + s\rho_s\gamma_s W_s + v\rho_v\gamma_v W_v + d\rho_d\gamma_d W_d$$
$$+ B^{Ts}Ts + B^{Tv}Tv + B^{Td}Td$$
$$+ B^{sv}sv + B^{sd}sd + B^{vd}vd$$

where W_T, W_s, W_v, and W_d indicate vectors of predetermined variables with corresponding vectors of coefficients γ_T, γ_s, γ_v, and γ_d, k is a constant, and ρ_T, ρ_s, ρ_v, and ρ_d indicate constants each greater than zero. If we let $B^{sT} = \rho_T\beta_{Ts} = \rho_s\beta_{sT}$, $B^{Tv} = \rho_T\beta_{Tv} = \rho_v\beta_{vT}$, $B^{Td} = \rho_T\beta_{Td} = \rho_d\beta_{dT}$, $B^{sv} = \rho_s\beta_{sv} = \rho_v\beta_{vs}$, $B^{sd} = \rho_s\beta_{sd} = \rho_d\beta_{ds}$, and $B^{vd} = \rho_v\beta_{vd} = \rho_d\beta_{dv}$ indicate cross-equation restrictions, then optimization yields a system of four equations:

$$T = \alpha_T + \beta_{Ts}s + \beta_{Tv}v + \beta_{Td}d + \gamma_T W_T$$
$$s = \alpha_s + \beta_{sT}T + \beta_{sv}v + \beta_{sd}d + \gamma_s W_s$$
$$v = \alpha_v + \beta_{vT}T + \beta_{vs}s + \beta_{vd}d + \gamma_v W_v$$
$$d = \alpha_d + \beta_{dT}T + \beta_{ds}s + \beta_{dv}v + \gamma_d W_d$$

The cross-equation restrictions reduce to four restrictions $\beta_{Tv}\beta_{vs}\beta_{sT} = \beta_{Ts}\beta_{sv}\beta_{vT}$, $\beta_{Tv}\beta_{vd}\beta_{dT} = \beta_{Td}\beta_{dv}\beta_{vT}$, $\beta_{Td}\beta_{ds}\beta_{sT} = \beta_{Ts}\beta_{sd}\beta_{dT}$, and $\beta_{sv}\beta_{vd}\beta_{ds} = \beta_{sd}\beta_{dv}\beta_{vs}$.

APPENDIX 4A.6

Table 4A.1   Contracts derived from filings to the FERC

Marketer	Generator	FERC docket no. or SEC filing
Alliant Energy	Minergy Neenah	ER00-89
Ameren Energy Marketing, Dynegy Power Marketing, LG&E Energy Marketing	Midwest Electric Power Inc.	ER00-3353-001
Aquila Energy Marketing Corporation and UtiliCorp United Inc.	Elwood Energy II LLC	ER01-2270
Aquila Energy Marketing Corporation and UtiliCorp United Inc.	Elwood Energy III LLC	ER01-2681
Aquila Power Corporation and UtiliCorp United Inc.	LSP Energy LP	ER00-3539
Attala Energy Company LLC	Attala Generating Company LLC	ER02-2165
Avista Energy	Rathdrum Power	ER02-216, ER01-2862
Central Illinois Light Company	AES Medina Valley Cogen	ER01-788
Central Illinois Light Company	Altorfer	ER01-1758
CinCap Duke Trenton	Duke Vermillion	ER01-2335
Commonwealth Edison Company (Coal Stations Agreement)	Midwest Generation LLC	ER00-1378
Commonwealth Edison Company (Collins Station Agreement)	Midwest Generation LLC	ER00-1378
Commonwealth Edison Company (Peaking Stations Agreement)	Midwest Generation LLC	ER00-1378
Commonwealth Edison Company	Midwest Generation LLC	ER02-289
Consolidated Edison Company of NY	Entergy Nuclear Indian Point 2 LLC	ER01-1721-001

Constellation Power Source Inc.	ER02-445
Constellation Power Source Inc.	Orion Power Holdings 2000 10-K
Constellation Power Source Inc.	ER02-339
Coral Energy Tenaska Gateway Partners	ER01-2903
Coral Power LLC Baconton Power LLC	ER00-3096
Coral Power LLC WFEC Genco LLC	ER01-1481
CPN Pleasant Hill LLC MEP Pleasant Hill LLC & MEP Pleasant Hill Operating LLC	ER01-905
Dominion Nuclear Marketing I and Dominion Nuclear Marketing II Pleasants Energy LLC	ER02-698
Duke Energy Corporation Rockingham Power LLC	ER00-2984-001
Duke Energy Trading and Marketing LLC Bridgeport Energy LLC	ER01-2352
Duke Energy Trading and Marketing LLC Casco Bay	ER01-216
Duke Energy Trading and Marketing LLC Duke Energy Moss Landing LLC	ER02-1662
Edison Mission Marketing and Trading Company Harbor Cogeneration	ER99-4018
El Paso Energy Marketing Company Berkshire Power Company LLC	ER00-498
El Paso Power Services Company Cordova Energy Company LLC	ER01-2595
Engage US LP Elwood Energy LLC	ER99-4100
Exelon Kincaid Generation	ER01-2274
Exelon University Park Energy	ER01-2725
Exelon Generation Company LLC AmerGen Energy Company LLC	ER02-786
Exelon Generation Company LLC Elwood Energy	ER01-1975
Exelon Generation Company LLC Southeast Chicago Energy Project LLC	ER02-2017

Table 4A.1 (continued)

Marketer	Generator	FERC docket no. or SEC filing
Florida Power & Light Company	DeSoto County Generating Company	ER02-1446
Holy Cross Energy and Public Service Company of Colorado	Public Service Company of Colorado	ER02-8
LG&E Energy Marketing Inc.	LG&E Power Monroe LLC	ER02-902
MidAmerican	Cordova Energy Company	ER00-1967
Mirant Americas Energy Marketing LP	Commonwealth Chesapeake Company	ER00-3703, ER02-1537
Mirant Americas Energy Marketing LP	Mirant Chalker Point LLC	ER01-2974
Mirant Americas Energy Marketing LP	Mirant Mid-Atlantic LLC	ER01-2981
Mirant Americas Energy Marketing LP	Mirant Peaker LLC	ER01-2975
Mirant Americas Energy Marketing LP	Mirant Zeeland LLC	ER01-2479
Morgan Stanley Capital Group Inc.	South Eastern Electric Development Corporation	ER99-3654
Municipal Energy Agency of Nebraska	Black Hills Power Inc.	ER01-2577
Niagara Mohawk Energy Marketing	Black River Power LLC	ER00-2044
Niagara Mohawk Power Corporation	Constellation Nuclear LLC	ER01-1654
NRG Power Marketing Inc.	NEO California Power LLC	ER02-1700
NRG Power Marketing Inc.	NRG Energy Center Dover	ER02-1698
Pacificorp	FPL Energy Vansycle	ER01-838
Pacificorp	Rock River I	ER01-2742
PECO Energy Company	AmerGen Energy Company LLC	ER00-1806
PG&E Energy Trading Power LP	DTE Georgetown	ER00-3054
PG&E Energy Trading Power LP	Lake Road Generating Company LP	ER02-2130
Public Service Company of Colorado	Indeck Colorado LLC (Arapahoe Station)	ER00-1952
Public Service Company of Colorado	Indeck Colorado LLC (Valmont Station)	ER00-1952

Company	Docket
Public Service Company of New Mexico	
Public Service Electric & Gas	
Select Energy Inc.	
Sempra Energy Trading Corporation	
Sempra Energy Trading Corporation	
The California Department of Water Resources	
Virginia Electric and Power Company	
Virginia Electric and Power Company	
Williams Energy Marketing & Trading Company	
Delta Person Limited LP	ER01-138
Cedar Brakes IV	ER01-2765
Northeast Generation Company	ER00-953
Ogden Martin Systems of Union Inc.	ER00-1155
Sunbury Generation	ER00-357
Pacificorp Power Marketing	ER01-2685
Doswell Limited Partnership	ER01-1182
LSP Energy LP	ER00-3539
AES Alamitos LLC, AES Huntington Beach LLC, AES Redondo Beach LLC	ER98-2184, ER98-2185, ER98-2186
Williams Energy Marketing & Trading Company	Cleco Evangeline LLC	ER00-3058-001
Wisconsin Electric Power Company	Badger Windpower LLC	ER01-1071
Wisconsin Power and Light Company	Northern Iowa Windpower	ER02-192
WPS Energy Services	Northeast Empire LP	ER01-2568
Yampa Valley Electric Association	Public Service Company of Colorado	ER01-1814

165

5. The financial structure of Commercial Revolution: financing long-distance trade in Venice 1190– 1220 and Venetian Crete 1278–1400

Well before economists had explicitly distinguished an economics of contracting, business historians had illuminated a role for principal–agent contracts in enabling gains from complex exchange. They had, for example, crafted a narrative about how merchants exploited a technology of contracting and innovations in accounting to mobilize investment for long-distance trade in the Late Middle Ages. The narrative depends on a sequence of four ideas: long-distance trade was a catalyst of European economic revival in the Mediterranean; merchants came to depend on agents to conduct transactions in geographically dispersed markets; equity-like schemes known generically as *commenda* contracts enabled merchants and their agents to share risk; and risk-sharing enabled merchants and their agents to attract investment for long-distance trade ventures.

The focus on principal–agent contracts and trade in the Late Middle Ages derived from a direct examination of the extant paper trail that commercial activity generated. Historians trolling through the archived records of European merchants could not but help notice the preponderance of documents pertaining to overseas trade and notice that many of these documents were *commenda* contracts. What the paper trail leaves out, however, is direct evidence of how merchants accommodated the prospect that their agents might cheat them. Indeed, working through networks of agents may have enabled merchants to distribute their investments and managerial energies across portfolios of ventures. Portfolio effects alone may have constituted an effective means of managing risks and encouraging merchants to invest in overseas trade in the first place, but agency secured under the terms of *commenda* contracts introduced a problem of asymmetric information. A difficulty with the equity-like compensation that *commenda* afforded is that it depended on agents' reports of transactions that merchants could neither observe nor verify *ex post*. Agents might cheat by under-reporting proceeds gained in intermediate transactions. Without some means of neutralizing or, at least, accommodating the problem of cheating, merchants might not be able to realize portfolio effects and mobilize investment for overseas trade.

Cheating is interesting, because it motivates questions about what might constitute some means of governing exchange. It motivates questions about the governance of contractual relations – questions for which the extant paper trail has yielded few answers. The structure of the governance problem is generic: gains from trade often depended on one party yielding to another party information that was relevant to both parties' payoffs. Information was susceptible to distortion, and distortion may have enabled agents to cheat. Anticipating this, vulnerable parties may have underinvested in a commercial venture or might have forgone exchange entirely thus denying all parties potential gains from exchange. To encourage investment, all parties together may have instituted governance structures that enabled those parties involved in transmitting information to credibly commit to maintaining the integrity of information.

To focus ideas, consider a *commenda* contract between a merchant and his trading agent in June of 1207. In Venice Matteo Marzolo advanced 100 Venetian lira, a sizable sum, to Domenico Gradenigo. Gradenigo would venture to Alexandria (Egypt), presumably to acquire a stock of pepper and other spices to be resold at a trade fair in Venice, but that was not explicit. Gradenigo was granted authority to trade as he saw fit all along the route to and from Alexandria. After returning to Venice the two parties would share profits, with three-quarters of the profit going to Marzolo and the remaining one-quarter going to Gradenigo. (See Morozzo della Rocca and Lombardo 1940, pp. 29–30.)

A truthful accounting of profit would have depended on a truthful accounting of transactions that the merchant, Marzolo, could not observe. Yet, why would not Gradenigo cheat by, say, reporting that the price of pepper acquired in Alexandria or the prices of other commodities acquired along the way were higher than they actually were? There is another complication. Gradenigo also secured parallel *commenda* contracts with three other parties for 50, 100, and 135 Venetian lira. Might Gradenigo favor one account over another by, say, assigning more profitable transactions to the one and less profitable transactions to the other? Or would Gradenigo assign proceeds (truthfully reported or not) in proportions commensurate with each party's investment?

One way to neutralize these potential hazards would be to dispense with the equity-like profit-sharing and to revert to simple debt contracts – that is, to simply lend money to Gradenigo with the expectation of recovering a fixed return. Debt would relieve each party of having to know anything about transactions conducted far out of view. In contrast, equity contemplates some type of (possibly very elaborate or costly) mechanism to support truthful reporting. Gradenigo's investors might, for example, meet their own demand for support mechanisms by supplying those mechanisms. Could they have implemented a costly auditing scheme? Or could they have implemented a costly monitoring scheme by, say, hiring a party to spy on their trading agent?

It is not obvious that Gradenigo's investors could have assembled auditing or monitoring mechanisms at anything but prohibitive cost. The contracts suggest, however, an informal type of peer-monitoring scheme. Specifically, the contracts between Gradenigo and his investors indicate that Gradenigo was to organize his travels around the Easter *muduam* (merchant convoy and corresponding trade fair in Venice) sponsored by the Republic of Venice. He was even instructed to venture to Alexandria on a specific vessel. He would thus be traveling with a number of other parties, including other investors' trading agents, who would be trading in the same commodities at the same sites at the same time. Information about the prices of commodities, then, would be commonly dispersed. Gradenigo's investors could expect independent reports about commodities prices, and they could use such reports to informally assess Gradenigo's self-reported performance.

This chapter takes up the question of how informal assessments could support investors' relationships with their trading agents, but it was not the type of question that the established economic history had been equipped to recognize. To my knowledge, it was not until the seminal work of Avner Greif on the Maghribi traders that economic historians had explicitly focused research on governance problems relating to long-distance trade in the Middle Ages. Historians had not been insensitive to the prospect that agents might cheat; they appealed to the idea that merchants would have relied on kinship relations to bind agents. Even so, I do something that business historians may have been less well equipped to do: I distinguish evidence from a dataset of contracts representing cross-sections of maritime activity. Specifically, I characterize discrete patterns exhibited in a dataset of 1823 principal–agent contracts that spans two environments.[1] One environment involves trade ventures extending from Venice to the Eastern Mediterranean and Black Sea in the years 1190–1220. The contract data from these years provides some insight into the role of kinship relations in enabling long-distance trade. The second

[1] I gathered all of the data from the State Archives of Venice in the summers of 1995, 1996 and 1997 and in spring 2003. Of the 1823 contracts, 1416 derive from unpublished sources.

environment involves the financing of long-distance trade extending from Venetian Crete to the Aegean, the Black Sea, and other parts of the Eastern Mediterranean in the fourteenth century. The contract data from both environments enable us to conduct quasi-experiments about the role of information in supporting trade ventures organized by means of *commenda* contracts and debt.

The data yield discrete patterns that are difficult to reconcile with the established narrative. First, 849 of the 1823 contracts (47 percent) in the dataset are debt contracts. Debt constituted an important tool in the merchant's contracting toolbox and, yet, the established narrative has little or nothing to say about it. That is not to say that important dimensions of the narrative, such as risk-sharing, were not important, but the narrative fails to indicate tradeoffs (if any) merchants and their agents may have perceived in choosing between debt financing and *commenda*. Second, the data indicate that appealing to kinship relations does provide clues to how merchants organized long-distance trade. It turns out, however, that the clues illuminate considerations the established narrative does not feature. Rather than exploit kinship relations to bind agents and mitigate cheating, merchants exploited trade ventures to enable family relations to build up capital of their own and to gain experience doing business overseas.

How might we understand these discrete patterns? The chapter advances a two-part contract selection hypothesis about the role of information and institutions in supporting long-distance trade. First, the choice between debt and *commenda* featured tradeoffs. *Commenda* may have afforded risk-sharing, but it also afforded agents opportunities to expropriate returns that otherwise would have obtained to their merchants. Debt may have denied contracting parties the advantages of risk-sharing, but it resolved the governance problem by finessing it. An agent may well misrepresent transactions, but debt yielded to merchants' payoffs that were invariant to agents' reports. Second, merchants and their agents aligned *commenda* and debt with underlying attributes of trade ventures in a discriminating way. *Commenda* lined up with ventures for which merchants had access to informal sources of information. Merchants used them, for example, to finance ventures that involved commodities, such as pepper, that agents commonly acquired in markets commonly attended by other agents. Informal information gave merchants some capacity to detect cheating if not to verify it. An agent might misrepresent transactions, but other agents, including other merchants' agents, might yield reports of commodities prices against which a merchant might compare any single agent's report. A deviant report might not constitute evidence of cheating that parties could exploit in formal enforcement processes, but it could provide a basis for informal sanctions. In contrast, debt emerges as the mode of financing of last resort: merchants and their agents used it to finance ventures in which merchants had no means of detecting (much less verifying) cheating.

The remainder of the chapter proceeds in five sections. The first of these characterizes the established historical narrative and outlines more recent contributions in economic history to the problem of mitigating cheating. The first section also links the contract selection hypothesis to literatures on financial structure and contract design. The second section describes the data and the environments from which they were generated. The third discusses salient patterns in the data and how the contract selection hypothesis provides a way of understanding these patterns. I include a discussion of how the financing of non-maritime activities interacted (if at all) with investor–trader relationships. Examination of a dataset of 291 contracts involving the financing of non-maritime activities suggests that contracting parties did not use these other transactions to support relationships over time. Instead, the individuals who participated in non-maritime activities were almost entirely different from those who (evidently) specialized in maritime activities. The discussion of this third section sets up the multinomial probit analyses of contract selection presented in the fourth section. The fifth section concludes.

HISTORICAL NARRATIVES

The Principal Historical Narrative

With Karl Marx having illuminated a trajectory along which societies evolve – a shining path extending from pre-history to an absorbing state called communism – historians in the late nineteenth century grasped the obvious research agendum: to map the evolution of society from its feudal heritage to its capitalistic stage of development. Hence the efforts to survey the archival records for clues about the emergence of a medieval proto-capitalism.

The principal historical narrative illuminates a role for principal–agent contracts in enabling a revival of trade in the Mediterranean in the Late Middle Ages. (See, for example, Pirenne 1925, p. 110; de Roover 1963, p. 43; Lopez 1971, p. 73; Kedar 1976, p. 25; Pryor 1983 p. 133; Hunt and Murray 1999, p. 55.) By the middle of the 1970s historians had synthesized from a century of archival research a thesis about how merchants and their agents enabled an expansion of trade in the Mediterranean. The kernel of the argument is that organizing trade ventures by means of *commenda* contracts enabled the functionaries of trade to share risk and, in turn, to realize gains that risk-averse parties operating alone with their own resources would otherwise have passed up.

The historical thesis joins concepts of trust and risk-sharing in explaining the role of *commenda* in enabling the revival of trade of the Commercial Revolution. Historians have been sensitive to the prospect that agents retained under the terms of a *commenda* contract might cheat their investors. The principal conclusion of the literature on this count is that investors could resort to *commenda* contracts if they could hire honest agents (Lopez and Raymond 1955; de Roover 1963; Lane 1964 [1965]; Hunt and Murray 1999) or family members (Byrne 1916; North 1991). Investors could trust honest agents to report gains or losses honestly, and family bonds, presumably, would again encourage agents to render truthful reports. The next part of the thesis indicates how *commenda* enabled an expansion of trade. The idea is that contracts featuring risk-sharing enabled contracting parties to participate in ventures yielding the most uncertain returns. (Lane 1973, p. 139; Kedar 1976, p. 25.) For example, in characterizing contracting practices in the thirteenth and early fourteenth centuries, both Frederic Lane and Benjamin Kedar distinguish between ventures conducted within a physically secure inner-core zone conforming to most of the Eastern Mediterranean and an outer zone conforming to the frontiers of the inner core and beyond into India and Central Asia. Agents venturing beyond the inner core would have faced both greater physical hazards and greater uncertainty over the availability of commercial prospects.

Taken together, trust and risk-sharing enabled the functionaries of trade to realize gains that risk-averse parties would have otherwise forgone. At least three difficulties with this thesis are (1) it does not explicitly address the trade-offs encountered in choosing *commenda* over debt contracts or vice-versa, (2) it neither recognizes nor rationalizes the role of yet other types of contracts that appear in the data, and (3) it is motivated by heavy interpretations assigned to no more than two anecdotes that have been heavily cited in the literature. The first anecdote relates to the experiences of the Venetian Giovanni Loredan in India. Lopez (1943) indicated that in 1338–39 Giovanni Loredan ventured to India via the Black Sea with financing provided by family members by *commenda* contracts. This example of traveling to the outer zone under a *commenda* has been presented in Lopez (1943, 1951, 1955, 1971), Lopez and Raymond (1955), Lane (1973), and Kedar (1976) as evidence of the role of the *commenda* in enabling long distance trade. Meanwhile, Kedar (1976) and Lopez (1951) indicate the venture of the Genoese Benedetto Vivaldi and his brother in 1315 to India under the terms of a *commenda* contract as further evidence. Kedar (1976, p. 25) explicitly outlines the thesis with these two examples:

> In the outer zone, the prevalent form of partnership was the *commenda*, or as
> the Venetians usually called it, the *colleganza* . . . This form of partnership . . .
> was perfectly suited to the commercial trips to the distant, only partially known
> lands of Further Asia. Indeed, both of the commercial voyages to India about
> which the financial details are known – the voyages of the Genoese Benedetto
> Vivaldi in 1315 and of the Venetian Giovanni Loredan in 1339 – were under-
> taken by men who entered into *commenda* contracts.

The two anecdotes are suggestive but alone do not provide a foundation
upon which to establish a theory of contract selection.[2] In contrast, this
chapter advances a simple contract-selection hypothesis, then does two
things that no study on medieval contracting has yet done: (1) it makes
the hypothesis stand up to a sizable, representative dataset of contracts,
and (2) it makes the hypothesis stand up to a large dataset of unpublished
contracts. The reader should not discount this second point. There is
a distinct bias in the selection of cartularies that have been published.
Editors tend to choose to edit cartularies that are short and that feature
less complex documents.[3]

The Governance Narrative

One reason the principal historical narrative may not have featured a role
for debt financing is that historians did not have tools for characterizing
tradeoffs between debt and equity. Historians had, for the most part, been
working implicitly out of a contract-as-promise framework. According to
such a perspective of contracting, one party to a contract may promise to
perform X, Y, and Z. Failure to perform invites appeals to (frictionless)
formal enforcement processes, and these processes enable counterparties
to redress breaches or to impose sanctions. Under such a framework, it is
not obvious how we might characterize tradeoffs between debt and equity.
In contrast, it would be natural for researchers working out of a contract-
as-framework perspective (Llewellyn 1931) to recognize tradeoffs. The
prospect that agents may cheat their merchants introduces broad scope
for governance by, for example, enabling a richer examination of the role
of both formal and informal enforcement processes. We need take only

---

[2]   Moreover, all we know is that the Vivaldi brothers never returned to Genoa.
They may have simply absconded with their investors' funds.
[3]   A transliteration of the cartularies of Giovanni Gerardo, for example, would
surely run into many volumes – more than a single researcher could, perhaps,
justify doing. Even so, the cartularies of Giovanni Gerardo and others maintained
at the State Archives of Venice are far more interesting than those that have been
published.

one further step to suggest that the choice of financial structure (debt or equity) can itself affect the form governance takes.

No researchers had taken up how the choice of financial structure could affect governance, but Greif (1989, 1993) explicitly takes up the problem of cheating with respect to long-distance trade and suggests how informal processes – specifically, reputation mechanisms – could enable merchants to accommodate the problem of cheating.

Reputation mechanisms constitute one class of mechanisms parties might use to support exchange. They depend on repeated interactions between parties, on flows of information parties use to detect cheating, and on sanctions parties use to redress or punish cheating (Stigler 1964; Bull 1987). Folk theorem results derived from the theory of supergames (Sorin 1992) suggest that it can be easy to rationalize any number of practices and institutions as reputation mechanisms. Theory can motivate multiple equilibria, leaving theorists stuck with looking for criteria according to which parties might select one candidate equilibrium over another. The upshot is that theory alone may provide little descriptive, predictive, or prescriptive content. Even so, empirical research suggests that people who were unencumbered with academic concerns about multiplicity of equilibria managed to institute and maintain reputation mechanisms. (See Greif 1989, 1993 for economic analysis of the experiences of the Maghribi traders documented in Goitein 1967, 1973. See Edwards and Ogilvie 2012 for a rejoinder.) Further research suggests that formal institutions such as the Law Merchant may have enabled parties to implement and maintain informal reputation mechanisms (Milgrom et al. 1990).

It is not obvious that reputation mechanisms served much of a role in ordering trade ventures that European merchants had organized – a topic that Greif (1994) takes up – but that raises the question of how European merchants accommodated the problem of cheating. North (1991, p. 106) suggests how we might build on the principal historical narrative and incorporate the governance problem:

> The traditional resolution of this [governance] problem in medieval and early modern times was the use of kinship and family ties to bind agents to principals. However, as the size and scope of merchant trading empires grew, the extension of discretionary behavior to others than kin of the principal required the development of more elaborate accounting procedures for monitoring the behavior of agents.

North's statement appeals to the role of kinship relations in enabling long-distance trade, but it also builds on the idea that reaching beyond kinship relations and making the shift to more impersonal exchange enabled merchants to expand trade. The statement also suggests that information, and the accounting mechanisms used to secure it, helped mitigate cheating.

Contract Selection

The principal historical narrative does not take up the governance problem. The existing governance narrative makes governance the focus of analysis, but it leaves out an account of how merchants detected cheating in the first place. Reputation effects, for example, would have depended on merchants being able to detect (if not verify) cheating. Indeed, as Bull (1987, p. 148) observes, "[R]eputation effects are only as strong as the information flows that support them," but it is not obvious what could have constituted accounting procedures that would have enabled merchants to detect distortions in agents' reports of transactions.

There do exist indications that accounting procedures may have served a role in mitigating other types of cheating – specifically, cheating derived from an agent's claim, say, that cargoes had been spoiled or otherwise compromised during transit. Italian merchant vessels often featured shipboard scribes who maintained records of the quantity and the condition of cargoes that agents both loaded and unloaded. Other than that, it is not obvious that contracting parties could have depended on accounting procedures to neutralize cheating. Information remained susceptible to manipulation, limiting parties to nothing more than suasion to discourage cheating. In some Italian jurisdictions, for example, notaries could have faced the prospect of being burned at the stake for falsifying documents (Brătianu 1927, p. 32).

The spectacle of a public execution might go some way toward preserving the integrity of information, but this study concentrates on the link between financial structure – a debt-versus-equity question – and the problem of mitigating cheating. The contract selection hypothesis builds on earlier research in economics on the relationship between financial structure and governance. Modigliani and Miller (1958) had noted that, while it is intuitively plausible to suggest that financial structure and governance are related, the standard tools of economics did not provide a way of characterizing the relationship. Their remarkable result was that, when viewed through the lens of established economic theory, the choice between debt and equity financing was irrelevant. Later research, such as Jensen and Meckling (1976), Myers (1977), and Myers and Majluf (1984), appealed to newer theory to suggest how problems of asymmetric information and moral hazard could rescue the relevance of financial structure by illuminating governance tradeoffs between the choice of debt or equity financing. Williamson (1988) appealed to a transaction costs logic to suggest how governance tradeoffs could motivate an empirically testable contract selection hypothesis.

Williamson (1988) ties the selection of debt and equity to the degree to which gains from exchange are relationship specific. In the environment he considers, the governance attending equity financing facilitates the efforts of parties to adapt their relationship to contingencies realized over the course of long-term exchange. In contrast, debt grants to an outside party (for example, the bank) some discretion over the decision to wrap up the parties' collaboration and to liquidate assets. Insofar as liquidating would entail dissipation of relationship-specific value, then equity might dominate, for it might be better to work things out internally (and preserve relationship-specific value) than grant an outside party, who is less well situated to appreciate the relationship-specific value, the option of marching in and destroying that value. The tradeoff, however, is that the governance attending equity might require costly institutional supports. Instituting and operating the processes by which parties "work things out" may be costly. Debt financing precludes these costs.

The environment examined here parallels those of the models of "costly state verification" inspired by Townsend (1979) and the model of costly state falsification introduced by Crocker and Morgan (1998). These environments feature a problem of *ex post* asymmetric information in that contracting parties must commit to terms of contract before some party learns certain payoff-relevant information – that is, before that party learns his "type".[4] Townsend and later authors consider relationships between financial structure and (costly) institutional supports such as auditing schemes. Crocker and Morgan examine the relationship between financial structure and agents' cheating technology. Insofar as cheating may entail some cost, agents might opt to reveal information truthfully. As long as a principal knows an agent's cheating technology, the parties might be able to design a contract isomorphic to a direct mechanism by which agents reveal private information.[5]

What happens, however, when auditing is infeasible at any cost or investors know nothing of agents' cheating technologies? That is, what happens

---

[4]   Problems of asymmetric information typically involve environments in which some party has already received payoff-relevant information (learns his "type") before parties commit to terms of contract.

[5]   An important innovation of Crocker and Morgan (1998) was the extension of the Revelation Principle to environments to which earlier authors (for example, Lacker and Weinberg 1989) suggested the revelation principle might not apply. Crocker and Morgan characterize a single-crossing condition by which agents sort themselves by type.

when contracting parties have no instruments other than the compensation scheme? The situation corresponds with the converse of the problem explored in Williamson (1988). Williamson (1988) is occupied with the endogeneity of institutional supports: why would parties to exchange bother to assemble costly mechanisms to support their relationships? When it is not possible, however, to craft support mechanisms – that is, when it would be prohibitively costly to assemble institutional supports such as costly auditing schemes – contracting parties are left with the prospect of abandoning exchange or with adapting the choice of contract to features of the environment. Some environments, for example, may feature informal sources of information of sufficient quality to enable contracting parties to support *commenda* with informal enforcement mechanisms.

The main point of Williamson (1988) is that equity shows up as the mode of financing of last resort (for investments in which relationship-specific value is at stake) given contracting parties maintain some capacity for assembling costly supports. The main issue here is that debt shows up as the mode of financing of last resort (for investments involving little or no relationship-specific value) given contracting parties maintain little or no capacity for assembling costly supports. In contrast, when parties can monitor agents' performance at low cost, then equity-like financing may supplant debt financing. That yet leaves open the question, however, of how parties structure contracts when monitoring entails less than prohibitive cost but may only yield noisy signals of agents' performance. Indeed, an expansive reading of Faure-Grimaud and Mariotti (1999) yields the deceptively simple point that, while debt contracts might be optimal when parties have no access to contract supports, the prospect that they could not economically assemble some type of support would seem to be exceptional. A whole host of informal instruments may be available around which parties could then organize the governance of equity-like schemes or more elaborate debt contracts.

On this last matter economic literature offers an array of options. (Dixit 2009, pp. 10–11 advances a three-part taxonomy of options.) Specifically, problems of *ex post* asymmetric information involving low-quality information can be more broadly construed as problems of imperfect monitoring about which there is both a prodigious theoretical and empirical literature. Fudenberg et al. (1994), for example, extend the theory of repeated games and a folk theorem to environments in which contracting parties commonly receive noisy signals relating to each other's performance. Such apparatus may rationalize the use of reputational schemes even when noise renders monitoring imperfect.

A limitation of such reputational monitoring schemes is that they depend on parties to exchange having the luxury of being able to perform over time. Absent such luxury, contracting parties have to incentivize performance by implementing payoffs and punishments within the scope of one-shot interactions. A more important limitation, however, of monitoring schemes (whether reputational or not) is that they depend on contracting parties receiving the same (possibly noisy) signal. In a Green and Porter-type mechanism (Green and Porter 1984), for example, firms participating in a collusive scheme to restrain competition commonly observe a market-wide indicator such as price (in a quantity-setting environment) or market-wide output. Firms may be able to use such indications to make common inferences about whether or not erstwhile conspirators had deviated from a collusive agreement to restrict output or raise price. Absent common signals, however, firms cannot make common inferences, and, absent common inferences, they cannot come to common understandings about each party's performance. Contracting parties effectively lose the ability to monitor performance.

Difficulties in monitoring performance suggest the outlines of a few hypotheses about the selection of contracts and the enforcement of *commenda* contracts. Specifically, peer monitoring could have supported *commenda* contracts in certain environments. These environments would have been more congenial to *commenda* contracting in that they afforded the financiers of overseas trade some means, formal or informal, of (imperfectly) monitoring agents' performance. In contrast, contracting parties would forgo contracting or would revert to debt contracts in environments that did not afford some means of monitoring performance.

A question remains about how it is that the environment might be more congenial. On this count theory does not offer much guidance. A suggestion advanced here, however, is that *commenda* dominated in environments in which agents were more likely to be trading commonly with other agents (their peers) at commonly visited sites in commonly traded commodities. (I would be tempted to appropriate the language of Lane 1973 and Kedar 1976 and suggest that these environments correspond closely to their geographic concept of the "inner-core zone".) In contrast, debt contracts tended to support activity on the informational frontiers of the trade economy. (I suggest that these environments correspond to something of Lane's and Kedar's "outer zone".) Further, debt tended to dominate when the local trade economy (if not the system-wide trade economy) was depressed. These patterns suggests that *commenda* prevailed in environments that were more congenial in that information about commercial prospects in a given overseas site was abundant whereas debt prevailed in environments in which information was sparing.

The environments of the inner core may have been congenial, because they afforded contracting parties access to institutions to support exchange. The maritime republics of the Mediterranean, for example, traditionally made a point of formalizing trading relationships with other important trade sites. Formalized relationships included terms by which visiting merchants could trade locally as well as agreements by which foreign merchants could set up a permanent, physical presence called a *fondaco*. The Venetian republic, for example, had already established a *fondaco* in Alexandria, Egypt by 1173, a site at which Venetian merchants could secure lodging and organize transactions (Constable 2003).

The Venetian republic also sponsored regular merchant convoys that traveled between Venice and Egypt, and it was the combination of regular (and regulated) commercial traffic (state-sponsored convoys) and a regular physical presence (a *fondaco*) in such important ports as Alexandria that afforded Venetian merchants some means to monitor their trading agents. Trading agents venturing from Venice to Egypt were operating in the presence of other agents who would be trading in the same commodities. They would have symmetrical access to facilities and information. Knowing this, investors situated in Venice could exploit the reports of other parties to gauge the performance of their own agents and detect, if not verify, cheating. Knowing that, agents could be expected to refrain from cheating. In such transparent environments, parties could afford to organize trade ventures under the terms of *commenda* contracts. In less congenial, less transparent environments, parties might forgo exchange or adopt debt financing.

Insofar as maintaining transparency involved maintaining both a regular stream of trade and a physical presence in an overseas site, then the trade between Venice and Egypt through most of the thirteenth century was exceptional. In contrast, most of the trade activity examined in this chapter was episodic. Local authorities might commit to formal trade treaties, but the inability or unwillingness of these same authorities to contain piracy or other predations could frustrate trade. Such was the experience, for example, with the important trade between Venetian Crete and Turkish *beyliks* in the Aegean. The *beyliks* of Aydin and Menteshe periodically renewed trade treaties with Crete. The renewals, however, were responses to breakdowns – breakdowns induced by larger events and currents such as fits of anti-Turkish crusading in the Aegean. Even the trade between Venice and Egypt itself eventually reverted to fitfulness and instability. After the Mamlukes of Egypt took over the last of the crusader holdings in the Levant (Acre) in 1291, the formerly stationary trade with Egypt reverted to the kind of episodic trade that became prevalent throughout the Eastern Mediterranean. Attending the reversion to episodic trade was a reversion from *commenda* financing to debt financing.

THE DATA

The data from 1278–1400 (1701 contracts) derive from the logbooks (cartularies) of 28 notaries maintained at the State Archives of Venice. (See Table 5.1.) All of these data pertain to trade ventures that merchants operating out of Crete had organized. The records of only five notaries have been published: Angelo de Cartura, Donato Fontanella, Leonardo Marcello, Pietro Pizolo, and Zaccaria de Fredo. The records of these five notaries account for 309 of the 1701 contracts (18.2 percent). We can find the records of notaries in the archival series *Notai in Candia* maintained at the State Archives.

The remaining data from the years 1190–1220 (122 contracts) derive from the archival series the *Cancelleria Inferiore* maintained at the State Archives. These data do not derive from notaries' cartularies but derive from contracts that individuals had maintained in family archives. Most of the contracts pertain to trade ventures originating in Venice, although a few ventures originated in other sites such as Constantinople. All of the contracts have been transliterated in a series titled the *Codice Diplomatico Veneziano*, and all but one of these contracts have been published in Morozzo della Rocca and Lombardo (1940) and Lombardo and Morozzo della Rocca (1953).

1278–1400

The data from 1278–1400 indicate that in some years the records of particular notaries featured a high proportion of maritime contracts – sometimes more than 15 percent of all contracts – but in other years very few maritime contracts appear.[6] From these data I indicate three types of contracts: *commenda*, debt, and contracts I have labeled "pooling contracts". The one dimension that distinguishes these types from each other is the rule by which principals and agents share total surplus. Under the terms of *commenda* contracts, parties split proceeds in fixed proportions such as half and half, two-thirds and one-third, and, less often, three-quarters and one-quarter. Debt contracts made agents the residual claimant; agents would guarantee fixed payoffs (principal plus interest) to their investors.

---

[6] The proportion that prevailed across all notaries in the entire dataset is 3.59 percent. The high was 22.52 percent (Giovanni Gerardo in 1352). Leonardo de Vegla achieved 13.47 percent (30 of 223 contracts) in 1348 although Giovanni Gerardo, the most prominent notary, achieved only 3.53 percent (44 of 1248 contracts) in that same year. Three other notaries achieved proportions in excess of 15 percent in 1304, 1305, and 1352.

Table 5.1   Distribution of contracts across notaries

	1278–81	1300–1304	1305–09	1310–14	1315–19	1320–24	1325–29	1330–34	1335–39
Andrea Nigro								32	2
Andrea de Bellamore							12		
Angelo Bocontolo									
Angelo Cariola			5						
Angelo Donno					6				
Angelo de Cartura			92						
Antonio Brixiano									
Bartholomeo Francisci									120
Donato Fontanella						3			
Filippo Malpes									
Francisco de Cruce									14
Giorgio Aymo									
Giorgio Candachiti									
Giorgio da Milano I									
Giorgio di Ligardo									1
Giovanni Catacalo									
Giovanni Gerardo							5	144	110
Giovanni Similiante							23	14	
Iacobus de Firmo									
Leonardo Marcello	29								
Leonardo Quirino					57	32			
Leonardo de Vegla									
Marco di Piacenza									5
Nicolo Brixiano									2
Nicolo Tonisto									
Pietro Pizolo		173	3						
Stefano Bono		58		14	2				
Zaccaria de Fredo									
Total	29	231	100	14	65	35	40	190	254

Pooling contracts read just like *commenda* and debt contracts, except that they indicate payoffs as a function of the number of shares (*partes*) in a vessel that the parties have purchased.[7] Pooling contracts show up in the records of many notaries starting in 1339, a year of renewed warring with Turks in the Aegean (Zachariadou 1983). The relative frequency of pool-

---

[7]   How shares translate into profit-sharing rules is ambiguous. An important aspect of these shares, however, is that they indicate that agents were operating alongside other agents representing the interests of other merchants. Alan Stahl and F.X. LeDuc agree with my interpretation (personal communication, February 2005).

1340–44	1345–49	1350–54	1355–59	1360–64	1365–69	1370–74	1385–89	1390–94	1395–1400	Total
										34
										12
	203	18								221
										5
										6
										92
		4								4
										120
										3
		1								1
										14
					65	19				84
									8	8
	10									10
										1
							26	29		55
6	144	41	87	2						539
										37
2										2
										29
										89
	39									39
4	5									14
										2
							21			21
										176
										74
		9								9
12	401	73	87	2	65	19	47	29	8	1701

ing contracts is greatest in 1347, the year in which the first wave of plague of the sequence of waves we know as the Black Death invaded the Aegean. Pooling contracts disappear in the succeeding few years.

Parties seem to have used pooling contracts in environments that were subject to extraordinary physical hazards. Investors may very well have been concerned that any one agent might not be able to return and to remit payments. More importantly, parties seem to have used pooling contracts in non-stationary environments in which negative shocks to the informational structure of the trade economy rendered commercial prospects difficult to ascertain.

All contracts feature the following types of information:

1. The identities and towns of residence of the investors.
2. The identities and towns of residence of the agents.
3. Investments on the part of investors in kind or in specie.
4. The rule by which parties share profits and losses.
5. The assignment of losses from spoilage or piracy to the investors or agents.
6. Date of enactment.
7. Contract duration: the time by which the agents must dispatch their obligations.
8. The identities of witnesses to the contract.
9. The identity of the notary assembling the contract.

Contracts often feature other terms:

10. An itinerary agents are supposed to follow.
11. An explicit indication that the agent surrenders the option to deviate from a stated itinerary.
12. The specific vessel by which an agent must travel.

The 1701 contracts from 1278–1400 number 777 *commenda*, 119 pooling contracts, and 805 debt contracts. Important destinations include Palatia (formerly Miletus), the principal port of the Turkish *beylik* of Menteshe on the Anatolian Peninsula (289 contracts), and Theologo (formerly Ephesus), the principal port of the Turkish Beylik of Aydin (47 contracts). Egypt (Alexandria or Damietta), Rhodes, and Cyprus show up in 123, 104, and 120 contracts, respectively. Most other contracts involve trade with islands in the Aegean. Contracts often would not indicate an itinerary or might even explicitly indicate that agents would reserve complete discretion over the selection of destinations.

These contracts span 760 lenders and 1610 agents. The matching of lenders and agents is many-to-many, in that any one contract may feature more than one lender or more than one agent. Altogether, the data span 2605 unique dyads (principal–agent pairs).

The Representativeness of the Data, 1330–55

Some of the data exercises presented in the following two main sections of the chapter depend on the data being sufficiently representative so that we might (1) characterize volumes of maritime commerce and (2) identify relationships, if any, that depended on repeated interactions. The contract selection exercise for Crete in the penultimate section, for example, identifies relationships that unfolded over the course of several interactions.

That same exercise, however, suggests that repeated interactions did not inform contract selection.

I use the contract data from 1330–55 to track repeated interactions between lenders and their agents. Specifically, an analysis of the matching of lenders and agents to notaries suggests that specific principal–agent pairs (dyads) tend to match up with particular notaries. The larger suggestion is that examining the records of any one notary can give a nearly complete record of how a particular principal–agent relationship unfolded over time. More generally, the data suggest that lenders tended to concentrate their contracts on particular notaries, and notaries tended to concentrate their business on particular lenders. Agents, for their part, appear to have followed the lead of their lenders when matching with notaries.

Consider, first, the matching of dyads to notaries. For each dyad I identify a "maximal" notary – whom the dyad selected more frequently or as frequently as any other notary. I then assign all of the non-maximal contracts to a composite notary "all other notaries". For example, the lender Iohannes Anaplioti was matched in three different contracts with the agent Giorgio Pisianello. The first of these contracts was assembled by the notary Giovanni Gerardo in 1346, and the two other contracts were assembled by the notary Angelo Bocontolo in January and October 1347. Thus, Angelo Bocontolo emerges as the maximal notary for the dyad composed of Iohannes Anaplioti and Giorgio Pisanello, and all other notaries assembled a single contract for this dyad. Meanwhile, the lender Constancio Cutaioti was matched in five different contracts with the agent Costas Bono. Each of these contracts had been assembled by the notary Bartholomeo Francisci. Other agents were involved in some of the contracts, and two of the contracts were effectively simultaneous, being signed three days apart, one involving Costas Bono alone and another involving the pair of agents, Costas Bono and Iani Calodha. In this case, Bartholomeo Francisci emerges as the maximal notary, and all other notaries assembled no contracts for this particular contracting dyad.

I pool all contracts together and estimate a single parameter, p, the probability by which dyads tended to match with their maximal notaries. The most obvious way to estimate the matching probability p would be to pose a binomial matching model by which number of times a dyad matched with the maximal notary is counted as a successful match to what is implicitly understood as the contracting parties' preferred notary. The number of times the dyad matched with all other notaries is counted as a failure to match with the preferred notary. Thus, for a given dyad i, the likelihood of observing n_i successful matches out of the dyad's set of K_i contracts would correspond to

$$\Pr(y_i = n_i | K_i) = \begin{bmatrix} K_i \\ n_i \end{bmatrix} p^{n_i} (1-p)^{K_i - n_i} = \left[\frac{K_i!}{n_i!(K_i - n_i)!} \right] p^{n_i} (1-p)^{K_i - n_i}$$

An advantage of this simple matching model is that it allows one to be agnostic about the number of other notaries that may have been available to any given contracting party. Instead, the model only depends on the binomial designations "maximal" and "all other notaries". A deficiency with this model is that it clumsily accommodates the large number of single-appearing dyads. Implicit in the model is the assumption that appearing a single time amounts to successfully matching one time with their preferred notary.

I adapt the binomial model so that it is agnostic about whether a match to a maximal notary constitutes a "successful" match to a preferred notary. This allows us to ask: what is the maximum number of contracts a dyad could be expected to secure either with a maximal notary or all other notaries? Again, an advantage of this approach is that it does not require us to identify all of the notaries that may have been available to a particular dyad.

In this case, the likelihood of observing a maximum of n_i matches with a maximal notary or all other notaries out of the dyad's set of K_i contracts would correspond to:

$$\Pr(y_i = n_i | K_i) = \begin{bmatrix} K_i \\ n_i \end{bmatrix} \{ p^{n_i} (1-p)^{K_i - n_i} + p^{K_i - n_i} (1-p)^{n_i} \} \left[\frac{1}{\text{int}(K_i / n_i)} \right].$$

The term $\text{int}(K_i / n_i)$ equals the integer value of the ratio of contracts K_i to maximal matches n_i.[8] Thus, given a dyad appeared only one time in the dataset – that is, given $K_i = 1$ – the likelihood of observing a maximum number of contracts of 1 is 1. Given a dyad appeared two times ($K_i = 2$), the likelihood of observing a maximum of 1 contract is $2p(1-p)$. The likelihood of that same dyad securing a maximum of 2 contracts would be $p^2 + (1-p)^2$. The likelihood of observing a maximum of zero contracts is zero. Finally, the expected maximum for a dyad that appeared two times is $2[1 - p(1-p)]$.

This expected maximum model assigns the likelihood p to a dyad matching with a maximal notary, but it does not bar the prospect that a dyad may choose all other notaries more frequently than a maximal notary. It turns out, however, that the maximal notaries for each of the 1405 dyads that

---

[8] The term $1/\text{int}(K_i / n_i)$ accommodates the double-counting that attends the tie between the maximal notary and all other notaries. The term equals 1/2 when $K_i = 2n_i$ and equals 1 otherwise.

appear in 1330–55 are not dominated by all other notaries. The three dyads that appear most frequently, for example, appear five times in the data, and each of these three dyads concentrate its contracts on a single notary. (One dyad concentrates its five contracts on the notary Angelo Bocontolo, and the other two dyads concentrate their contracts on the notary Bartholomeo Francisci.) Similarly, the three dyads that appear four times in the data concentrate their contracts on (three different) single notaries. Of the 18 dyads that appear three times, 17 concentrate their contracts on a single notary. No situation exists by which, say, a dyad appears three times but distributes its three contracts across three notaries, in which case any single notary would be maximal but all other notaries would account for a contrived maximum of two contracts.

Pooling the data across all dyads (indexed $i = 1$ though to I) and applying the expected maximum model implies a log-likelihood function:

$$\ln L = \sum_{i=1}^{I} \left\{ \ln \begin{bmatrix} K_i \\ n_i \end{bmatrix} - \ln(int(K_i/n_i)) + \ln(p^{n_i}(1-p)^{K_i-n_i} + p^{K_i-n_i}(1-p)^{n_i}) \right\}.$$

Maximum likelihood estimation is applied to the full dataset from 1330–55 as well as to a random subsample comprising about 80 percent of these data. Estimation is also applied to a subsample generated by excluding one of the most prominent notaries, Angelo Bocontolo.

Estimation across the two subsamples constitutes two quasi-experiments informing the robustness of the estimate performed on the full dataset. The random subsample was generated by assigning a random integer between 0 and 9 to each of the 1405 dyads in the full dataset and selecting those assigned a value between 0 and 7. (The 8s and 9s were excluded.) Applying estimation to this subsample suggests how robust estimation to the full sample might be if it were subject to a similar process of data censoring. The other subsample implies an alternative means of censoring data: what happens when the entire cartulary of a prominent notary is lost or otherwise excluded?

Maximum likelihood estimates of p (with estimated standard errors) are presented in Table 5.2 in the column labeled "Dyads". Estimation across the full dataset and two subsamples yield tight estimates between 94.21 percent and 96.53 percent (with estimated standard errors less than 1.61 percent). The suggestion is plain: insofar as we can interpret matching with the maximal notary as matching with a contracting party's preferred notary, then contracting parties managed to match with their preferred notaries about 95 percent of the time.[9]

---

[9] The singleton dyads contribute nothing to the likelihood function

Table 5.2　Probability of matching with a preferred notary

	Dyads	Principals	Agents
Expected maximum model	95.23%	87.98%	75.95%
	1.32%	1.33%	1.49%
	N = 1405	N = 395	N = 912
Expected maximum model random subsample	94.21%	87.97%	75.83%
	1.60%	1.53%	2.18%
	N = 1134	N = 328	N = 768
Expected maximum model subsample excluding Angelo Bocontolo	96.53%	92.91%	82.83%
	1.31%	1.20%	1.74%
	N = 1072	N = 298	N = 747
Linear regression	98.63%	85.32%	75.10%
	0.38%	4.68%	3.52%
	N = 1405	N = 395	N = 912
Linear regression random subsample	99.30%	85.32%	76.76%
	0.31%	4.68%	3.74%
	N = 1134	N = 328	N = 768
Linear regression subsample excluding Angelo Bocontolo	99.05%	91.37%	84.89%
	0.36%	3.25%	2.03%
	N = 1072	N = 298	N = 747
Binomial model	99.17%	91.90%	87.48%
	0.23%	0.90%	0.85%
	N = 1405	N = 395	N = 912

To benchmark the results I apply the binomial model to the full dataset.[10] I also apply a linear regression model of the form $y_i = \beta K_i + \varepsilon_i$ where ε_i corresponds to a normally distributed error process.[11] As above, y_i corresponds to the maximum between the count of contracts assigned to a maximal notary and the count of contracts assigned to all other notaries. Both estimation methods yield matching probabilities in excess of 98 percent.

---

corresponding to the expected maximum model. Estimation amounts to ignoring those data. Instead, the results are largely driven by the dyads that appear two times. Of these dyads, 89 concentrate their contracts on a single notary, and 12 split their contracts between two notaries.

[10]　The maximum likelihood estimate of the matching probability p under the binomial model is simply the ratio of the number of successes to the number of draws $\sum_{i=1}^{I} n_i / \sum_{i=1}^{I} K_i$.

[11]　I estimate the equation by ordinary least squares (OLS) with robust (White) standard errors to accommodate heteroskedasticity derived from the fact that observations with larger K_i can yield larger errors.

The estimated value of β amounts to an estimate of the matching probability p in that pK_i corresponds to the expected number of matches to a preferred notary in a binomial process featuring K_i independent draws. Thus, the regression model amounts to a binomial model with a normally distributed error process.

I also apply the matching analysis separately to principals and agents. (See the columns labeled "Principals" and "Agents" in Table 5.2.) The expected maximum model yields estimates between 87 percent and 93 percent for the probability by which lenders match with their maximal notaries. Further, we can interpret these results as corresponding to matches with preferred notaries rather than merely maximal notaries in that each lender's maximal notary is not dominated by all other notaries for all but one of the 395 lenders that appear in the full dataset from 1330–55.[12] The lender Nicolo de Clarencia appears in three contracts distributed across the years 1342, 1347 and 1348. Each contract was drawn up by a different notary, so it is not obvious that we could identify a preferred notary. In contrast, the lender Constancio Cutaioti appeared in 57 contracts, 46 of which were assembled by the maximal notary Bartholomeo Francisci. The remaining 11 contracts were assembled by all other notaries, and it would be difficult to suggest that Bartholomeo Francisci was not Constancio Cutaioti's preferred notary.

The expected maximum model also yields estimates between 75 percent and 83 percent for the matching of agents to maximal notaries. Again, we can interpret these matches to maximal notaries as matches to preferred notaries in that the maximal notaries are not dominated for all but eight agents out of the 912 agents that appear in the dataset from 1330–55. Further, the maximal notaries strictly dominate all other notaries for 206 agents.

Taking a global perspective of the matching data suggests a more sophisticated interpretation than the interpretation that the agent matching data or lender matching data alone suggest. Specifically, the entire body of matching data suggest the following interpretations:

Result 1:   Lenders really did maintain preferences over notaries.

Result 2:   Lenders would direct their agents to match with their preferred notaries.

That agents appear to match less frequently with a seemingly preferred notary is consistent with their selection being dictated by lenders.

---

[12]   Further, the maximal notaries strictly dominate all other notaries in 101 of the 395 instances.

Moreover, the suggestion that lenders tended to maintain preferences for particular notaries suggests that examining the records of those same notaries in isolation can provide a good perspective of a lender's career as a financier of overseas trade ventures. I pose the larger suggestion as a distinct result:

Result 3:   In general, the records of a single notary provide a good perspective of specific principal–agent relationships, including those that unfolded over the course of more than one interaction.

I provide two further types of evidence to substantiate that lenders tended to concentrate their contracts on particular notaries. In Table 5.3 I exhibit the distribution of the most active lenders' contracts across notaries. Table 5.3 demonstrates that five of the six most active lenders who appear in the data tended to concentrate most (88 percent) of their contracts on a single notary. For example, the lender Stephano Anafioti concentrated 38 of his 40 contracts on the notary Giovanni Gerardo, and the remaining two contracts appeared in the cartulary of the notary Francisco de Cruce. Meanwhile, the sixth lender, Stamatio Brixiano, concentrated all but one of his 40 contracts on two notaries. He concentrated 23 on the notary Angelo Bocontolo and 16 on Giovanni Gerardo.

Table 5.4 demonstrates that notaries can be diverse. Some notaries, for example, averaged more than several contracts in a day whereas others averaged a single contract once every several days. Yet others, such as Marco da Piacenza, assembled a large volume of contracts (1346) but contributed a disproportionately small share of maritime contracts (12). Bartholomeo Francisci, in contrast, contributed a disproportionately high share of maritime contracts in a relatively short time that spanned one of the frenzied peaks of trade with Turkish *beyliks* (1338–39). Leonardo de Vegla also contributed a disproportionately large number of contracts in a short interval. He contributed 39 contracts in the frenzy of trade activity in 1347–48.

The patterns exhibited in Tables 5.3 and 5.4 suggest the following result:

Result 4:   A small proportion of career notaries managed disproportionately large shares of contracting.

Angelo Bocontolo and Giovanni Gerardo maintained long careers and provided notarial services during periods of both low activity and high activity. Other notaries tended to show up during periods of intense commercial activity and tended to serve the demands of less active lenders. The exception is Bartholomeo Francisci, who dedicated most of his notarial services to the lenders Constancio Cutaioti and Marco Benbo of Venice.

Table 5.3   The matching of active lenders to preferred notaries

Notary	Constancio Cutaioti	Marco Benbo de Venecium	Stamatio Brixiano	Stephano Anafioti	Iohannes Anaplioti	Iohannes Filielo	Single-appearing lenders	All other lenders	Notary's maritime contracts
Angelo Bocontolo	1		23		7		74	117	221
Antonio Brixiano			1				2	1	4
Bartholomeo	46	50					10	14	120
Francisci							1		1
Filippo Malpes									
Francisco de Cruce	3			2			5	4	14
Giacobo de Firmo							2		2
Giorgio da Milano I							6	4	10
Giorgio de Ligardo							2		2
Giovanni Gerardo	7		16	38	15	24	136	218	451
Giovanni Similiante							4	10	14
Leonardo de Vegla		2			2		17	19	39
Marco da Piacenza							11	1	12
Nicolo Brixiano							2		2
Zaccaria de Fredo							3	6	9
Distinct Contracts	57	52	40	40	24	24	275	394	901

Table 5.4 Differentiation in notary contract counts and notary-days

Notary	Maritime contracts	Total contracts	Notary-days	Share of maritime contracts (%)	Share of total contracts (%)	Share of notary-days (%)
Angelo Bocontolo	221	4105	1916	24.53	22.91	10.71
Antonio Brixiano	4	238	212	0.44	1.33	1.19
Bartholomeo Francisci	120	942	592	13.32	5.26	3.31
Filippo Malpes	1	80	15	0.11	0.45	0.08
Francisco de Cruce	14	488	396	1.55	2.72	2.21
Giacobo de Firmo	2	164	153	0.22	0.91	0.86
Giorgio da Milano I	10	376	1003	1.11	2.10	5.86
Giorgio di Ligardo	2	102	215	0.22	0.57	1.20
Giovanni Gerardo	451	8352	8760	50.06	46.62	52.07
Giovanni Similiante	14	145	336	1.55	0.81	1.88
Leonardo de Vegla	39	305	425	4.33	1.70	2.38
Marco da Piacenza	12	1346	2827	1.33	7.51	17.24
Nicolo Brixiano	2	1188	91	0.22	6.63	0.51
Zaccaria de Fredo	9	85	91	1.00	0.47	0.51
Totals	901	17915	17890	100.00	100.00	100.00

190

1190–1220

An advantage of the data from 1190–1220 is that they tend to feature more detail than the data from the fourteenth-century notaries' cartularies. They tended to indicate whether or not the agent was to coordinate travel with a state-sponsored *muda* (merchant convoy and trade fair). Also, contracts tended to be more explicit about family relations, if any, between the contracting parties. Even so, some of the data derive not from contracts but from receipts by which parties to a venture formally acknowledged the accounting of the results of a venture. Receipts sometimes left out details that would otherwise have been relevant to the analysis.

The contracts are much like those from 1278–1400, with two important exceptions. The data do not include any pooling contracts, and they include two types of *commenda*. One type, which authors sometimes recognize as unilateral *commenda*, were just like those used from 1278–1400. Authors recognize other commenda as bilateral *commenda*, the principal difference being that agents also contributed some share, usually one-quarter, of the financing to the venture. Normally agents participating in a unilateral *commenda* could expect to receive one-quarter of the proceeds. Agents contributing one-quarter of the financing usually secured one-half of the reported profits.

Fifty-six of the 122 documents are original contracts with the remaining 66 being composed of receipts. Fifty-two, 26, and 44 of the documents corresponded, respectively, to unilateral *commenda*, bilateral *commenda*, and debt.

HYPOTHESIS TESTING

The data enable us to operationalize tests of three hypotheses about contract selection:

1. Repeated interactions supported *commenda* contracts.
2. Peer monitoring supported *commenda* contracts.
3. Kinship relations supported *commenda* contracts.

Repeated Interactions

To examine the first hypothesis I identify every unique investor–agent pair (dyad) that shows up anywhere in the entire set of contracts. A given contract may feature more than one dyad in that contracts sometimes featured more than one agent or, even, more than one investor. Thus a contract featuring two investors and two agents will feature four distinct dyads.

I examine dyads through two sets of exercises. First, I recount the frequency with which unique individuals as well as unique dyads show up in the contract data. It turns out that over three-quarters of dyads and over two-thirds of individuals appear only once in the data. Most relationships span no more than a single venture, and yet many of those one-shot interactions involved *commenda* contracts.

In the next main section, on Crete, I apply the frequency of dyads to probit analyses of the selection of dimensions of contract.

Peer Monitoring

To address the question of peer monitoring, I assemble three variables for use in multinomial probit analysis. These variables provide some measure of the quality of information supporting each trade venture. These variables are proxies for the volume of Venetian trade in the Eastern Mediterranean. Higher volume may reflect more voluminous streams of information, but the variables also give some indication of the institutional structure in which each venture was embedded. The first variable, *galley volume*, indicates the number of galleys (large vessels organized in convoys by the Venetian republic) sent from Venice to sites in the Aegean or to sites in the furthest eastern reaches of the Mediterranean, including Cyprus, Lesser Armenia (what is now coastal Syria) and Egypt. In some years the Venetian republic assembled as many as 20 galleys. Less commonly, the Republic sent no galleys. During 1350–55, for example, the Venetian republic was engaged in a war with Genoa (the Third War with Genoa) over access to the Black Sea. The Venetian republic suspended galley traffic in those years.

Contracts in the dataset do not indicate whether or not ventures were organized around state-sponsored convoys, but the variable *galley volume* does capture the point that ventures directed to ports served by state-sponsored convoys were more likely to have been supported by convoys in the years that the Republic of Venice had organized sizable convoys. The second proxy variable, *Genoese war*, serves a similar role. *Galley volume* is integer valued (ranging from 0 to 20) whereas *Genoese war* is binary. It distinguishes the six-year interval spanned by the Third War with Genoa from all other years. It captures the point that commercial traffic was likely lower during the war as any traffic may have been more susceptible to physical hazards.

These first two variables reflect global conditions in the trading environment. The third variable, *local trade volume*, reflects local conditions in Crete. I assemble a proxy for trade volume originating locally in Candia, the principal Venetian port on Crete. For each trading cycle (each calendar year) I calculate the rate at which notaries crafted contracts relating to overseas trade. (I calculate the number of contracts notaries crafted, on average, per day in a given year.) In 1334, for example, notaries crafted about as many as one contract every three days (0.378 contract per day). In 1342 and 1343, notaries crafted only about one contract per year. In 1354 they crafted no contracts at all.

These three variables go some way toward distinguishing three types of ventures: those that tagged along with state-sponsored convoys; those that visited ports on convoy routes, albeit without the support of a state-sponsored convoy; and those that deviated from established convoy routes. The principal argument is that contracting parties could enlist peer monitoring to support ventures embedded in state-sponsored convoys. (Again, I would suggest that these three variables go some way toward distinguishing environments that have much the flavor of the inner core and outer zone of Lane 1973 and Kedar 1976.) Trading agents would likely be trading alongside other agents in commonly traded commodities in commonly visited ports. Trading agents would have common access to robust streams of information, including information about prevailing prices. In contrast, trading agents conducting ventures directed to ports along convoy routes without the support of state-sponsored convoys would have been operating in environments in which information was more thinly dispersed. Fewer peers would have been available to support monitoring. Finally, trade deviating from convoys and convoy routes likely generated the least robust and most thinly dispersed streams of information. Even fewer peers, and possibly no peers at all, would have been present to support monitoring.

I also conduct two quasi-experiments. In the first, I conduct a quasi-experiment involving trade with Egypt. Differences in the trade during 1190–1220 from the trade after 1291 suggest how contracting parties probably had an easier time operationalizing peer monitoring in the earlier period. In the second, I examine differences in the data from 1190–1220 between ventures aligned with state-sponsored convoys and all other ventures. Differences in contract selection suggest how parties were able to operationalize peer monitoring along convoy routes but found themselves operating without the benefit of peer monitoring along other routes.

Kinship Relations

To examine the role of kinship relations, I appeal again to the data from 1190–1220 to examine the distribution of kinship relations in contracts across state-sponsored convoys and contract type. The results suggest not that investors depended on kin to mitigate cheating, but that agents depended on kin to sponsor their own trade activity.

Peer Monitoring and the Trade with Egypt

The data from 1278–1400 and 1190–1220 allow us to conduct a quasi-experiment. The two data sets reveal the financial structure of trade with Egyptian ports in two different environments. (See Table 5.5.) The data from 1190–1220 indicate that 18 of the 123 contracts involved trade with Egypt. Eleven of these 18 documents indicate explicitly that contracting parties coordinated their trade ventures with state-sponsored convoys, although it is likely that all or nearly all of the 18 trade ventures were coordinated around the convoys.[13] What is striking is that 15 of the 18 contracts (83 percent) were *commenda*. Even more striking is the contrast of these data with the data from 1278–1400. One hundred and twenty-three of the 1701 from 1278–1400 explicitly involved trade ventures to Egypt. One hundred of these 109 contracts (89 percent) were debt contracts.

The contract selection hypothesis provides a way of understanding the stark contrast between contract selection in the 1190–1220 interval and in the 1278–1400 period. Egyptian trade in 1190–1220 constituted a stationary environment, and *commenda* contracts prevailed. Egyptian trade in 1278–1400 was subject to much disruption, and debt contracts dominated. The remainder of this subsection is occupied with substantiating the following interpretation:

Result 5: Egyptian trade of 1190–1220 could support peer monitoring. In contrast, the Egyptian trade of the fourteenth century was less con-

Table 5.5   The trade with Egypt

	1190–1220	1278–1400
Commenda	15	9
Pool	0	5
Debt	3	109
Total	18	123

[13]   Thirteen of the 18 documents are receipts, and five are original contracts. Four of the five original contracts explicitly mention state-sponsored convoys, whereas only seven of the 13 receipts explicitly indicate convoys. The suggestion is that receipts were less likely to indicate whether or not contracting parties had coordinated completed ventures with state-sponsored convoys.

ducive to peer monitoring; Egypt had been incorporated into the secure inner-core zone but reverted to the outer zone post-1291.

Egypt had always been a nexus of intra and extra-Mediterranean trade. As the principal granary of the Eastern Mediterranean for millennia, and as a conduit for goods coming from India and other parts further east, it was natural for Venetian merchants and other European merchants to have developed commercial relations and experience in Egypt going back centuries.[14] By 1190–1220, the Venetian republic already had an established history sponsoring annual merchant convoys that would make the round trip from Venice, to Egypt, the Levant and back to Venice.

Over the centuries, the Republic of Venice variously regulated the convoys, but what is important for our purposes is that the Republic coordinated trade fairs in Venice and convoys with seasonal commodities markets in Egypt and the Levant. Merchants' agents ended up traveling together to participate collectively (if not cooperatively) in commodities markets at sites such as Alexandria and Dammieta. They generally returned with these convoys to resell commodities, such as pepper, they had acquired in trade fairs in Venice. Other European merchants, including other Italians, would acquire these goods for distribution elsewhere in Europe. By the fourteenth century the Republic started to sponsor convoys that traveled between Venice and northern Europe, thus affording merchants the opportunity to re-export goods acquired from the Eastern Mediterranean to European ports beyond the Mediterranean.

In 1190–1220, trade relations between Venice and the authorities in Egypt were secure, and state-sponsored convoys were routine.[15] Agents would end up traveling together to participate in the trade of the same commodities (principally pepper), and they would end up commonly informed about commodities prices. An agent might represent specific transactions he had conducted on behalf of merchants in Venice, but other agents might yield to those same merchants parallel reports of transactions they had conducted. An agent might cheat, but parallel reports would provide some scope for detecting information. Informal reports of prices may not have enabled merchants to appeal to formal processes to police cheating,

---

[14]   Venice's commercial relationship with Egypt extends at least to the ninth century. Indeed, part of the lore of Venice is that, in 828, Venetian merchants absconded from Alexandria with the remains of Saint Mark the Evangelist.

[15]   The Fourth Crusade of 1202–04 may have put a pause on some trade activity, but it did not disrupt the formal trade relations between Egypt and Venice, even though the original plan for the Crusade had been to invade Egypt. Instead, the crusaders ended up partitioning the Greek Latin Empire and supplanting the regime in Constantinople with one favorable to Venice's commercial interests.

but they may have enabled parties to appeal to informal processes such as reputation mechanisms or violence. Informal mechanisms, in turn, could have supported contracts featuring risk-sharing.

The interval 1190–1220 constituted a stationary environment in which to conduct trade in Egypt. In contrast, in most of the interval 1278–1400 the trade with Egypt was subject to a great deal of flux. In 1291 the Mamlukes overran the remaining Crusader holdings in the Levant. Trade with Egypt itself was suspended. Thus, at one stroke European traders lost their two principal points of East–West exchange. The Venetians responded with two parallel initiatives. They made efforts to renew trade relations with the authorities in Egypt, and they fought a war with the Genoese for control of access to the one remaining nexus of East–West exchange, the Black Sea. The Pope had banned trade with the Mamlukes, but by 1300 the Venetians had gone ahead and established trade relations with the Mamluke Sultan in Egypt and had settled on an uneasy peace with the Genoese.

By 1322 the Venetians bowed to papal pressure to suspend merchant convoys to Egypt. The Republic did not sponsor any other convoy to Egypt until 1344. By that time, much of Italy had already suffered years of severe famine. Much of the Republic of Venice's energies were occupied with securing grain. Grain supplies from the Black Sea had already been compromised, because in 1343 the Khan of the Golden Horde had expelled the Venetians and other western merchants from the Venetian trade colony at Tana and had started the siege of the Genoese colony at Caffa on the Crimea. The situation enabled the Venetians to convince the Pope to allow them to send a merchant convoy to Egypt.

Between 1344 and 1369 the Venetians periodically managed to secure approvals from the Pope to organize convoys. Ashtor (1976) suggests that these convoys were not always well attended, but by 1370 Venice managed to normalize trade relations with the Mamluke Sultan in Egypt. The Pope had lifted the ban on trade with the Mamlukes, thus relieving the Venetians of having to secure Papal approvals for each proposed convoy.

Merchants operating out of Crete did organize ventures to Egypt in both the intervals 1344–69 and 1370–1400. War and plague conspired to complicate and sometimes frustrate long-distance trade. The first wave of the sequence of plagues we know as the Black Death invaded the Aegean from Central Asia and the Black Sea in 1347. The Venetian authorities in Crete had been occupied with organized naval fleets to fight against coalitions of Turkish *beyliks* in the Aegean, but by spring 1347, the rate and volume of mortality had been so great that the authorities had to shift their attention to the problem of disposing of the dead (Vidulich 1976). Plague went on to ravage Italy in 1348 and the remainder of Western

Europe in the succeeding years. A major outbreak occurred again in the 1360s.

During 1350–54 the Venetians fought another war with Genoa, the Third Genoese War, over access to the Black Sea. Hostilities included both parties harassing and seizing the commercial traffic of the other. The Fourth Genoese War of 1376–81 brought the focus of hostilities virtually to Venice itself. Venice ended up ceding many of its holdings along the Dalmatian coast of the Adriatic, but Venice did hold on to other sites, such as Corfu, through which it could continue to service its naval and commercial fleets as they entered and exited the Adriatic. Historians suggest that it was only after this Fourth Genoese War that Venice's trade with the East really began to take off. (See, for example, Ashtor 1975, 1976.) By that time, the Venetians had already diverted some traffic through new links of new chains of East–West trade, such as its Beirut convoy line.

Peer Monitoring and Trade along Convoy Routes

The contract data from 1278–1400 do not explicitly indicate whether or not contracting parties coordinated their trade ventures with maritime convoys, but the 56 contracts in the data from 1190–1220 are explicit. Thirty-three of the 56 contracts involved ventures coordinated around convoys. Of these 33 contracts, 32 were *commenda*. (See Table 5.6.) In contrast, 23 contracts do not indicate convoys. Of these 23, 12 were *commenda* and 11 were debt contracts.

Result 6: Commerce supported by state-sponsored convoys was financed by *commenda*.

The larger suggestion is that state-sponsored convoys could support peer monitoring and that, therefore, contracting parties did not need to resort to the mode of financing of last resort (debt). Agents traveling with other agents along convoy routes to commonly trade in commodities enabled merchants to tap into informal sources of information. The

Table 5.6   The financial structure of contracts organized around the convoys, 1190–1220

	Convoy	No convoy	Total
Commenda	32	12	44
Debt	1	11	12
Total	33	23	56

information enabled them to detect, if not verify, cheating. The ability to detect cheating enabled them and their agents to commit to terms of contract by which merchants' payoffs depended on agents' reports of transactions that merchants could neither observe nor verify. In contrast, merchants could neither observe, verify nor detect transactions conducted off of the convoy routes, in which case they appealed to debt contracts, the mode of financing of last resort.

The Role of Kinship Relations

Many authors have suggested that family relations played a central role in ordering principal–agent relations. For example, it is striking that the Italian merchant-banking houses were centered on family relationships, but even these operations depended on non-family members to conduct transactions that merchants could neither observe nor verify. The puzzle remains: How did merchants mitigate cheating?

The data from 1190–1220 reveal the role of family relations in mitigating cheating in principal–agent contracts. The data indicate that 18 of 122 contracts (15 percent) featured contracts between principals and agents who were related or, at least, shared the same surname.[16] (See Table 5.7.) Of these 18 contracts, 16 (89 percent) were *commenda*. In contrast, of the remaining 104 contracts, 62 (60 percent) were *commenda*.

Family members tended to secure the agency services of family members not through debt but through *commenda* contracts. This pattern alone is consistent with the idea that merchants exploited family relationships in environments in which cheating could be a problem. Further examination, however, suggests that we should qualify such candidate conclusions. Table 5.8 works off of the subset of 56 original contracts and indicates the

Table 5.7   The financial structure of contracts organized around kinship relations, 1190–1220

	Family relation	No relation	Total
Unilateral *commenda*	13	39	52
Bilateral *commenda*	3	23	26
Debt	2	42	44
Total	18	104	122

[16] Original contracts and receipts sometimes explicitly indicated family relationships. Other times they did not. I assume that contracting parties with the same surname maintained some family relationship.

Table 5.8   The distribution of kinship relations and convoys, 1190–1220

	Family relation	No relation	Total
Convoy	10	23	33
No convoy	4	19	23
Total	14	42	56

cross-tabulation of family relations by convoy. Of the 14 original contracts that featured family relationships, ten were coordinated with convoy traffic. Even so, each of these 14 contracts were *commenda*. Four of the 14 contracts were not obviously coordinated with convoys, but a larger pattern becomes clear: contracting parties tended to assign family relations to *commenda* contracts for ventures conducted along convoy routes.

The data also reveal other structure specific to family relationships. Table 5.7 indicates not merely that family relations tended to line up with *commenda* but also that agents who were related to principals tended to be assigned to unilateral rather than bilateral *commenda*. Taken together, the data suggest a simple narrative. Contracting parties appear to have used the unilateral *commenda* as a way to give younger family members, who may not have had much capital of their own to contribute to bilateral *commenda*, opportunities to build up capital and to gain experience. Yet they gained their experience less in trade ventures that deviated from convoy routes but gained it mostly in the most secure types of trade – trade conducted along established convoy routes. Family relationships did serve an important role in mitigating cheating, but it would have been easier to suggest that the principal role of family relationships was to mitigate cheating if family members tended to be assigned to *commenda* contracts for ventures that did deviate from convoy routes.

Result 7:   Investors did not depend on kinship relations to support exchange. Instead, trading agents depended on kin to sponsor their incipient careers in long-distance commerce.

Contracting Dyads and Repeated Interactions

The data on principal–agent dyads demonstrate that, while repeated interactions were not infrequent, one-shot interactions dominated. It is not obvious, then, that mechanisms that depended on repeated interactions supported exchange. We might argue, however, that principals and their agents interacted in spheres of business other than maritime trade and that the prospect of repeated interactions in these other spheres could have supported exchange. I accommodate the prospect that relationships may have depended on interactions in other spheres by examining other, non-maritime commercial contracts. The data demonstrate, however, that there was virtually no intersection between the parties involved in non-maritime financing and the parties involved in the financing of maritime activities. There is almost no evidence that the activities of particular principal–agent dyads that show up in maritime trade extended to non-maritime trade.

Thus, there is almost no evidence that activity involving non-maritime trade supported principal–agent relations that were involved in maritime activity.

Non-maritime financing
We might suggest that the paper trail afforded by maritime contracts fails to capture all dimensions of parties' relationships that those same parties may have used to support exchange. In this subsection I examine other financial activities that parties might have used to support their relationships. The data reveal, however, almost no intersection between this other body of financial activity and maritime contracting. The results are consistent with the proposition that parties involved in maritime activity did not maintain commercial relationships outside of maritime activity. Also, insofar as that maritime activity did not involve more than one-shot interactions, their relationships did not extend beyond one-shot interactions. More generally:

Result 8: Commercial activity outside of maritime commerce did not support relationships involving maritime commerce.

I examine a dataset of 292 commercial contracts involving the financing of non-maritime activities – contracts extracted from a subset of the same notarial records from which the maritime contracts derive. These contracts were either loans or non-maritime *commenda* for local commerce. A distinguishing feature of the non-maritime *commenda* was that they would assign to investors losses from fire or theft (*ignis et latronum*) if clearly proven (*clarefactum*). In contrast, maritime contracts would assign to investors losses derived from shipwreck, piracy (*periculo maris et gentis*), or other such disruption.

The first objective is to determine the intersection of two sets of contract dyads: the set of dyads spanning the non-maritime contracts, and the set of dyads spanning the maritime contracts. The maritime contracts span 2579 unique dyads, and the non-maritime contracts span 424 unique dyads. Only a single dyad belongs to both sets of dyads. Further, that single dyad only extends to a single maritime contract and a single non-maritime contract.

The single dyad is composed of the investor Nicolis Pascaligo and the agent Giovanni de Rohdo. The cartulary of the notary Marco da Piacenza shows that, on February 13, 1339, Nicolis Pascaligo advanced to Giovanni de Rohdo (and to his partner Agnes C.) 40 Cretan hyperpers for local commerce of no specified type. The records of that same notary show that four days later Nicolis Pascaligo advanced to Giovanni de Rohdo another 80 hyperpers and 8 grossos in *commenda* for a venture to Turchia (Turkey). The two parties would share proceeds from the venture half-and-half, and remittance would be due within six months. As usual, the investor would bear losses, if clearly proven, from shipwreck or from artificial interventions such as piracy.

So far, the identification of dyads alone suggests that non-maritime transactions did not support exchange over time. We might object, however, that the set of non-maritime contracts is simply incomplete and may miss much of the intersection between maritime and non-maritime activity. I note two other pieces of evidence to suggest that the set of non-maritime contracts does offer a representative perspective. First, I collected both all non-maritime contracts and all maritime contracts from the cartulary of one of the two most important notaries in the dataset, Angelo Boccontolo. The records of Angelo Boccontolo span five years and include 222 maritime contracts and 40 non-maritime contracts. No dyads are common to both sets of contracts. Further, 586 unique individuals appear in the non-maritime contracts. Only 67 of these individuals appear in both the maritime contracts and the non-maritime contracts.

A larger dataset of non-maritime contracts would surely reveal a larger intersection of individuals involved in both maritime and non-maritime commerce, but it actually revealed more individuals who specialized only in local commerce. The larger suggestion remains: a substantial portion of individuals appear to have devoted their energies to maritime commerce, and a distinct set of individuals appear to have devoted their energies to non-maritime commerce. There appears very little in the way of the comingling of maritime and non-maritime investments. There is no evidence that contracting parties folded non-maritime activities into larger relationships that involved (and could have supported) maritime commerce.

Repeated interactions in maritime contracts

I now return to an exclusive focus on maritime contracts. The data from 1278–1400 include every contract available in the State Archives for the 30-year interval 1325–55. In this subsection I use a subset of that interval, 1330–55, to identify the frequency of contract dyads.

The principal result that comes out of this section is:

Result 9:   One-shot interactions dominated the maritime trade emanating out of Crete.

Results 8 and 9 suggest a larger result: whether or not peer-monitoring supported exchange, it is not obvious that the prospect of repeated interactions supported commercial exchange relations.

Two other results that obtain are:

Result 10:   A small proportion of career investors financed a disproportionately large share of maritime ventures.

Result 11:   Career investors tended to support distinct sets of trading agents.

The data from 1330–55 spans 900 contracts. Each contract featured at least one agent and one investor, but the prospect of repeated contract dyads (investor–agent pairs) implies that the 900 contracts might span fewer than 900 unique dyads. It turns out, however, that a contract joining m trading agents with n investors would span $m \times n$ dyads. Contracts often did feature more one trading agent or more than one investor. Accordingly, the set of 900 contracts might then span more than 900 unique dyads. It turns out that the set of 900 contracts spans 1405 unique dyads.

I assign to each unique dyad an indication of the number of times it appeared in the entire set of 1701 contracts. Table 5.9 reports the frequencies with which dyads appeared in the 900 contracts featured in the interval 1330–55. Of the 900 contracts from 1330–55, 680 (75.6 percent) involved dyads that appeared only once in the entire dataset.[17] These

Table 5.9   Repeat relations: 1330–55

Dyad frequency	*Commenda*	Pool	Debt	Total	Share (%)
1	210	91	379	680	75.6
2	41	15	93	149	16.6
3	11	6	27	44	4.9
4	7	0	5	12	1.3
5	6	3	6	15	1.7
Total	275	115	510	900	100.0

[17]   Over the entire set of 1701 contracts from 1278–1400, 78.0 percent (1326 contracts) appear as one-shot dealings.

Table 5.10   Repeat appearances: 1330–55

Frequency	Agent count	Investor count	Person count
1	648	289	874
2	131	40	177
3	59	22	79
4	26	11	37
5	15	7	20
6	9	5	16
7	11	6	12
8	3	5	11
9	6	2	10
10	3	1	7
11		2	1
13			1
15		1	2
21	1		1
24		2	2
40		2	2
52		1	1
57		1	
58			1
Total count	912	397	1254

single-appearing dyads indicate instances of one-shot dealings between trading agents and investors. Meanwhile, one-sixth of the contracts (149 or 16.6 percent) involved at least one dyad that appeared in one other contract, and only one other contract, in the complete dataset. Similarly, 44 contracts feature dyads that appeared three times in the dataset; 12 contracts featured dyads that appeared four times; 15 contracts feature dyads that appeared five times. No contracting dyad appeared more than five times in the entire dataset.

In Table 5.10 I turn from the frequency of unique dyads to the frequency of unique trading agents and investors. The 900 contracts featured in the interval 1330–55 span a set of 1254 individuals. Most of these individuals appear exclusively as trading agents or exclusively as investors, but there are 55 individuals who show up as both an agent and investor at least one time. Accordingly, the sum of the columns "Agent count" and "Investor count" does not correspond to the column "Person count". Instead the 55 individuals are double-counted in that they are included in the counts of 912 unique trading agents and 397 unique investors.

The principal observation is that more than 70 percent of agents and

70 percent of investors appear in only one contract. Specifically, 648 of 912 agents only appear one time, and 289 of 397 investors only appear once. Overall, more than 90 percent of unique individuals appear three or fewer times anywhere in the set of 900 contracts. Yet, a small number of individuals finance a disproportionate share of all contracts. Constantino Cutaioti, for example, appears as an investor in 57 contracts. (He also appears one time as a trading agent.) His 57 appearances as an investor span 93 unique dyads, 73 of which were one-shot interactions. It is not obvious that he depended on repeated interactions to support his relationships. Similarly, Constantino's father, Iohannes Cutaioti appears 52 times as an investor. His 52 appearances span 82 unique dyads and 76 one-shot interactions. Meanwhile, the ten investors who appear most frequently do so in as many as 284 of the 900 contracts (31.6 percent). Meanwhile, the

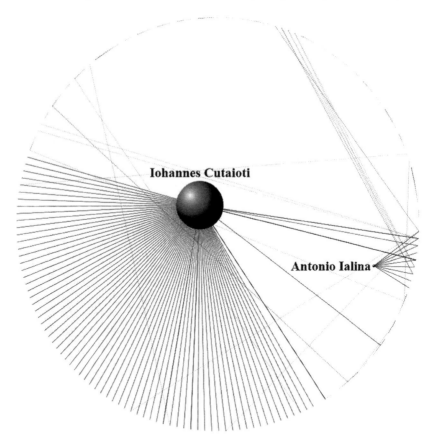

Figure 5.1   Prominent investors, 1320–29

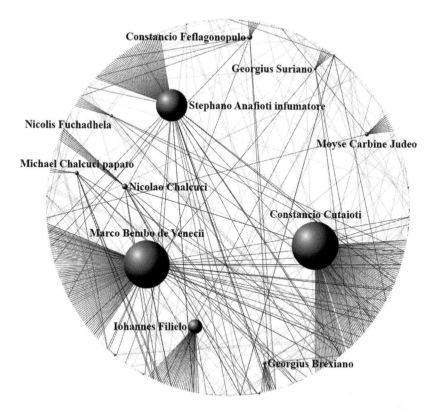

Figure 5.2   Prominent investors, 1330–39

ten most active agents appear in as many as 105 of the 900 contracts (11.7 percent).

Figures 5.1 to 5.4 indicate one way to graphically represent networks of investors and trading agents as well as the frequency of repeated interactions.[18] Each line in each graph is an arrow connecting a point representing a distinct investor to another point representing a distinct agent, but in Figures 5.1, 5.2 and 5.3, the points are sized to indicate the relative prominence of the financiers of overseas trade. In Figure 5.4, the points are sized to indicate the relative prominence of trading agents.

In each figure, most individuals are indicated as points situated on a circle. In Figures 5.1, 5.2, and 5.3 the most prominent investors are

---

[18]   The graphs were prepared with NodeXL (http://nodexl.codeplex.com/, accessed 13 November 2018).

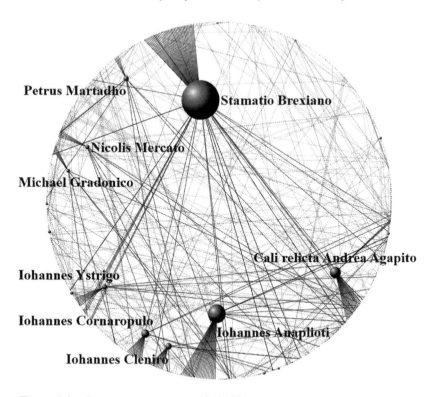

Figure 5.3   Prominent investors, 1340–55

indicated by solid black circles situated in the interior of the circle. Black arrows indicate the dyads to which these most prominent investors belonged, whereas all other dyads are indicated by gray arrows. Similarly, in Figure 5.4 the most prominent agents are also indicated by solid black circles, and black arrows indicate the dyads to which they belonged.

The most prominent investors are those who were party to at least ten dyads in a given interval of time, and each such prominent investor is explicitly identified. Figure 5.1, for example, indicates the one investor, Iohannes Cutaioti, who was party to at least ten unique dyads in the 1320s. Figure 5.2 indicates the 11 investors who were most prominent in the 1330s, and Figure 5.3 indicates the nine investors who were most prominent in 1340–55. Finally, Figure 5.4 indicates the three trading agents who were most prominent in 1330–55.

Figure 5.1 graphically displays 162 unique dyads in the 1320s, ten of which appear two times and one other that appears three times. The inves-

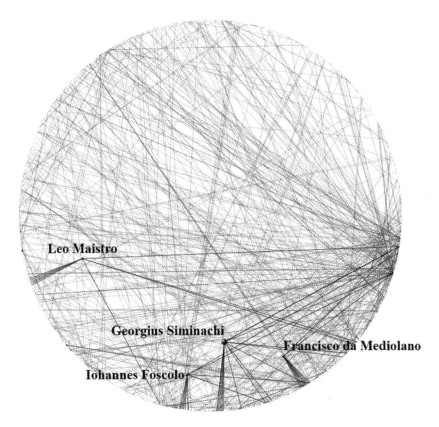

Figure 5.4   Prominent trading agents, 1330–55

tor Iohannes Cutiaoti appears most prominently by virtue of having been party to 48 contracts that spanned 76 of these 162 dyads. More striking than Cutaioti's prominence, however, is the fact that his relationships spanned so many dyads. He did not rely on a small number of agents to conduct the bulk of his affairs. It turns out that 69 of these 75 dyads only appear once. Four dyads each appear twice, and one dyad appears three times – that is, Iohannes Cutaioti did not contract the services of any one agent more than three times, and he contracted the services of most agents only one time.

Figure 5.2 identifies a larger number of prominent investors in the 1330s, a decade that involved fitful but important trade with the Turkish *beyliks*. The graph features 657 unique dyads, 238 of which involve the investors Constancio Cutaioti (the son of Iohannes Cutaioti), Stephano Anafioti, and Marco Bembo. Sixty of these 238 dyads appear more than once, and two appear five times each, but the remaining 178 dyads appear only one time – hence the graphical pattern, again, of arrows fanning out broadly from each of the points representing these prominent investors.

Figure 5.3 identifies about the same number of prominent investors in 1340–55, but it demonstrates that smaller investors played a larger role overall. The graph represents 749 unique dyads, only 53 of which appeared more than one time. Less prominent investors – investors who were party to ten or fewer dyads – were party to 566 of the 749 unique dyads.

I suggest three qualitative points to take from Figures 5.1, 5.2, and 5.3. First, the most prominent investors tended to invest with a broad set of agents; emanating from each point indicating a prominent investor is a fan of black lines rather than, say, a small number of black lines. Second, I note that these fan-shaped networks do not generally overlap. Investors tended to invest with distinct sets of agents. Finally, these fans of black lines may indicate a non-trivial proportion of dyads, but after 1340 the network of dashed lines indicates an even larger volume of relationships.

Finally, Figure 5.4 turns the focus from investors to agents. It explicitly identifies all three agents who were party to at least ten unique dyads in the entire interval 1330–55. The activities of these agents are dwarfed by the mass of all other activity. Taken together with Figures 5.2 and 5.3, the suggestion is plain: most investor–agent relations did not involve parties who participated more than a few times either as agents or investors.

In multinomial probit analyses I include variables that exploit the frequencies of dyads, agents, and investors. I also include variables that intendedly measure agents' and principals' experience, the suggestion being that more experienced trade functionaries may have had time to develop networks of relationships that span overseas markets, and these networks may have constituted sources of information that they could use to motivate and support contracting. What we find is that more active agents and investors were more likely to finance ventures with debt rather than with equity-like *commenda*, but the effects are modest.

CONTRACT SELECTION AND PROBIT ESTIMATION: CRETE 1330–55

This section joins three types of variables in analyses of selection along three dimensions of contract. The variables include the peer monitoring variables (*galley volume*, *Genoese war*, and *local trade volume*), a repeated interaction variable (a count of dyad frequencies labeled *repeated interaction*), and a set of investor and agent attributes. The principal focus is on the selection of the mode of financing (*commenda*, debt or pooling), which is identified with the sharing rule. Two other analyses focus on ways contracting parties would grant discretion to agents over the conduct of ventures. One way involved the selection or amendment of itineraries. Some contracts granted agents the option of selecting their own itineraries, whereas others restricted agents to specific itineraries. Similarly, some contracts indicated the specific vessels on which agents were expected to travel, whereas others imposed no such restrictions.

The analysis is limited to 1330–55, because the data from this interval are representative of the volume of economic activity, although I note that all results reported here obtain in estimations involving other intervals including 1320–70 (1167 contracts), 1320–60 (1082 contracts), and 1330–70 (1059 contracts). The construction of some regressors depends on a discrete measure of time (calendar years) whereas others depend on a much finer partition of time (a time index measured in days). Measuring certain quantities on an annual basis is reasonable in that trade activity was seasonal. It was seasonal, because many of the commodities being traded were agricultural and thus subject to seasonal patterns of production. Further, seaborne transportation was also subject to seasonal patterns. Seaborne commercial traffic, therefore, followed annual patterns.

The multinomial probit analyses characterize selection of three types of contracts: equity-like schemes (*commenda*), pooling contracts, and debt. Two other probit analyses focus on binary dimensions of contract that pertain to the discretion of the agent to choose or amend itineraries.

I list the regressors here:

- *Repeated interaction:* the maximum of the frequencies with which agent–investor dyads featured in a contract appeared anywhere in the entire dataset of maritime contracts.
- *Investor experience:* the maximum among investors in the contract of the number of appearances any one investor has made to date operating as an investor.
- *Agent experience:* the maximum among agents in the contract of the number of appearances any one agent has made to date operating as a trading agent.
- *Common investor:* indicates whether or not the contract features an investor common to other, simultaneous contracts.
- *Common agent:* indicates whether or not the contract features an agent common to other, simultaneous contracts.
- *Genoese war:* a binary indication illuminating the years 1350–55 as years in which Venice was engaged in war with Genoa.
- *Galley volume:* indicates the number of state-sponsored galleys sent out in a given year.

Table 5.11   Univariate statistics, 1330–55

N = 897	Mean	Std dev.	Minimum	Median	Maximum
Commenda	0.303	0.460	0	0	1
Pool	0.128	0.335	0	0	1
Debt	0.569	0.496	0	1	1
Agent discretion	0.204	0.403	0	0	1
Vessel specified	0.770	0.421	0	1	1
Repeated interaction	1.371	0.783	1	1	5
Investor experience	7.893	11.960	1	2	57
Agent experience	2.786	2.649	1	2	21
Common investor	2.266	2.334	1	1	11
Common agent	1.339	0.671	1	1	4
Genoese war	0.056	0.230	0	0	1
Galley volume	14	4	0	14	20
Local trade volume	0.1490	0.0746	0.0026	0.1463	0.3780

- *Local trade volume:* the average number of maritime contracts per notary-day in a given year.

Tables 5.11 and 5.12 feature descriptive statistics and correlations involving the regressors applied to the multinomial probit analysis for the interval 1330–55. (Nine hundred contracts correspond to the interval 1330–55, but values for some regressors are missing in three cases thus reducing to 897 the number of data points applied to the probit analyses.) Agents participated in an average of nearly three ventures in 1330–55, but most of them participated in only one or two ventures. (See *agent experience*.) Investors participated in an average of nearly eight ventures, but, again, most participated in only one or two ventures. (See *investor experience*.) Most agents participated only in one venture in any given 30-day interval (*common agent*), but some signed up for as many as four. Similarly, most investors participated in only one venture in any (*common investor*), given 30-day interval, but one investor invested in as many as 11 ventures.

The correlation table (Table 5.12) shows some unsurprising results as well as a few non-obvious clues about how trade was organized. Unsurprisingly, *agent experience* is positively correlated with *common agent*, and *investor experience* is positively correlated with *common investor*. All four of these same variables are correlated with *repeat relation*, a measure of the frequency of contract dyads. Specification tests applied to the probit analyses (likelihood ratio tests, not reported) indicate that *repeat relation*, *agent experience*, and *investor experience* contribute

Table 5.12 Correlation table, 1330–55

N = 897	Commenda	Pool	Debt	Agent discretion	Vessel specified
Commenda	1.000				
Pool	-0.253	1.000			
Debt	-0.757	-0.440	1.000		
Agent discretion	0.581	0.005	-0.542	1.000	
Vessel specified	-0.476	0.178	0.322	-0.434	1.000
Repeated interaction	0.022	-0.016	-0.010	0.078	0.059
Investor experience	0.035	-0.054	0.003	0.115	0.101
Agent experience	-0.118	0.093	0.047	-0.030	0.098
Common investor	-0.019	-0.127	0.103	0.032	0.110
Common agent	-0.073	0.040	0.041	0.000	-0.009
Genoese war	-0.107	-0.035	0.123	-0.099	0.086
Galley volume	0.127	-0.127	-0.033	0.150	-0.106
Local trade volume	-0.005	-0.098	0.070	-0.036	-0.182

	Repeated interaction	Investor experience	Agent experience	Common investor	Common agent
Repeated interaction	1.000				
Investor experience	0.386	1.000			
Agent experience	0.218	0.066	1.000		
Common investor	0.313	0.474	0.014	1.000	
Common agent	0.149	0.057	0.364	0.029	1.000
Genoese war	-0.072	-0.037	0.133	-0.111	-0.050
Galley volume	0.108	0.163	-0.161	0.317	0.036
Local trade volume	-0.059	-0.059	-0.003	-0.030	0.079

	Genoese war	Galley volume	Local trade volume
Genoese war	1.000		
Galley volume	-0.758	1.000	
Local trade volume	0.001	0.038	1.000

Table 5.13   Discretionary itineraries: 1330–55

N = 897 Specification	1	2
Repeated interaction	2.28%	2.17%
	1.23	1.17
Investor experience	0.31%***	0.34%***
	2.50	2.74
Agent experience	−0.46%	−0.68%
	−0.73	−1.07
Common investor	−1.42%**	−0.76%
	−2.12	−1.17
Common agent	0.00%	0.10%
	0.00	0.05
Genoese war		−16.78%***
		−5.15
Galley volume	1.69%***	
	4.46	
Local trade volume	−18.65%	−14.61%
	−1.05	−0.81
Log-likelihood	−435.47	−440.97

Notes: The notations ***, **, and * indicate statistical significance at the 1 percent, 5 percent, and 10 percent levels, respectively.

little information in addition to the information that *common agent* and *common investor* already contribute.

Table 5.13 pertains to agent discretion with respect to the selection or amendment of itineraries. (The binary choice variable is labeled *discretionary itineraries*.) Two specifications are reported. The specifications vary only in that they include either *Genoese war* or *galley volume* but not both since the two variables are highly correlated. Table 5.14 focuses on the decision of the parties to limit agent discretion by specifying the vessel on which agents were to travel. (The binary choice variable is *vessel specified*.) Meanwhile, Tables 5.15 and 5.16 feature marginal effects estimated from two specifications relating to the choice of mode of financing (*Commenda*, *Pool*, or *Debt*).

The principal results are as follows:

Result 12:   *Repeated interactions* did not inform the selection of the mode of contracting. Trade activity was organized mostly through one-shot interactions.

Increasing *repeated interaction* by a single interaction had the appearance of increasing the likelihood of choosing a *commenda* contract by

Table 5.14   Vessel specified: 1330–55

N = 897 Specification	1	2
Repeated interaction	−1.06%	−0.74%
	−0.49	0.02
Investor experience	0.20%	0.18%
	1.37	1.23
Agent experience	1.71%***	1.90%***
	2.52	2.79
Common investor	2.94%***	2.40%***
	3.42	2.84
Common agent	−2.35%	−2.56%
	−1.06	−1.15
Genoese war		15.34%***
		3.95
Galley volume	−1.36%***	
	−3.67	
Local trade volume	−84.55%***	−89.57%***
	−4.79	−5.08
Log-likelihood	−449.42	−452.49

Notes: The notations ***, **, and * indicate statistical significance at the 1 percent, 5 percent, and 10 percent levels, respectively.

2.93 percent or 2.76 percent in the two specifications, but both results are statistically insignificant, and they are small given that no dyad appeared more than five times and that most appeared only one time. See Tables 5.15 and 5.16.

The result is consistent with the observation that trade activity was organized mostly through one-shot interactions. Again, peer monitoring may have been important, but long-term relationships between a given agent and given investor did not obviously support exchange.

The next three results show that the peer monitoring variables do inform the analysis of contract selection. During those years in which the Venetian republic sponsored convoys to the Eastern Mediterranean, contracting parties would substitute out of debt contracts and into *commenda*. In contrast, contracting parties substituted out of *commenda* and into debt through the duration of the Third Genoese War. The larger suggestion is that *commenda* prevailed in environments that were more congenial to peer monitoring. Finally, I note that contracting parties tended to shift out of pooling contracts and into debt as trade volumes, measured by *local trade volume*, increased.

Table 5.15   Specification 1: 1330–55

N	272	115	510
	Commenda	Pool	Debt
Repeated interaction	2.93%	0.43%	−3.37%
	1.30	0.28	−1.39
Investor experience	0.19%	0.00%	−0.19%
	1.23	−0.03	−1.12
Agent experience	−2.21%***	0.86%**	1.35%*
	−2.81	2.14	1.77
Common investor	−1.58%*	−2.59%***	4.17%***
	−1.87	−3.17	4.39
Common agent	−3.16%	1.19%	1.98%
	−1.19	0.71	0.72
Genoese war			
Galley volume	1.63%***	−0.64%***	−0.99%***
	3.93	−2.69	−2.36
Local trade volume	1.50%	−55.17%***	53.68%**
	0.07	−3.23	2.32
Log-likelihood		−809.32	

Notes: The notations ***, **, and * indicate statistical significance at the 1 percent, 5 percent, and 10 percent levels, respectively.

Result 13:   Contracting parties substituted out of debt and into *commenda* as galley traffic increased.

In a year supported by an extra ten galleys in galley traffic, the share of *commenda* increased about 16 percent, and the share of debt contracts decreased about 10 percent. The results are statistically significant at the 1 percent level. See Table 5.15.

Result 14:   During the Genoese war, contracting parties substituted out of *commenda* and pooling contracts into debt.

The share of *commenda* decreased by about 22 percent in 1350–55, and the share of debt increased 28 percent. The results are statistically significant at the 1 percent level. See Table 5.15.

Result 15:   As *local trade volume* increased, contracting parties substituted out of pooling contracts and into debt.

As *local trade volume* increased from one maritime contract per week to one such contract every four days, the share of pooling contracts would

Table 5.16   Specification 2: 1330–55

N	272	115	510
	Commenda	Pool	Debt
Repeated interaction	2.76%	0.02%	−2.79%
	1.23	0.02	−1.15
Investor experience	0.22%	0.01%	−0.23%
	1.42	0.11	−1.36
Agent experience	−2.34%***	1.17%***	1.16%
	−2.97	2.82	1.51
Common investor	−0.93%	−3.13%***	4.06%***
	−1.13	−3.86	4.36
Common agent	0.15%	0.42%	2.67%
	0.06	0.25	0.97
Genoese war	−21.89%***	−6.53%**	28.43%***
	−4.74	−2.26	5.42
Galley volume			
Local trade volume	3.96%	−51.67%***	47.71%**
	0.19	−3.12	2.07
Log-likelihood		−810.02	

Notes: The notations ***, **, and * indicate statistical significance at the 1 percent, 5 percent, and 10 percent levels, respectively.

tend to fall by about 10 percent and the share of debt contracts would increase by about 10 percent. The results are statistically significant at the 1 percent level. See Tables 5.15 and 5.16.

Result 16:   Agent discretion was not increasing in *repeated interaction*.

The agent discretion variables, *discretionary itineraries* and *vessel specified*, are not discernibly responsive to *repeated interaction*. The signs of the marginal effects of repeated interaction are consistent with the idea that contracting parties assign more discretion to agents in relationships that were supported by repeated interactions, but the effects are both small and statistically insignificant. See both Tables 5.13 and 5.14.

Result 17:   Agent discretion increases as measures of maritime trade increase. Agent discretion decreases as the trade environment deteriorates.

The agent discretion variables, *discretionary itineraries* and *vessel specified*, respond to the peer monitoring variables *Genoese war*, *galley volume*, and *local trade volume*. Contracting parties are more likely to grant discretion over itineraries in the absence of war with Genoa. The marginal effect is -16.78 percent and is significant at the 1 percent level. (See Table 5.13.) That is, during the war of 1350–55, contracting parties were about 17 percent less likely to grant agents discretion over itineraries. The other specification reported in Table 5.13 indicates a marginal effect of 1.69 percent (also significant at the 1 percent level) on *galley volume*. That is, an increase in galley volume of ten galleys in a given year would also feature an almost 17 percent increase in the likelihood of contracting parties granting agents discretion over itineraries.

Table 5.14 indicates consistent results of similar magnitude. Specifically, contracting parties are more likely to require agents to travel via specific vessels when galley volumes are low or when Venice was engaged in its war in the Aegean with Genoa. (See Table 5.14.) With war raging, contracting parties were 15.35 percent more likely to determine up front the vessel on which agents were to travel. Similarly, a decrease in galley volume of ten galleys amounted to nearly a 14 percent increase in the likelihood that contracting parties would restrict agents to specific vessels.

Altogether the results suggest that contracting parties agree to restrict agents' degrees of freedom as the trading environment deteriorates. However, now consider the third peer monitoring variable, *local trade volume*. The marginal effects also suggest that agent discretion increases as trade activity increases, but the results are not statistically significant with respect to *discretionary itineraries*. (See Table 5.13.) Meanwhile, the results in Table 5.14 suggest that contracting parties were more than 8 percent less likely to impose restrictions on agents' choice of vessel as notaries' output of maritime contract increased from one contract every week to one contract every four days.

Result 18:   More experienced agents were less likely to have been financed by *commenda* contracts.

Experienced agents appear to have advanced their services when pooling contracts (or even debt contracts) were most earnestly deployed – to the detriment of *commenda*. An agent who had more than ten ventures of experience than another agent was more than 22 percent less likely to participate in a venture supported by a *commenda* contract. See both Tables 5.15 and 5.16.

Result 19:   Investor experience does not inform contract selection.

The marginal effects corresponding to *investor experience* are both small and statistically insignificant in both multinomial probit specifications.

Experienced investors do not distinguish themselves in the way they selected contracts. See both Tables 5.15 and 5.16.

Result 20:   Investors who financed more than one simultaneous venture depended more heavily on debt and less on pooling and *commenda* contracts.

The marginal effects reported in both specifications are consistent with the proposition that investors who financed simultaneous ventures were more likely to appeal to debt financing over *commenda* financing and pooling contracts. The marginal effects reported in Table 5.15 and 5.16 for *common investor* indicate that an investor financing three simultaneous ventures would substitute out of *commenda* and pooling contracts and into debt, with the likelihood exceeding 12 percent.

CONCLUSION

The research presented here provides clues to how parties enabled exchange in what Dixit (2004) might recognize as lawless environments. While it is uncontroversial to suggest that both formal and informal institutions can go some way toward enabling merchants to organize complex exchange, it is also reasonable to suggest that contracting parties could enable exchange in environments in which formal enforcement processes and even certain informal enforcement processes may not have been feasible. This is what makes the appeal of debt to finance trade ventures interesting: it required little institutional support, and it constituted an important means of mobilizing investment for overseas trade ventures. Debt financed activity on the informational frontiers of the trade economy.

The contrast in the experiences Venetian traders had between participating in state-sponsored convoys and deviating from convoy routes tells much of the story. In environments in which parties could tap into peer monitoring, they could invest themselves with some capacity to detect (if not verify) cheating. They could, in turn, support equity-like schemes (*commenda*) and share risk. The suggestion is that risk-sharing was, indeed, an important feature of contracting – why else would *commenda* show up at all in the notarial records? Even so, risk-sharing was not the most important aspect of contracting. The integrity of information – or the lack of integrity – had a more fundamental role in informing contract design. Indeed, the data suggest that in environments in which parties could not detect cheating, debt financing prevailed. Debt thus shows up as the default mode of financing.

In all of this we should keep in mind that formal institutions did exist.

The Venetian republic, for example, did maintain courts and other institutions for supporting economic activity. We might characterize governance in Venice as "government of the merchants, by the merchants, and for the merchants". Even so, we do not know much about how formal Venetian institutions supported relationships between investors and their trading agents. We do not know much, for example, about how merchants used courts to process claims relating to maritime commerce. While formal processes surely did serve some purposes, the evidence here suggests how merchants and their agents could have enabled exchange in environments situated well beyond the shadow of these formal processes.

Altogether, the results tell a story about how merchants and their trading agents used formal processes (contracting) and informal processes (peer monitoring) to mobilize investment for overseas trade ventures. The results also tell a story about processes that merchants and their trading agents did not enlist to mobilize investment. The evidence presented here shows that about three-quarters of the commercial ventures emanating out of Crete through the middle and late fourteenth century had been organized through one-shot interactions between merchants and their trading agents. There is no evidence in the records that contracting parties enlisted the prospect of future exchange (in maritime ventures or local, terrestrial ventures) between a specific investor and a specific agent to support exchange. Instead, over 70 percent of investors and 70 percent of agents show up no more than one time in the maritime contracts. They make their money and withdraw from the business. In contrast, a small number of investors show up prominently in the contract data. They effectively set themselves up as banks in their communities, and they have the appearance of serving distinct communities. One investor would support one set of trading agents. Other investors would support other, distinct sets of trading agents. Similar patterns show up with respect to notaries. A small number of notaries show up prominently in the contract data, and they also have the appearance of serving distinct communities in that they tended to serve distinct sets of investors and agents.

The results also tell a story about how merchants and their trading agents used these processes to adapt (to a limit) to changing circumstances in the trading environment. The late twelfth century closed with merchants operating out of Venice trading mostly around the Adriatic or venturing with state-sponsored convoys to Egypt and the Levant. A number of stalwarts such as Romano Mairano would venture to Constantinople which was then governed by a regime not always favorable to Venetian interests. (Mairano shows up in the records compiled by Morozzo della Rocca and Lombardo 1940 as leading an escape of Venetians by sea from Constantinople with ships of the Byzantine navy in pursuit.) Venice exploited the Fourth Crusade of 1202–04 to radically improve its position in the Eastern Mediterranean. In the settlement of 1204, the Venetians supplanted the regime in Constantinople with a regime favorable to its interests. Among other things, the change of regime enabled Venice to secure regular access to the Black Sea. Venice also secured islands in the Aegean, including Crete itself. These islands went on to serve for some centuries as points along important trade routes for securing merchant fleets and naval fleets. The trade that had been mostly restricted to the Adriatic now extended into the Aegean and the Black Sea. That trade was supported by much the same contracting practices albeit with some amendment. Unilateral *commenda* almost entirely displaced bilateral *commenda*, but, otherwise, the distribution of debt and equity appears little changed. *Commenda* prevailed on the convoy routes. Debt financed trade that deviated from state-sponsored convoys.

By 1300 the world had changed. In 1261 the Genoese had a hand in supplanting the regime in Constantinople with a regime favorable to their interests. They thereby established themselves as gatekeepers to the Black Sea. Then, in 1291, the Mamlukes of Egypt conquered the last of the crusader holdings in the Levant. Venice found itself cut off from trade with the East through Egypt and the Levant, so it should be no surprise that Venice then found itself challenging Genoa for access to the Black Sea. The Black Sea afforded access to Central Europe (by way of the Danube), to Central Asia and to the trade caravans arriving on the south coast of the Black Sea. The Second Genoese War, 1295–99, concluded with another uneasy settlement between Venice and Genoa.

The great dislocation of the late thirteenth century proved merely to be prelude to the dislocation that absorbed most of the fourteenth century. Global cooling may have had something to do with it. (Some researchers had disputed whether or not the "Medieval Warm Period" or "Medieval climate anomaly" was a global phenomenon, but others argue that it gave way to a global cooling "AD 1300 event".[19]) Researchers puzzle over the role of solar activity and volcanic activity in inducing climate events in the Late Middle Ages, but the main point remains: the trading environment was subject to much flux decade to decade or even year to year. The 1340s may have encompassed the worst of it. The decade opened with some years

---

[19]   See, for example, Keller (2004) and Crowley and Lowery (2000) on global phenomena in the Late Middle Ages generally; Yang et al. (2009) on climate anomalies in Central Asia; Favier-Dubois (2007) on southern Patagonia; Nunn (2012) and Masse et al. (2006) on equatorial, western Micronesia; and Mauquoy and Barber (1999) on Northern England and the Scottish Borders.

of famine across Italy. Venetian fleets scoured the Eastern Mediterranean and Black Sea for grain. (In 1342 the Venetians even managed to secure a one-time dispensation from the Pope to send a fleet to Egypt to secure grain.) By that time, tales of plague raging in Central Asia and further east may have already reached the Mediterranean, and by 1347 the plague itself (the Black Death) invaded the Aegean before moving on via trade routes to the rest of Western Europe.

Through all of that, the merchants of Crete and their trading agents demonstrated their pluckiness by trading vigorously through almost all of the disruption. Many of them were local Cretans. Others were resident Venetians, and even the occasional Genoese shows up in the notarial records. Many of their counterparts overseas were Turks of various *bey-liks* of pre-Ottoman Anatolia. The contracting technology afforded some flexibility in contract design, and contracting parties would substitute out of certain types of contracts and into others as the demands of each trading season merited. However, the records do provide hints about how the financing and organization of trade might have changed. Already a number of trading agents found themselves venturing forth on vessels owned and operated by prominent, noble families of Venice. (They also sometimes ventured out on galleys owned by the Republic but managed by Venetian nobles.) Some of these same noble families went on to manage and own sugar plantations on Cyprus. These families may have gone on to integrate within family enterprises the production or procurement of commodities with the shipping of those same commodities. The paper trail of maritime financing may have changed in that venture-specific, pairwise contracting by means of *commenda* or debt contracts may have given way to processes internal to the family firm.

6. Knowledge spillovers and industrial policy: evidence from the Advanced Technology Program and the Department of Defense

For more than a generation the federal government has maintained programs promoting research joint ventures (RJVs). The ostensible motivation late in the going was to promote inter-firm knowledge spillovers. Knowledge spillovers (positive informational externalities) represent a share of the social returns to research and development (R&D) that exceed the private returns to the parties who generated that knowledge.[1] Trade secrets or know-how, for example, might leak out to competitors, or firms might actively induce spillovers by poaching another firm's knowledge-able employees or reverse-engineering that other firm's technologies. Either way the problem of appropriating returns to investment in R&D might be severe enough to discourage private parties from investing at all. The appropriability problem thus induces underinvestment.[2] In turn, the germ of a public policy rationale obtains: subsidizing private R&D initiatives may mitigate the appropriability problem;[3] further, insofar as collaborative R&D might be even more conducive to spillovers, collaborative ventures might constitute richer targets for public supports.

In the beginning, the real motivation for supporting RJVs was less sophisticated. Promoting RJVs was part of a larger sequence of policy initiatives aimed at stemming the perceived decline of American competitiveness, especially with respect to Japan. Knowledge spillovers had already become an important subject of academic research[4] even with respect to RJVs,[5] but it would be several years yet before the concept

---

[1] See, for example, Griliches (1979, 1992, p. 43), Jaffe (1998) and Campbell et al. (2009) on this count.

[2] See, for example, Arrow (1962) for an early account of the appropriability problem.

[3] See, for example, Campbell et al. (2009) and Siegel et al. (2003) on this count.

[4] See, for example, Griliches (1979).

[5] Early theoretical contributions include Spence (1984), Katz (1986), and

would explicitly inform RJV-specific policy debate.[6] Even then, however, it is not obvious that federal government initiatives had any effect with respect to competitiveness or spillovers. It is not obvious, for example, that public initiatives were good at identifying RJVs that would be best situated to generate spillovers. If anything, federal initiatives appear to have channeled resources to ventures that involved little in the way of spillovers – that is, to just the kind of ventures that private parties could have been expected to pursue absent government supports.

The conclusion derives from examination of the structure of 171 RJV contracts. Research joint ventures involving more highly appropriable technologies tended to exploit contractual mechanisms to mitigate, rather than encourage, spillovers. It turns out that government-subsidized ventures tended to aggressively exploit those same contractual mechanisms. In contrast, non-subsidized ventures as a whole have tended to be less aggressive about exploiting those mechanisms. We are left with the curious result that, insofar as any ventures were occupied with inducing knowledge spillovers between RJV partners – with what RJV partners would alternatively call knowledge transfers – they tended to be non-subsidized ventures. Further, non-subsidized ventures tended to involve technologies that were more conducive to spillovers to parties external to the ventures.

Ultimately, subsidized RJVs, and RJVs more generally, have tended not to look like the private RJV between the genomics firm Human Genome Sciences (HGS) and the pharmaceuticals firm SmithKline Beecham (SKB). It is broadly understood, for example, that tacit knowledge can only be transferred by means of personnel transfers (Teece 1986; Anand and Galetovic 2000). The various R&D collaboration agreements and licensing agreements between HGS and SKB featured explicit provisions according to which SKB reserved the right to detail a few of its personnel to HGS facilities to work with HGS personnel.[7] By working alongside HGS personnel, SKB personnel could absorb know-how that would allow

---

d'Aspremont and Jacquemin (1988). These studies illuminate a problematic aspect of spillovers, the prospect that R&D partners might free-ride on the R&D efforts and knowledge contributions of others.

[6] Jaffe (1998, 2008) and Klette et al. (2000) illuminate important issues about assessing spillovers and public initiatives to induce spillovers. Meanwhile, Grindley et al. (1994) show that the cooperative venture SEMATECH was plagued with free-rider problems. Other empirical research on RJVs includes Oxley (1997b), Sakakibara (1997, 2001, 2003), Branstetter and Sakakibara (1998, 2002), Majewski and Williamson (2004), Link et al. (2005), and Röller et al. (2007).

[7] Contracts are included as exhibits in the HGS quarterly report (SEC Form 10-Q) dated August 20, 1996. The two parties made a National Cooperative Research Act 1984 (NCRA) filing in 1993.

them to apply the HGS technology to the development of pharmaceuticals. In contrast, most other contracts in the dataset do not provide such visitation rights. Indeed, R&D partners may restrict the physical proximity of researchers in order to frustrate unintended knowledge spillovers.

A preoccupation with spillovers would miss a larger result. It is not obvious that the problems of either channeling spillovers or containing spillovers constituted important aspects of collaboration. Neither is it obvious that the principal problem of enabling collaboration was to contain misappropriation of intellectual properties by their R&D partners. Rather, the principal problem has involved securing rights of way to conduct collaborative R&D. That is, the principal problem has involved forbearance: how to secure commitments from potential R&D partners to refrain from strategically advancing claims of misappropriation and thereby secure rights of way for R&D partners to freely collaborate. In this way RJV contracts have more the spirit of multi-lateral commitments not to sue and less the spirit of mechanisms to selectively channel knowledge transfers or contain unintended spillovers.

IN THE BEGINNING

Japan had caught up with the West. This was widely perceived. The Japanese, however, would have to anticipate the prospect that other nations would yet endeavor to catch up with them. Such was a message from the new premier, Yasuhiro Nakasone, in early 1983.

This was preamble to the Prime Minister's larger message. "During the process of modernization, when Japan was busily trying to catch up with the advanced nations of the West," the role of the central government "was to guide, supervise, and control." Yet, having caught up, this traditional role had become "a hindrance to the free activities of the private sector". In the future, private enterprise would have to look more to private, decentralized initiatives and less to centralized administration.[8]

The Prime Minister's speech marked the beginning of a larger campaign to inject and sustain a decentralization meme in policy debate in Japan – and not too soon. Various, new, big public initiatives were already in place. The Japanese government, for example, had already launched its Fifth Generation Computing project, the latest installment in a long sequence of initiatives designed to enable Japanese firms to leapfrog American firms, most notably IBM, in the development and commercialization

---

[8] Nakasone (1983, pp. 12–18).

of semiconductors and other computing technologies,[9] or so it was understood by interested parties and their congressmen in Washington.[10] They argued that American industry could expect foreign competitors to overtake it absent an affirmative policy response to Japanese (and even European) industrial policy.

These parties, largely supplicant firms from Silicon Valley, went up Capitol Hill several times in 1983 and 1984 to argue that, similar to Japanese and European firms, they should be permitted to collaborate in RJVs. Collaboration, they reported, had enabled Japanese and European firms to avoid duplicative costs. Why invent the wheel ten times over when a single effort would suffice? Further, a collaborative effort could induce important knowledge-sharing between RJV partners. Knowledge-sharing, in turn, might allow RJV partners to engineer a superior wheel than any single entity's effort alone could yield.

The argument, ultimately, was that collaboration afforded foreign firms a competitive advantage. Collaboration, they argued, could also enhance the competitiveness of American firms. Not unreasonably, however, the prospect of organizing RJVs between competing entities could attract antitrust scrutiny. The prospect of antitrust liability could discourage parties from organizing RJVs, many of which could be procompetitive.

Through the 1980s the federal government did launch programs to address antitrust concerns and subsidize RJVs. After all this time, however, little is understood either about how firms have exploited such programs or, ultimately, about how we should evaluate such programs. Was cost-sharing the principal objective of some RJVs, or did firms organize RJVs to pursue other objectives? Was knowledge-sharing an important

---

[9]   West (1996), p. 253.

[10]   See, for example, *Japanese Technological Advances and Possible United States Responses using Research Joint Ventures: Hearings before the Subcommittee on Science, Research and Technology of the House Committee on Science and Technology*, 98th Congress (June 29 and 30, 1983); *Research and Development Joint Ventures: Hearing before the Subcommittee on Science, Research and Technology of the House Committee on Science and Technology*, 98th Congress (July 12, 1983); *Joint Research and Development Legislation: National Cooperative Research Act of 1984: Hearings before the Subcommittee on Monopolies and Commercial Law of the House Committee on the Judiciary*, 98th Congress (September 14, 22 and 29, 1983); *The National Productivity and Innovation Act and Related Legislation: Hearings before the Senate Committee on the Judiciary*, 98th Congress (June 29, October 26, 1983 and March 12, 1984); *Antitrust Policy and Joint Research and Development Ventures, Hearing before the Joint Economic Committee*, 98th Congress (November 3, 1983).

aspect of RJV participation? More importantly, did subsidies mitigate underinvestment in R&D?

The research presented here exploits a unique perspective to answer these questions. Many RJVs filed papers with the Antitrust Division of the US Department of Justice under the terms of the National Cooperative Research Act 1984 (NCRA). Filings show that cost-sharing had been the principal objective of many RJVs. Collaboration in those same RJVs, however, had not generally extended to knowledge-sharing. Insofar as RJV partners contributed knowledge inputs at all – what they call "background intellectual property" – they contributed them so that their RJV partners might secure rights of way to freely collaborate and use each other's technologies.

National Cooperative Research Act filings also suggest that government-subsidized ventures tended to involve little in the way of knowledge-sharing. In these ventures RJV partners tended to contribute background intellectual property that was more appropriable in that it was less susceptible to unintended spillover. Highly appropriable intellectual properties, however, constituted the kinds of knowledge assets firms could be expected to contribute to an RJV absent external inducements. Thus, government subsidies ended up chasing RJVs that RJV partners would likely have formed absent those same subsidies. It is not obvious, then, that there was much underinvestment.

A larger conclusion is that government-subsidized ventures tended to look like those that involved highly appropriable technologies whereas non-subsidized ventures were more likely to involve less appropriable technologies. Specifically, government-subsidized ventures tended to look more like those involving chemicals, whereas non-subsidized ventures tended to look more like electronics. It is broadly understood, for example, that intellectual properties involving chemicals are less susceptible to unintended spillover than those involving electronics. This dichotomy between chemicals and electronics shows up distinctly in certain dimensions of RJV contracts. These dimensions include the duration of nondisclosure restrictions. Research joint venture partners have tended to assign very long-term restrictions on the disclosure of intellectual property relating to chemicals, and they have tended to impose short-term restrictions or no restrictions at all on the disclosure of intellectual property relating to electronics. It turns out that government-subsidized ventures have tended to look like chemicals in that they project much the same contract profile as chemicals. Among other things, they tend to feature long-term nondisclosure restrictions. In contrast, non-subsidized ventures have tended to look more like electronics in that they have tended to feature nondisclosure restrictions of much shorter duration.

These conclusions derive from examination of RJV contracts featured in 171 NCRA filings. This particular dataset of contracts is interesting, because it is just that: a dataset of actual contracts. Most research on R&D joint ventures has to work out of datasets that describe selected features of joint ventures. This dataset is also interesting, because the contracts allow us to identify distinctions between government-subsidized joint ventures and joint ventures that received no public support. Specifically, 57 of the 171 contracts involved government subsidies, with 20 contracts involving funding from the Advanced Technology Program (ATP), and another 23 involving funding from the Defense Advanced Research Projects Agency program (DARPA) maintained by the Department of Defense (DOD). Yet another 20 involved funding from other government entities.

THE NATIONAL COOPERATIVE RESEARCH ACT AND NONDISCLOSURE AGREEMENTS

The NCRA constituted only one of a handful of initiatives that the federal government rolled out in the 1980s to promote the competitiveness of American industry.[11] Proponents of the Act and of other initiatives argued that American firms should be permitted to collaborate on R&D in ways similar to those of their Japanese and European competitors. Collaboration, it was argued, would allow firms to share costs (and thus avoid duplicative R&D efforts) and to share knowledge.[12]

---

[11] Flamm and Nagaoka (2007) note that "The Stevenson–Wydler Technology Innovation Act of 1980 encouraged industry and government researchers to work together in Cooperative Research and Development Agreements (CRADAs). The Bayh–Dole University and Small Business Patent Act of 1980 was designed to encourage university researchers to transfer their technology to commercial companies". By the late 1980s the focus of federal policy had moved beyond making passive accommodations for private initiatives in joint research to actively subsidizing private initiatives and organizing initiatives of its own. (Mowery and Rosenberg 1989 elaborate on this point.) The government, for example, ever worried about preserving the perceived "lead" of American firms in the commercialization of semiconductors, launched the SEMATECH consortium to support SEMiconductor MAnufacturing TECHnology. One year later (1988), Title V of the Omnibus Trade and Competitiveness Act situated a new program, the ATP, in the Department of Commerce. The ATP started with a small appropriation of $10 million to support discrete projects. Most projects were to be pursued by single firms, but RJVs were selected to pursue others. By 1995, the ATPs annual appropriation exceeded $340 million.

[12] See, for example, the Senate Report on The National Cooperation Research Act of 1984, S. REP. NO. 98-427, reprinted in 1984 U.S.C.C.A.N. 3105, 3106.

The NCRA contemplated RJVs that would be horizontal in that they would join actual or potential competitors.[13] Allowing competitors to collaborate – and to do so in contractually formalized joint ventures – would pose obvious antitrust concerns, but the Act qualified the approach by which the antitrust authorities would evaluate RJVs. Proposed joint ventures could yet be subject to challenge, but they would be relieved of the automatic condemnation that would otherwise attend application of the per se rule in antitrust litigation. Instead, courts would be required to fold potential pro-competitive effects into their analyses of the overall effects of given joint ventures. Further, some provision was made to limit the damages that could obtain in private antitrust litigation to actual damages rather than extended to the treble damages normally afforded to injured parties under section 4 of the Clayton Antitrust Act.

Figure 6.1 features the distribution by year of NCRA filings from the inception of the NCRA through to August 2009. In all, 1343 filings have been made. Many of these filings do not pertain to collaborative R&D. The implementation in 1993 of the National Cooperative Research & Production Act encouraged some parties to report production joint ventures. These ventures may have anticipated knowledge spillovers but did not necessarily contemplate important R&D. In 2004 the Act was further extended to "Standards Development Organizations" (SDOs). Two types of entities have appealed to SDO status: familiar entities such as the Institute of Electrical and Electronics Engineers (IEEE) that coordinate the inclusion of existing intellectual properties in technological standards, and certification authorities that promote professional standards in service industries. Since 2004, 260 SDOs have made NCRA filings. The 171 RJVs examined in this chapter compose more than one in seven (15.8 percent) of the 1083 non-SDO filings submitted since 1984 through August 2009.

Evidence from NCRA filings submitted since 1984 suggests that RJVs have promoted both cost-sharing and knowledge-sharing although not

---

[13]   Cost-sharing and the types of knowledge-sharing that proponents had in mind anticipated collaborations that were horizontal in that they would join firms that were potential or even actual competitors. Evidence suggests that cost-sharing has, indeed, been an important dimension of some research collaborations organized under the terms of the NCRA, and there is evidence that knowledge-sharing has been important in yet other research joint ventures (Majewski and Williamson 2004; Röller et al. 2007). The evidence suggests, however, that knowledge-sharing prevails in ventures that are more vertical in that they join parties who are situated to contribute complementary know-how and capabilities (Majewski and Williamson 2004). It turns out that not even Japanese research consortia conformed to the purportedly Japanese style of collaboration in that they too tended to assume vertical, rather than horizontal, structures (Sakakibara 2003).

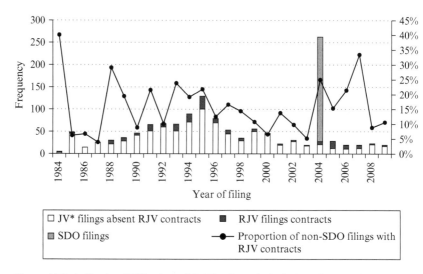

Note: * The indication 'JV' in place of 'RJV' reflects the inclusion of production joint ventures starting in 1993.

Figure 6.1   Distribution of NCRA filings over time

necessarily in ways anticipated by the proponents of the Act (Majewski and Williamson 2004; Röller et al. 2007). Even so, this chapter takes up a dimension of collaboration without which no cost-sharing or knowledge-sharing of any kind would obtain: the problem of securing rights-of-way to conduct R&D – or what Grindley and Teece (1997) would recognize as the freedom to operate – within the context of a collaborative venture. At first sight, the problem involves nothing more than resolving hold-out:[14] parties to a candidate collaborative venture may maintain property rights, including intellectual property rights, that would allow them to block joint R&D or to block the subsequent commercialization of technologies that might proceed from joint R&D. These rights might not even embody interesting knowledge, but parties might use them strategically in order to extract rents. With each rights-holder in a sequence of rights-holders hold-ing out for a better deal, collaboration may be delayed or even frustrated. In an environment in which property rights are well defined, the solution is simple: before undertaking any joint R&D, the parties commit to a grand cross-licensing agreement by which each party implicitly grants to all other members rights of way to exploit within the context of the collaboration

---

[14]   Again, see Grindley and Teece (1997). See also Merges (1996).

whatever intellectual properties with which joint R&D may potentially make contact.

Resolving hold-out is an important problem, and in environments involving well-defined property rights, hold-out may constitute the only important hazard that contracting parties must anticipate. In contrast, environments in which property rights are uncertain support a richer set of strategic behaviors and attending hazards. The problem derives from the fundamental fact that property rights imply legal process – a formal process to which parties may appeal to sort out property rights violations. Characterizing violations depends on delineating property, yet that alone may constitute a nontrivial problem. A line in the sand might go far toward delineating the bounds of beachfront properties, and delineating properties will go some way toward allowing parties to demonstrate violations to third parties (for example, the court or an arbitrator), but intellectual property rights may be uncertain in that neither contracting parties nor enforcement authorities may be able to distinguish fine lines between intellectual properties. That leaves open questions about whether one party would be able to detect violations let alone prove violations to enforcement authorities. Moreover, practical difficulties encountered in delineating properties may frustrate efforts to characterize what might constitute violations in the first place. It gets worse. Practical difficulties may enable the owners of intellectual properties to falsely assert misappropriations of intellectual property on the part of others and to game legalistic processes. Specifically, asserting misappropriations can enable the owners of intellectual properties to draw other parties into protracted legal processes, all in an effort to frustrate the efforts of these others to pursue R&D and to commercialize technologies (Lanjouw and Lerner 2001; Lanjouw and Schankerman 2001; Majewski and Williamson 2004). Claims of misappropriation might not have much merit, but demonstrating the merits (or demerits) of a claim to a third party (for example, the court) can be costly (Williamson 1999).

The gaming of legalistic processes and problems of contract enforcement constitute opposite sides of the property rights coin. At first sight, much of the action in designing RJV contracts involves resolving generic hold-out problems: R&D partners will grant to each other rights of way to exploit intellectual properties that they each contribute to their ventures. That is, they grant rights of way to what they formally recognize as background intellectual property. Research and development partners will also grant rights of way to exploit intellectual properties innovated within the context of collaboration (foreground intellectual property). (That is, what R&D partners do in each of the 171 RJVs examined in this chapter.) Yet, while granting rights of way may neutralize hold-out, rights of way may also facilitate unintended knowledge spillovers. Spillovers, in turn, may diminish the ability of parties to appropriate returns from investments in the R&D that yielded their intellectual properties. It is natural, then, that R&D partners might institute mechanisms that qualify rights of way.

Research and development partners principally use nondisclosure agreements (NDAs) and licensing restrictions to qualify rights of way. Parties might, for example, reserve vetoes over the licensing of either background or foreground intellectual property to third parties. Restricting licensing may mitigate spillovers, but one tradeoff is that it may also frustrate the efforts of R&D partners to commercialize technologies after collaboration has ended. Similarly, parties might impose restrictions on the disclosure of intellectual property to third parties. Insofar as NDAs are enforceable, then they may help parties contain spillovers, but, again, restricting disclosures may frustrate the efforts of parties to commercialize technologies.

While the enforceability of NDAs speaks to the appropriability of intellectual property, remedies to the appropriability problem may allow parties to expropriate returns from their R&D partners. Appropriability depends on the ability of parties to detect violations and to demonstrate violations to third parties. In contrast, parties can exploit NDAs by asserting violations on the part of R&D partners. Just as violations may be hard to detect, so too, false claims may be difficult to distinguish from genuine claims. Making claims alone may be adequate for drawing R&D partners into protracted legalistic processes, all in an effort to expropriate rents. Anticipating the prospect of such gamesmanship, contracting parties might qualify the use of NDAs. We thus end up with a compounded sequence of qualifications: Parties remedy appropriability problems by qualifying rights of way (through NDAs), but the qualifications themselves introduce distortions that also invite qualifications.

Contracting parties qualify NDAs by limiting their duration. Arora and Merges (2004, p. 461) observe that "nondisclosure agreements between independent parties are difficult to enforce, owing in part to the complexity of defining the information to be kept secret and separating it from the pre-existing information of the parties" – which is part of the point. If NDAs were easy to enforce, there might be no reason to limit their duration. As it is, the duration of such restrictions varies widely. In some instances parties commit to NDAs that last a few years after the termination of collaboration. In other instances, NDAs may last indefinitely, and in yet others parties may impose no restrictions. Ultimately, the duration of NDAs exhibits variation that is amenable to "survival analysis".

The hypothesis maintained here is that the duration of NDAs reflects tradeoffs between appropriability and legalistic gamesmanship.

Specifically, parties assign NDAs of longer duration intellectual properties that are more appropriable and NDAs of shorter duration intellectual properties that are more amenable to legalistic gamesmanship. The real interest in conducting survival analysis of NDAs, however, is less in testing the hypothesis than in using the hypothesis to reveal differences (if any) between the background intellectual properties and foreground intellectual properties the parties contribute to government-subsidized ventures and to non-subsidized ventures. The exercise depends on differences in the appropriability of intellectual properties pertaining to chemicals and electronics. Chemicals are widely understood to be more appropriable than electronics (for example, Arora 1997), and the prediction that proceeds from the hypothesis would be that NDAs pertaining to chemicals would exceed those assigned to electronics, which they do by significant margins. Just as the Chemicals/Electronics dichotomy manifests itself in the duration of NDAs, so too does a dichotomy between government-subsidized ventures and non-subsidized ventures. Specifically, NDAs assigned to background intellectual property in government-subsidized ventures tend to be longer than NDAs assigned to background intellectual property in non-subsidized ventures. An interpretation that parallels the Chemicals/Electronics dichotomy becomes plain: government-subsidized ventures tend to involve more appropriable background intellectual property, not the type of intellectual property that would be more susceptible to unintended spillover.

THE ADVANCED TECHNOLOGY PROGRAM

The ATP was inspired by concerns that American firms had proven less capable than foreign (especially Japanese) competitors at commercializing technologies that those same American firms had first developed. (See, for example, Ruegg and Feller 2003, pp. 3–4.) It was established by Title V of the Omnibus Trade and Competitiveness Act 1988 and started funding projects in 1990 with an annual appropriation of $10 million. By 1995 the ATP budget grew to $341 million with most funding directed to single-firm projects – a fact that had attracted criticism – but the ATP also had an explicit mandate to promote collaborative R&D (GAO 1996; Idelson 1996). The ATP was subject to some reform in 1997, and the America COMPETES Act 2007 initiated the process of supplanting the ATP with the Technology Innovation Program (TIP), a program that is more heavily focused on collaborative ventures and small and medium-sized firms (Schacht 2009). The TIP was dismantled in 2012.

By the mid-1990s the ATP found itself waging a defensive political battle to justify its annual budget appropriations. A central problem was that it was not obvious what the ATP's mission was supposed to be or that the ATP could execute it. Indeed, the principal concern that American firms were failing to commercial technologies did not suggest an obvious mission. Over time, however, the ATP and its proponents came to characterize its mission as supporting the development by American firms of intendedly "early stage, high-risk", "pre-competitive", "enabling technologies" that yield "broad-based economic benefits".[15] While it might not be obvious what such incantations means, a reading of Jaffe (1998) suggests that we could recast the mission statement with the language of theoretically recognized concepts as spillovers and appropriability. The ATP intendedly sponsored joint ventures pursuing the development of technologies that would be less amenable to appropriation (hence, high-risk and likely pre-competitive) but would yield a high volume of knowledge spillovers (thus enabling the realization of broad-based benefits).

Opposition to the ATP started to mount by 1995. In that year, the Clinton administration proposed expanding the ATP's annual appropriation to $750 million by 1997. The proposal invited a response. The Republican-controlled Committee on Science of the House of Representatives requested an evaluation of the program by the General Accounting Office (GAO). The GAO criticized ATP's self-evaluation methods, observing that some of the ATP's methods amounted to little more than bean-counting (GAO 1995, pp.6, 9). The ATP would, for example, report numbers of applications for ATP funding as well as numbers of ventures the ATP had selected for funding. Conceivably, we could fold these numbers into an analysis illuminating the volume of collaborative R&D that would not have been assembled but for ATP sponsorship, and the ATP did, in fact, present these numbers as evidence demonstrating the effectiveness of the program. Yet, absent defensible counterfactual benchmarks, such numbers reveal little.

The ATP had made some effort to engineer counterfactuals. It surveyed parties that had applied for ATP sponsorship – both those to which the ATP had denied funding as well as those that had secured funding. Would the winners or losers have pursued collaborative R&D even absent ATP sponsorship? The GAO report of 1995 as well as a succeeding GAO report

---

[15]   See, for example, the stream of testimony featured in the Hearing before the Subcommittee on Environment, Technology and Standards of the Committee on Science, House of Representatives, June 14, 2001 and chapter 4 of the National Science Board (1998) report. See also Laidlaw (1998), Powell (1998), Chang et al. (2002), Feldman and Kelley (2003), Ruegg and Feller (2003), and Campbell et al. (2009).

of 1996 used the answers to such questions to generate results of its own – results that observers characterized as "mixed." Specifically, both reports indicated that the ATP had financed projects that private parties would have financed absent the ATP subsidies as well as projects that parties would have abandoned (or did abandon) absent subsidies. Opponents of the ATP illuminated the former results, and proponents illuminated the latter. Yet, before judging the ATP, we might prefer to fold the results into an analysis that demonstrates some awareness of the ATP's technology for screening applications. The GAO's criticisms, for example, amounted to finding that the screening technology would sometimes yield false positives; instances in which the ATP chose to fund ventures that likely yielded highly appropriable returns and would therefore have been able to secure private financing. The ATP's self-reported successes, meanwhile, also ignore the prospect of false positives: that some projects would not have secured private financing does not establish that they should have received sponsorship. Instead, even though such ventures may not have yielded sizable private benefits, neither would they necessarily have yielded much in the way of knowledge spillovers.

That the ATP's screening technology would, like any screening technology, have yielded false positives, and false negatives should be no surprise. Thus, merely counting perceived failures and successes again amounts to little more than bean-counting. As a matter of course, highly appropriable ventures will have sometimes secured funding, and less appropriable ventures that would otherwise have yielded a large volume of knowledge spillovers will sometimes have been passed over. A difficulty for the ATP, however, was that it could not demonstrate that its screening technology was any good at avoiding errors. It was not well equipped to identify and measure spillovers. The best it could do was commission a draft report[16] that indicated that "'controlling for the effect of intra-industry information flows on appropriability, intraindustry R&D information flows complement firms' own R&D efforts, underscoring the social welfare benefits of such flows.' These findings are consistent with fundamental propositions leading to ATP's establishment" (Ruegg and Feller 2003, p. 228).

An ATP-commissioned study by Mowery et al. (1998) that used patent-citation to identify spillovers to assess knowledge spillovers in ventures sponsored by the ATP between 1991 and 1995 was ignored. The authors examined the intensity of patent citations between candidate RJV partners before application for ATP sponsorship. Insofar as patent citations

---

[16]   Cohen and Walsh (2000).

measure potential for knowledge spillovers in collaborative ventures, the results presented in the study suggest that the ATP did not select ventures that were better situated to generate spillovers than ventures to which ATP denied funding.[17]

That was not the end it. The ATP may have had difficulty characterizing the spillovers induced by ATP-sponsored ventures. Outside reviewers, meanwhile, had less difficulty cataloguing instances in which the ATP ended up sponsoring ventures that should probably have been passed over. In a 2000 report, for example, the GAO evaluated three projects – not a large number – but determined that in each case entities competing with the joint venture partners had already been engaged in the commercialization of competing technologies for some time (GAO 2000, p. 4). The GAO concluded that ATP had not been situated "to ensure that it [had been] consistently . . . funding existing or planned research that would [have not been] conducted in the same time period in the absence of ATP financial assistance" (GAO 2000, p. 5).

The GAO report opened with the observation that there had been "continuing debate over whether the private sector has sufficient incentives to undertake research on high-risk, high-payoff emerging and enabling technologies without government support, such as ATP" (GAO 2000, p. 3). This chapter does not take up the debate, but maintains that knowledge spillovers are important phenomena. The chapter does take up questions that might yet inform debate: entities such as the ATP may have difficulty identifying and measuring knowledge spillovers, but organizational inputs (contracts) provide clues about how joint-venture partners have accommodated the spillover of knowledge inputs (background intellectual properties) as well as the spillover of the knowledge outputs of collaborative R&D (foreground intellectual property).

DATA

The data derive from RJV contracts included in 171 NCRA filings.[18] Contracts are not work plans, but are documents that set up rules and processes through which R&D partners manage background intellectual

---

[17]   Mowery et al. (1998) explicitly note that patent citations might not gauge all spillovers. Specifically, they might fail to pick up spillovers of tacit knowledge and know-how, the type of items that defy codification in a patent application.

[18]   About one in seven NCRA filings include contracts relevant to collaborative R&D. I have no basis for suggesting that parties' decisions to include, rather than exclude, contracts from NCRA filings reflect selection biases. Additionally, I have

property and foreground intellectual property. First and foremost, contracts provide rights of way: they universally feature implicit cross-licenses between R&D partners on background intellectual property and foreground intellectual property. There is no variation on this count. Instead, important variation in contracts shows up across three dimensions: the assignment of R&D efforts (who conducts R&D), the assignment of rights over the licensing of intellectual properties (who assumes rights to license background or foreground intellectual property to third parties), and the nature of personnel transfers (who maintains rights to visit the sites of important R&D). Variation also shows up in the duration of NDAs. All contracts feature NDAs on either background intellectual property or foreground intellectual property. Most feature NDAs on both.

We might expect that parties who conduct R&D and develop foreground intellectual property would dictate the terms by which that foreground intellectual property could be licensed. In some cases, however, R&D partners agree to assign to another party – possibly one of their own partners – the right to license foreground intellectual property to non-member entities. Research and development partners might do this, for example, to promote the adoption of the RJVs' technologies by nonmembers. Meanwhile, it is well understood that parties to collaborative R&D require personnel transfers in order to induce transfers of certain tacit knowledge (Teece 1986; Anand and Galetovic 2000). Of the 171 sets of contract examined here, just over 25 percent (44 RJV contracts) explicitly indicate the rights of at least one RJV member to visit the work site of another party who conducts R&D.

I assemble binary indicators for each of the three dimensions. The first indicator, labeled *Member R&D*, indicates whether or not at least one RJV member conducts R&D. (A positive indication does not rule out R&D efforts by entities external to the RJV, such as a government or university laboratory.) The second indicator, *Third-party licensing*, indicates whether or not R&D partners assign to some other party the right to license their foreground intellectual property. Research and development partners might, for example, formally incorporate the RJV and assign it rights to license intellectual property. The third indicator, *Visitation*, indicates whether or not at least one R&D partner has the right to visit the site at which some other party conducts R&D. That party might be an RJV member or an entity external to the RJV.

I apply the three binary indicators to probit analyses to discern

---

no basis for suggesting that decisions to make NCRA filings selection reflect biases that would skew the results of the survival analyses.

differences between government-subsidized ventures and non-subsidized ventures. I also subject NDAs on background intellectual property and foreground intellectual property to separate survival analyses (Cox regressions). Conceivably, the binary indicators and the duration of NDAs will also vary with the attributes of intellectual properties underlying each RJV as well as with the attributes of RJV partners themselves. It is well understood that attributes span many dimensions – such as the codifiability of intellectual property or the degree to which intellectual property is tacit (Winter 1987; Contractor and Ra 2002). It is also well understood that some parties will be better equipped than others to absorb and exploit another party's knowledge (Sampson 2004). While it is not likely that one could assemble controls that would allow us to precisely measure all attributes for each contract, we can assemble controls that go some way toward capturing these various dimensions.

Altogether, I assemble five dependent variables: the three binary indicators, the duration of NDAs applied to background intellectual property, and the duration of NDAs applied to foreground intellectual property. I also assemble 12 independent variables, 11 of which are binary. Three of the binary variables indicate government entities: *ATP*, *DOD* (Department of Defense), and *All other government*. Five of the binary variables are two-digit Standard Industrial Classification (SIC) codes assigned to the technologies that were the subject of the RJVs. Only those SICs appearing more than ten times in the dataset of 171 RJVs are included, but they are included in order to pick up some of the variation across attributes of the underlying intellectual property. The included SICs represent *Gas and oil extraction (SIC 13)*, *Chemicals (SIC 28)*, *Industrial and commercial machinery (SIC 35)*, *Electronics (SIC 36)* and *Business services (SIC 73)*. I include another binary variable labeled *Pollution abatement* to indicate whether or not the RJV technology pertains to pollution abatement. Two other binary variables elaborate the role of third-parties in collaborative R&D. The variables *Federal laboratory* and *University* indicate whether or not a government laboratory or a university contributed R&D efforts. Finally, I include a variable indicating the year in which the RJV made its NCRA filing (*File year*). *File year* controls for trends over time (if any) in the way parties craft NDAs.

Some readers may wonder about differences between equity joint ventures and contractual arrangements that readers might recognize as alliances. I exclude an indicator variable distinguishing equity joint ventures, because only four RJVs were organized as equity joint ventures. Finally, I did craft two other variables to isolate the effects of two entities that are represented more than ten times each in the set of 171 RJVs. Research joint venture partners frequently contracted each of these two entities to conduct R&D, but inclusion of them in any of the survival analyses did not add information beyond what industry variables already contributed.

The government variables require some elaboration. The 20 ATP-sponsored ventures featured in the dataset made NCRA filings between 1989 and 1999. That ten-year interval leaves out ATP activity from the past decade, but it turns out that it largely conforms to the interval of ATP-ventures examined by Dyer et al. (2007). This could be important, because I use the results presented here to qualify the principal conclusions featured in Dyer et al. (2007). In that paper the authors examine all ventures assembled between 1990 and 2001. Meanwhile, the NCRA filings of the 23 DOD-sponsored ventures in the dataset span a longer interval, 1985 through to 2004. Department of Defense-sponsored ventures tended to be driven by DOD demands for technologies with specific capabilities. In contrast, the process of identifying ATP-sponsored ventures was more decentralized in that private parties had a greater hand in proposing R&D projects.

Table 6.1 indicates the distribution of the three binary contract dimensions across each of the 11 binary independent variables. It indicates that, for example, of 14 contracts that involved *Gas and oil extraction (SIC 13)*, six (42.9 percent) involved some type of visitation rights. Five contracts involved R&D efforts by RJV members, which means that nine contracts exclusively involved R&D efforts by non-members. Specifically, these nine RJVs involved efforts by some entity or entities contracted by R&D members to undertake prescribed projects. None of the 14 contracts involved third-party licensing.

Now consider ATP-sponsored ventures. Of 22 such ventures, 18 (81.8 percent) involved R&D efforts by member firms, yet only two of the 22 contracts (9.1 percent) involved some type of visitation rights. The suggestion is plain: parties to ATP-sponsored ventures tended to engage R&D efforts, but they engaged efforts in separate facilities as opposed to working side by side with researchers from other member firms. Thus far, the ventures appear to have involved little in the way of knowledge transfers. Contrast these results with all non-ATP ventures featured in the dataset (not reported in Table 6.1). Less than half of the non-ATP ventures – only 64 of 149 ventures (43.0 percent) – involved member firm R&D efforts; the ATP-sponsored ventures involved heavier hands-on participation by member firms. Even so, non-ATP ventures involved visitation (42 of 149 ventures). Whether or not member firms engaged R&D efforts, more of them were permitted to visit the sites at which some party did engage important R&D.

Advanced Technology Program-sponsored ventures aside, other

Table 6.1   Contract dimensions: visitation, member R&D and third-party licensing

	Observations	Visitation	Member R&D	Third-party licensing
SIC 13 – Gas and oil extraction	14	6 / 42.9%	5 / 35.7%	0 / 0.0%
SIC 28 – Chemicals	41	8 / 19.5%	20 / 48.8%	1 / 2.4%
SIC 35 – Machinery	37	7 / 18.9%	7 / 18.9%	4 / 10.8%
SIC 36 – Electronics	13	3 / 23.1%	11 / 84.6%	3 / 23.1%
SIC 73 – Business services	26	7 / 26.9%	15 / 57.7%	6 / 23.1%
Government sponsorship	57	13 / 22.8%	39 / 68.4%	6 / 10.5%
ATP	20	2 / 9.1%	18 / 81.8%	1 / 4.5%
DOD	23	7 / 30.4%	17 / 73.9%	4 / 17.4%
All other government	20	6 / 30.0%	10 / 50.0%	5 / 25.0%
Federal laboratory	13	5 / 38.5%	9 / 69.2%	2 / 15.4%
University	37	10 / 27.0%	17 / 45.9%	2 / 5.4%
Pollution abatement	55	4 / 7.3%	12 / 21.8%	4 / 7.3%
All contracts	171	44 / 25.7%	82 / 48.0%	16 / 9.4%

government-sponsored ventures appear, thus far, to have involved some volume of knowledge transfers. Over 30 percent of the ventures sponsored by either the DOD or "All other" government entities featured visitation. Department of Defense-sponsored ventures also tended to feature a relatively high volume of member R&D efforts (73.9 percent).

Now note an apparent pollution abatement effect: member firms tended to contract out R&D efforts in that only 12 of 55 ventures (21.8 percent) involved member R&D. Also, only four of the 55 ventures (7.3 percent) involved visitation. That is, member firms tended to assign discrete tasks to contractors who worked absent observation in their own facilities. The ventures appear to have involved little in the way of the transfer of knowledge assets. Instead, member firms simply pooled financial resources and paid an outside party to perform a prescribed task.

Tables 6.2 and 6.3, respectively, summarize the duration of NDAs applied to background intellectual property and foreground intellectual property. The data feature NDAs of both zero duration and indefinite duration. The longest NDAs of definite duration for either background

Table 6.2   Duration of NDAs: background intellectual property

	N (obs.)	Average* duration (years)	Minimum duration (years)	Observed maximum (years)	Indefinite NDAs (count)
SIC 13 – Gas and oil extraction	14	3.85 1.32	0	5	1 7.1%
SIC 28 – Chemicals	41	10.85 1.19	0	35	7 17.1%
SIC 35 – Machinery	37	6.49 1.18	0	10	2 5.4%
SIC 36 – Electronics	13	3.92 1.32	0	5	0 0.0%
SIC 73 – Business services	26	12.10 1.24	0	35	5 19.2%
Government sponsorship	57	17.71 1.17	0	20	15 26.3%
ATP	20	17.53 1.29	0	10	5 25.0%
DOD	23	15.44 1.27	0	20	5 21.7%
All other government	20	22.15 1.32	0	5	7 35.0%
Federal laboratory	13	10.09 1.35	0	10	2 15.4%
University	37	10.13 1.19	0	35	5 13.5%
Pollution abatement	55	5.15 1.15	0	20	3 5.5%
All contracts	171	8.99 1.09	0	35	21 12.3%

Note: * The average corresponds to $\sum_{i=1}^{N} t_i \big/ \sum_{i=1}^{N} \delta_i$ where $\delta_i = 1$ indicates finite NDA (zero otherwise) and $t_i = 35$ for NDAs of indefinite duration.

Table 6.3   Duration of NDAs: foreground intellectual property

	N (obs.)	Average* duration (years)	Minimum duration (years)	Observed maximum (years)	Indefinite NDAs (count)
SIC 13 – Gas and oil extraction	14	2.86 1.31	1	5	0 0.0%
SIC 28 – Chemicals	41	18.13 1.20	0	35	10 24.4%
SIC 35 – Machinery	37	4.46 1.18	0	10	2 5.4%
SIC 36 – Electronics	13	4.54 1.32	3	5	0 0.0%
SIC 73 – Business services	26	12.43 1.24	0	20	5 19.2%
Government sponsorship	57	15.45 1.16	0	20	13 22.8%
ATP	20	11.94 1.27	0	10	3 15.0%
DOD	23	10.50 1.25	0	20	3 13.0%
All other government	20	31.64 1.35	0	10	9 45.0%
Federal laboratory	13	10.45 1.35	0	10	2 15.4%
University	37	9.48 1.19	0	10	4 10.8%
Pollution abatement	55	8.37 1.15	0	20	6 10.9%
All contracts	171	9.07 1.08	0	35	20 11.7%

Note: * The average corresponds to $\sum_{i=1}^{N} t_i \left/ \sum_{i=1}^{N} \delta_i \right.$ where $\delta_i = 1$ indicates finite NDA (zero otherwise) and $t_i = 35$ for NDAs of indefinite duration.

intellectual property or foreground intellectual property run for 35 years. In 21 and 20 of the 171 contracts, respectively, the NDAs applied to background intellectual property and foreground intellectual property were indefinite.

The second column of Tables 6.2 and 6.3 indicates the average duration of NDAs across the various binary variables. This requires some explanation. Absent instances of indefinite duration, we might simply summarize the duration of NDAs by reporting averages and attending standard deviations. Yet, instances of indefinite duration frustrate this. We can, however, understand indefinite duration as data truncation, and it turns out that methods of dealing with duration data are well equipped to accommodate such truncation.

For each subset of the contract data indicated by the 11 binary indicators, I apply a duration model that requires nothing more than estimation of a single parameter, a constant hazard rate. More generally, a hazard function constitutes one way of modeling the prospect of a single, discrete event occurring at a given instant in time, given the event has not yet occurred. The event of interest is the termination of an NDA at time t.

Appealing to the termination of an NDA as a single, discrete event enables us to appeal to the standard tools of survival analysis according to which the hazard rate $h(t) = f(t)/[1 - F(t)]$, where $f(t)$ indicates a probability density function, $F(t)$ indicates the corresponding cumulative density function, and the term $1 - F(t)$ indicates the probability that the duration of the NDA under examination exceeds t. Imposing a constant hazard rate $h(t) = \lambda$ amounts to imposing the exponential density function $f(t; \lambda) = \lambda e^{-\lambda t}$ and survival function $S(t; \lambda) = 1 - F(t; \lambda) = e^{-\lambda t}$. This allows us to express the corresponding likelihood function as

$$L = \prod_{\substack{finite \\ restrictions}} f(t_i; \lambda) \prod_{\substack{indefinite \\ restrictions}} S(t; \lambda) = \prod_{\substack{finite \\ restrictions}} \lambda e^{-\lambda t_i} \prod_{\substack{indefinite \\ restrictions}} e^{-\lambda t_i}$$

$$= \prod_{i=1}^{N} (\lambda e^{-\lambda t_i})^{\delta_i} (e^{-\lambda t_i})^{1-\delta_i}$$

where i indexes each contract in a set of N contracts and

$$\delta_i = \begin{cases} 0, & \text{NDA}_i \text{ is indefinite} \\ 1, & \text{NDA}_i \text{ is finite} \end{cases}.$$

The corresponding log-likelihood is

$$\ln L = \sum_{i=1}^{N} (\delta_i \ln \lambda - \lambda t_i),$$

and the maximum likelihood estimate of the hazard rate corresponds to

$$1/\lambda = \sum_{i=1}^{N} t_i \Big/ \sum_{i=1}^{N} \delta_i.$$

Note, that if there is no truncation (no NDAs of indefinite duration), then $\delta_i = 1$ for all i and a familiar result obtains: the average duration of the NDAs corresponds to the reciprocal of the hazard rate – that is,

$$1/\lambda = \sum_{i=1}^{N} t_i \Big/ N.$$

The average duration (years) reported in the first column of Table 6.2 corresponds to

$$1/\lambda = \sum_{i=1}^{N} t_i \Big/ \sum_{i=1}^{N} \delta_i,$$

where $t_i = 35$ for NDAs of indefinite duration. Standard errors are also reported. The other three columns indicate the minimum observed duration (almost always zero years), the maximum of the NDAs of definite duration (observed maximum), and the count of NDAs of indefinite duration (indefinite duration).

Many formative results are apparent. The Chemicals/Electronics dichotomy obtains in the NDAs for background intellectual property. The duration of NDAs corresponding to *Chemicals (SIC 28)* average 10.85 years, whereas for *Electronics (SIC 36)* the average is 3.92 years. The longest NDA for electronics was five years, whereas the longest NDA of definite duration for *Chemicals* was 35 years. Furthermore, seven of the NDAs with respect to *Chemicals* were indefinite. None of the NDAs for *Electronics* were indefinite.

Government-sponsored ventures appear to assign to background intellectual property NDAs of longer than average duration. They average 17.71 years, whereas the average across the entire dataset of 171 contracts is 8.99 years. Meanwhile, ventures involving R&D inputs from *Federal laboratories* do not feature such long NDAs. Those NDAs average 10.09 years.

Table 6.3 yields some parallel results and some different results pertaining to foreground intellectual property. The Chemicals/Electronics dichotomy is more pronounced. Meanwhile, the distinction between ventures sponsored by the ATP and the DOD and all other contracts is greatly diminished. In contrast, the 20 ventures involving *All other government* entities tend to impose NDAs of very long duration on foreground intellectual property. They average 31.64 years, whereas the average across the entire dataset is 9.07 years.

Tables 6.2 and 6.3 enable elaboration of the apparent pollution abatement effect. Ventures involving the development of pollution abatement technologies tend to feature NDAs of shorter than average duration on background intellectual property and NDAs of average duration on foreground intellectual property. The results are consistent with a view that such ventures tend to involve less in the way of important knowledge inputs and more in the way of task-oriented R&D around which member firms pool financial resources to cover the costs of contracting the R&D efforts of an outside party.

RESULTS

The descriptive statistics featured in Tables 6.1, 6.2, and 6.3 suggest a number of results, but the succeeding five tables feature more systematic (regression) analyses, though I must stress that the results I illuminate involve correlations between the dependent and independent variables, not causal relationships. Specifically, I am not examining treatment effects. The variables *ATP* and *DOD*, for example, do not identify treatments that induce certain effects, although I will indulge in some abuse of language and speak of such things as an ATP effect or DOD effect. Even so, all of the results reported here are more descriptive in that they indicate how ventures sponsored by such entities as the ATP or DOD tended to organize themselves.

Tables 6.4–6.6 present probit analyses pertaining to the various binary dimensions of contract. Tables 6.7 and 6.8 present survival analyses of the NDAs. I model the duration of NDAs with the Cox relative risk model. In its simplest form, the Cox model corresponds to a proportional hazards model by which the hazard rate conforms to $\lambda(t;x_i) = \lambda_0(t)e^{x_i'\beta}$ where i indexes each RJV, x_i indicates a vector of covariates measured at time $t = 0$, β is a vector of regression coefficients, and $\lambda_0(t)$ indicates an arbitrary baseline hazard rate common to all RJVs. I separately estimate Cox models for NDAs on background intellectual property and NDAs on foreground intellectual property. In both models I accommodate NDAs of indefinite duration by treating them as survival times known only to have exceeded 35 years.

While the Cox model can be adapted to accommodate non-proportional hazards, I only report results for Cox proportional hazard models. There is some evidence that hazards may not be proportional across the two values of the covariate *University*, but all of the results obtain in Cox regressions that either accommodate or ignore the potential for non-proportional hazards. I also note that all of the qualitative results I report are robust to estimation by each model in the nested sequence of fully parametric models comprised of the gamma, Weibull, and exponential hazard models.[19]

Given a covariate $x_{ij} \geq 0$ and coefficient β_j, a coefficient estimate $\hat{\beta}_j$

---

[19] Estimating Cox models amounts to ignoring the baseline hazard rate and applying maximum likelihood to the remaining part of the model to yield a partial likelihood. One technical point remains: the simplest Cox models apply to survival data that feature unique survival times. The partial likelihood estimation must be adapted to accommodate ties in the survival data. While there is no unique way to accommodate ties, I follow the suggestion of Kalbfleisch and Prentice (2002, pp. 105–6) and apply the Efron approximation of the average partial likelihood.

Table 6.4   Probit analysis: visitation

Visitation	(1)	(2)	(3)
SIC 13 – Gas and oil extraction	0.085	0.068	0.055
	0.144	0.140	0.139
SIC 28 – Chemicals	−0.001	0.025	0.018
	0.102	0.106	0.107
SIC 35 – Machinery	−0.037	−0.043	−0.046
	0.099	0.098	0.098
SIC 36 – Electronics	−0.106	−0.094	−0.076
	0.095	0.098	0.106
SIC 73 – Business services	−0.088	−0.078	−0.085
	0.083	0.084	0.082
File year	0.018***	0.017***	0.018***
	0.007	0.006	0.007
ATP		−0.188***	−0.195***
		0.054	0.054
DOD			−0.079
			0.084
All other government			0.014
			0.100
Federal laboratory			0.092
			0.134
University	0.043	0.042	0.053
	0.082	0.079	0.082
Pollution abatement	−0.304***	−0.315***	−0.320***
	0.057	0.057	0.058
Likelihood	−83.31	−80.59	−80.04

Note: The notations ***, **, and * indicate significance at the 1 percent, 5 percent and 10 percent levels, respectively.

would indicate a hazard ratio $e^{x_{ij}\hat{\beta}_j}$, which is a hazard rate of proportion $e^{x_{ij}\hat{\beta}_j}$ of the baseline hazard rate $\lambda_0(t)$. Positive coefficients indicate hazard rates that exceed the baseline rate and thus imply shorter survival times (NDAs of shorter duration). Negative coefficients indicate smaller hazard rates and therefore imply longer survival times (NDAs of longer duration).

The probit analyses and survival analyses illuminate four sets of results. First, the Chemicals/Electronics dichotomy bears out in the survival analyses. The duration of NDAs involving *Chemicals* are significantly longer than those involving *Electronics*. The results are consistent with hypothesis that more appropriable intellectual properties map into NDAs

Table 6.5   Probit analysis: member R&D

Member R&D	(1)	(2)	(3)	(4)
SIC 13 – Gas and oil	−0.350***	−0.348***	−0.320**	−0.323**
extraction	0.105	0.113	0.125	0.127
SIC 28 – Chemicals	−0.037	−0.054	−0.032	−0.008
	0.122	0.126	0.126	0.123
SIC 35 – Machinery	−0.366***	−0.370***	−0.360***	−0.356***
	0.096	0.097	0.099	0.099
SIC 36 – Electronics	0.164	0.150	0.100	0.108
	0.184	0.186	0.185	0.185
SIC 73 – Business services	−0.168	−0.187	−0.203	−0.195
	0.125	0.124	0.125	0.127
File year	−0.007	−0.007	−0.006	−0.006
	0.008	0.008	0.008	0.008
ATP		0.371***	0.401***	0.391***
		0.108	0.103	0.106
DOD			0.230*	0.235*
			0.127	0.129
All other government				−0.097
				0.146
Federal laboratory				0.146
				0.186
University	−0.065	−0.066	−0.106	−0.116
	0.099	0.101	0.105	0.107
Pollution abatement	−0.387***	−0.363***	−0.339***	−0.337***
	0.084	0.089	0.093	0.093
Likelihood	−96.59	−92.83	−91.34	−90.89

Note: The notations ***, **, and * indicate significance at the 1 percent, 5 percent and 10 percent levels, respectively.

of longer duration. The ATP effect comes second. Advanced Technology Program-sponsored ventures tend not to involve visitation and tend to involve the input of background intellectual properties that are highly appropriable. Altogether, the results parallel those of Mowery et al. (1998) in that they suggest that ATP-sponsored ventures tended to involve little in the way of spillovers of knowledge inputs. Third, there is a parallel but less elaborate DOD effect. Department of Defense-sponsored ventures also feature highly appropriable knowledge inputs in that, similar to *Chemicals*, the duration of NDAs on background intellectual property tend to be long. Fourth, and finally, the pollution abatement effect bears out. Ventures involving pollution abatement technologies tended to

Table 6.6   Probit analysis: member R&D × visitation

Member R&D × Visitation	(1)	(2)	(3)
SIC 13 – Gas and oil extraction	−0.031	−0.041	−0.034
	0.070	0.063	0.063
SIC 28 – Chemicals	0.059	0.078	0.099
	0.082	0.085	0.090
SIC 35 – Machinery	−0.029	−0.033	−0.024
	0.067	0.064	0.063
SIC 36 – Electronics	−0.098**	−0.094**	−0.090**
	0.043	0.042	0.041
SIC 73 – Business services	−0.088*	−0.076	−0.078*
	0.047	0.049	0.045
File year	0.003	0.003	0.002
	0.005	0.005	0.005
ATP		−0.085**	−0.084**
		0.040	0.038
DOD			0.013
			0.073
All other government		−0.060	−0.095***
		0.052	0.033
Federal laboratory			0.252*
			0.151
University	−0.018	−0.014	−0.034
	0.054	0.052	0.044
Pollution abatement	−0.227***	−0.230***	−0.216***
	0.045	0.045	0.044
Likelihood	−62.88	−61.36	−59.38

Note: The notations ***, **, and * indicate significance at the 1 percent, 5 percent and 10 percent levels, respectively.

concentrate on cost-sharing by means of contract R&D. These ventures involved little in the way of the sharing of knowledge inputs.

I take up these results in turn:

Result 1:   The Chemicals/Electronics dichotomy bears out in the duration data.

Tables 6.7 and 6.8 feature the Cox regressions of NDAs against the industry codes and the government indicators. Both tables feature a set of three nested regressions with the first illuminating the relationship of ATP sponsorship and DOD sponsorship to the duration of NDAs involving background intellectual property, and the second table illuminating the

Table 6.7   Duration of NDAs: background intellectual property Cox regression coefficients

Background intellectual property	(1)	(2)	(3)
SIC 13 – Gas and oil extraction	1.222***	1.029**	1.006**
	0.471	0.479	0.476
SIC 28 – Chemicals	0.031	−0.013	0.053
	0.215	0.218	0.214
SIC 35 – Machinery	0.024	−0.070	−0.187
	0.303	0.296	0.322
SIC 36 – Electronics	0.816***	1.055***	1.076***
	0.204	0.225	0.227
SIC 73 – Business services	0.180	0.231	0.235
	0.270	0.286	0.286
File year	−0.026*	−0.028*	−0.026*
	0.016	0.015	0.016
ATP		−0.535**	−0.506**
		0.246	0.229
DOD		−0.631**	−0.683**
		0.246	0.268
All other government			−0.513
			0.334
Federal laboratory			0.563
			0.371
Pollution abatement	0.198	0.139	0.265
	0.256	0.262	0.265
Likelihood	−444.21	−440.90	−439.14

Note: The notations ***, **, and * indicate significance at the 1 percent, 5 percent and 10 percent levels, respectively.

relationship of *All other government* entities to the duration of NDAs involving foreground intellectual property. Positive coefficient estimates indicate higher hazard rates (and therefore shorter duration), and negative coefficient estimates indicate lower hazard rates (and therefore longer duration).

In all six Cox regressions, the coefficient estimates pertaining to *Chemicals* is significantly lower than the coefficient estimates pertaining to *Electronics*. Likelihood ratio tests suggest that specification (3) in each table adds little information that is not already captured by specification (2) in each table. The difference between the coefficient estimates is 1.068 – a difference significant at the 1 percent confidence level – which in turn implies that *Electronics* features a hazard rate with respect to

Table 6.8   Duration of NDAs: foreground intellectual property Cox regression coefficients

Foreground intellectual property	(1)	(2)	(3)
SIC 13 – Gas and oil extraction	0.683**	0.610*	0.547
	0.328	0.333	0.342
SIC 28 – Chemicals	-0.655***	-0.590***	-0.562**
	0.227	0.223	0.231
SIC 35 – Machinery	0.478	0.413	0.409
	0.316	0.330	0.326
SIC 36 – Electronics	0.434**	0.433**	0.543**
	0.202	0.205	0.225
SIC 73 – Business services	-0.067	0.124	0.171
	0.303	0.294	0.318
File year	-0.006	-0.004	-0.002
	0.016	0.016	0.016
ATP			-0.262
			0.261
DOD			-0.292
			0.237
All other government		-0.764**	-0.847**
		0.371	0.390
Federal laboratory			0.297
			0.353
Pollution abatement	-0.058	-0.018	-0.061
	0.249	0.258	0.260
Likelihood	-452.45	-449.46	-448.46

Note: The notations ***, **, and * indicate significance at the 1 percent, 5 percent and 10 percent levels, respectively.

background intellectual property that is $e^{1.068} = 2.911$ times greater than the *Chemicals* hazard rate. Specification (2) in Table 6.8 yields a similar result. The difference in coefficient estimates is significant at the 1 percent level and implies a hazard rate $e^{1.023} = 2.780$ times greater than the *Chemicals* hazard rate.

Result 2:   Advanced Technology Program-sponsored ventures may have involved the sharing of knowledge outputs, but they involved little in the way of the transfer of knowledge inputs. The result delimits the conclusions of ATP-sponsored research.

Tables 6.4, 6.5, and 6.6 present results from the binary probit analyses. The feature results pertaining to *Visitation, Member R&D*, and for the interacted variable *Member R&D × Visitation*. I do not report results for *Third-party Licensing*, because they contributed little information.

These tables feature marginal effects rather than coefficient estimates. Likelihood ratio tests suggest that specifications (2) in Tables 6.4 and 6.5 as well as specification (3) in Table 6.6 constitute the best specifications.

Table 6.4 indicates important correlations between *Visitation* and the variables *File year, ATP*, and *Pollution abatement. DOD* and *All other government* are inconsequential, but specification (2) indicates that ATP-sponsored ventures featured visitation 19.5 percent less frequently than the baseline venture, a result that is significant at the 1 percent level. *Machinery (SIC 35), ATP* and *Pollution abatement* are featured prominently in Table 6.5 with respect to *Member R&D*. Specification (2) indicates that ATP-sponsored ventures depended on member R&D efforts 37.1 percent less frequently than the baseline venture, a result that is also significant at the 1 percent level.

Now consider the interaction term *Member R&D × Visitation*. The term identifies 27 instances in which RJVs featured visitation rights and at least one member firm contributed important R&D efforts. Such instances should reflect circumstances more conducive to the transfer of knowledge inputs or knowledge outputs. A modest, negative ATP result obtains: ATP-sponsored ventures featured the combination of member R&D efforts and visitation by other member firms 8.4 percent less frequently than the baseline venture.

Now consider the duration of NDAs. Specification (2) in Table 6.7 indicates that ATP-sponsored ventures imposed NDAs on background intellectual property characterized by hazard rates $e^{-0.535} = 58.6\%$ as large as the hazard rate prevailing in the baseline venture, a result that is significant at the 1 percent level. Meanwhile, Table 6.8 indicates no discernible correlation between *ATP* and the duration of NDAs on foreground intellectual property.

The survival analysis suggests that ATP-sponsored ventures tended to feature background intellectual properties more like *Chemicals* than *Electronics*: more amenable to appropriation and less amenable to unintended spillover. Meanwhile, the results pertaining to *Visitation* and *Member R&D × Visitation* suggest that ATP-sponsored ventures were less likely by design to be motivated by the prospect of important transfers of knowledge inputs.

These results are interesting, because they allow one to qualify the conclusions of ATP-sponsored research. Dyer et al. (2007), for example, examined 142 ATP ventures organized between 1990 and 2001. They observe that ATP ventures appear more vertical than horizontal in that member firms purportedly contributed complementary assets and capabilities, and they further suggest that these ventures were focused on knowledge sharing.

The results presented here are consistent with the findings of Dyer et al. (2007), but the results delimit what knowledge sharing likely entailed. It may have entailed the sharing of knowledge outputs – as noted by other ATP-sponsored research (Feldman and Kelley 2003) – but there is little indication that member firms were sharing knowledge inputs. They were certainly providing the rights of way that member firms required to collaborate, but the ventures do not look like the ventures that really did require transfers of knowledge inputs, such as that between HGS and SKB.

Result 3:   DOD-sponsored ventures have involved knowledge inputs that are less amenable to spillover.

The one salient *DOD* result parallels the counterpart *ATP* result: DOD-sponsored ventures imposed NDAs on background intellectual property characterized by hazard rates $e^{-0.631} = 53.2\%$ as large as the hazard rate prevailing in the baseline venture, a result that is also significant at the 1 percent level. Table 6.8 indicates no discernible correlation between *DOD* and the duration of NDAs on foreground intellectual property.

Again, the survival analysis suggests that DOD-sponsored ventures tended to feature background intellectual properties more similar to *Chemicals* than *Electronics*, that is, more amenable to appropriation and less amenable to unintended spillover.

Result 4:   Ventures involving the development of pollution abatement technologies have concentrated on cost-sharing, not on the transfer of knowledge assets.

The results relevant to *Pollution abatement* derive entirely from the probit analyses. The survival analyses indicate no discernible correlations between the duration of NDAs and *Pollution abatement*. Specification (2) in Table 6.4 indicates that ventures organized around developing pollution abatement technologies featured visitation 31.5 percent less frequently than the baseline venture. Specification (2) in Table 6.5 indicates that *Pollution abatement* featured *Member R&D* 36.3 percent less frequently than the baseline venture. Finally, specification (3) in Table 6.6 indicates that these same ventures featured the combination of member R&D efforts and visitation 21.6 percent less frequently than the baseline venture. All of these results are significant at the 1 percent level.

The results are consistent with *Pollution abatement* involving little in the way of member firm R&D efforts, little in the way of knowledge inputs by member firms, and more in the way of sharing the costs of contracting out R&D efforts to a party external to the venture.

WHENCE COMPETITIVENESS?

In all of this we might wonder what had become of the competitiveness agenda, for it was mercantilistic notions such as national competitiveness that initially motivated industrial policies to counter Japanese and European industrial policies.[20]

More generally, we may observe that episodes of economic distress have concentrated attention in policy circles on innovation and the competitiveness of American industry. The episode of the late 1970s concentrated concern on the perceived loss of leadership to Japanese firms in the development and production of semiconductors and other computer hardware (Corey 1997, p. 111). The experience of the late 1980s and early 1990s brought much of the same, with proponents of activist policy raising concerns over Japanese investments in superconductivity and high-definition television (HDTV) (Mowery and Rosenberg 1989; Bingham and Papadakis 1998).[21] Meanwhile, in the 2010s, debate about the role of public investment in technology has resurged, with some policymakers concerned about the perceived lead that China has achieved in commercializing green technology.

The China episode has yet to fully play out, but the Japanese episode proved to be overtaken by developments unanticipated in the policy debate. It turned out that, over time, the private strategic initiatives of American firms would make a mockery of the competitive advantages that public initiatives in Japan and Europe purportedly afforded to foreign firms. With the model of IBM in mind, public initiatives endeavored to promote innovation at the cutting edge of specific technologies so that American firms might maintain their lead in those same technologies. In contrast, private initiatives focused more on the innovation of new products if not on the innovation of new technologies *per se*. Indeed,

---

[20] See West (1996). Further, I would suggest that public initiatives appear to have been predicated on the notion that assuming a lead in the commercialization of technologies involved assuming a lead in the innovation of technologies. Further, these initiatives seemed predicated on the Schumpeterian notion that innovation involved substantial costs and risks that only large entities such as IBM or consortia of smaller entities could afford to bear.

[21] Yet, the HDTV failed, and the promise of room-temperature superconducting materials remains unrealized.

product innovation often involved deploying existing technologies rather than deploying cutting-edge technologies. New products even diminished the commercial significance of the cutting-edge technologies and yet inspired other firms to develop technologies to complement those same new products.

Public initiatives, for example, missed important market developments (if not technological developments *per se*) involving both computer hardware and software. For example, it was small and nimble entities such as Commodore, Atari, Radio Shack, and Apple Computer that were realizing a new market for microcomputers, and they were doing it largely by commercializing existing technologies.[22] Thus, much of the action, it turned out, involved not leapfrogging IBM's capabilities in high-end (mainframe) computing but in commercializing existing, and even off-the-shelf, technologies to serve more pedestrian demands.

Ironically, it was IBM's own latent smallness and nimbleness that set the stage for the eventual commoditization of computer hardware. After failing in 1980 to make an effective entry into microcomputing with its 5120 computer, IBM authorized a small team to bypass internal company protocols and roll out a microcomputer prototype in short order. The effort involved using off-the-shelf components and contracting with a privately owned software company named Microsoft to assemble the operating system for what turned out to be the 5150 computer, the IBM personal computer (PC).[23]

The commercialization of the PC in 1983 would mark the beginning of a Microsoft software empire. The strategic opportunities to exploit network effects and lock-in would prove to be concentrated less in hardware and more in software.[24] IBM implementation of an open architecture amounted to launching what would turn out to be a low-margin industry of IBM-compatible clones populated by any number of manufacturers, including Japanese manufacturers.

---

[22] For example, Xerox made the first attempt to commercialize a microcomputer with a mouse and a graphical interface, but it was Apple with its Macintosh computer that first managed to successfully commercialize such technologies.

[23] Microsoft "went public" in March, 1986.

[24] By the mid-1990s Japanese firm Toshiba may have even secured a leading market position in the commercialization of microcomputers and memory chips (Fong 1998, p. 343), but, as West (1996, p. 257) observed at the time with respect to memory chips, "profits are far from assured, however, in a market that has been chronically plagued by under- and overcapacity due to the large investments and long lead times necessary to expand production capacity".

CONCLUSION

How do private entities exploit government programs to support R&D? What types of projects do government sponsors choose? The chapter examined 171 research joint ventures identified in NCRA filings made between 1984 and 2009. While the NCRA is itself an important government program, it turns out that the data extracted from NCRA filings provides an important perspective on how firms exploit both the NCRA and other government programs. The data also provide indications of the kinds of projects government sponsors choose. One-third of the 171 contracts (57) involved RJVs that received subsidies from various federal programs. Another 13 involved R&D efforts contributed by federal laboratories.

The two bodies of programs best represented in the data are the ATP and various DOD programs including DARPA. The most important results in this chapter amount to comparing and contrasting the organization of ventures sponsored by the ATP and the DOD with the baseline venture typified by the entire body of data.

Ventures sponsored by the ATP and the DOD appear much like ventures organized around the development of chemicals. Intellectual properties involving chemicals have been long understood to be more appropriable than other bodies of intellectual property. Indeed, a contrast is often made between chemicals and electronics, with the former being amenable to all types of remedies to unintended spillovers and the latter being unavoidably subject to spillovers. The ATP and DOD-sponsored ventures featured background intellectual properties that were subject to more restrictive protections. Specifically, they were subject to non-disclosure agreements of long duration suggesting that the parties to such ventures tended to contribute the kinds of intellectual properties that were less susceptible to spillover.

Further results suggest that ATP-sponsored ventures tended to involve projects that did not require transfers of knowledge inputs. Instead, member firms would dispatch R&D tasks in their independent facilities. This is in contrast to the long-running, non-subsidized collaboration between HGS and SKB. SmithKline Beecham reserved the right to detail personnel to HGS facilities so that these same personnel might absorb some of the HGS know-how SKB would then need to develop new drug therapies. Thus, whereas the transfer of knowledge inputs was an explicitly designed feature of the HGS/SKB collaboration, such transfers were explicitly precluded in ATP-sponsored ventures.

The NCRA data also speak to cost-sharing. A large number of ventures (55 of 171) involved the development of pollution abatement technologies.

The structures of the contracts corresponding to these ventures suggest that they involved little in the way of R&D efforts by member firms. Instead, member firms tended to contract out, to parties external to the venture, well-defined, discrete tasks. The purpose of these ventures amounted to cost-sharing: member firms would share the costs of compensating contract researchers. These ventures involved little in the way of transfers of knowledge inputs.

References

AES Ironwood, LLC (2002), "Form 10-K 2001", SEC EDGAR website, accessed February 18, 2019 at https://www.sec.gov/edgar.shtml.

Alchian, Armen and Harold Demsetz (1972), "Production, information costs, and economic organization", *American Economic Review*, **62**, 777–95.

Alvarez, Michael and Garrett Glasgow (1999), "Two-stage estimation of nonrecursive choice models", *Political Analysis*, **8**, 147–65.

Anand, Bharat N. and Alexander Galetovic (2000), "Uncertain property rights and holdup in R&D", *Journal of Economics and Management Strategy*, **9**, 615–42.

Areeda, Phillip (1983), "Intraenterprise conspiracy in decline", *Harvard Law Review*, **97**, 451–73.

Arora, Ashish (1997), "Patents, licensing, and market structure in the chemical industry", *Research Policy*, **26**, 391–403.

Arora, Ashish and Robert P. Merges (2004), "Specialized supply firms, property rights and firm boundaries", *Industrial and Corporate Change*, **13**, 451–75.

Arrow, Kenneth (1951), "An extension of the basic theorems of classical welfare economics", *Proceedings of the Second Berkeley Symposium on Mathematical Statistics and Probability*, Berkeley, CA: University of California Press, pp. 507–32.

Arrow, Kenneth (1951), *Social Choice and Individual Values*, 3rd edn 2012, New Haven, CT: Yale University Press.

Arrow, Kenneth (1969), "The organization of economic activity: issues pertinent to the choice of market versus non-market allocation", in *The Analysis and Evolution of Public Expenditure: The PPB System*, vol. 1, U.S. Joint Economic Committee, 91st Congress, 1st Session, Washington, DC: US Government Printing Office, pp. 47–64.

Arrow, Kenneth J. (1962), "Economic welfare and the allocation of resources for invention", in Kenneth J. Arrow, *The Rate and Direction of Inventive Activity: Economic and Social Factors*, Princeton, NJ: Princeton University Press, pp. 609–26.

Arrow, Kenneth (1977), "Optimization, decentralization, and internal pricing in business firms", in Kenneth Arrow and Leonid Hurwicz (eds), *Studies in Resource Allocation Processes*, Cambridge: Cambridge University Press, pp. 134–45.

Ashtor, Eliahu (1975), "The volume of Levantine trade in the Later Middle Ages (1370–1498)", *Journal of European Economic History*, **4**, 573–612.

Ashtor, Eliahu (1976), "Observations on Venetian trade in the Levant in the XIVth century", *Journal of European Economic History*, **5**, 533–86.

Ashworth, Tony (1980), *Trench Warfare 1914–1918: The Live and Let Live System*, London: Macmillan.

Aumann, Robert (1976), "Agreeing to disagree", *Annals of Statistics*, **6**, 1236–9.

Axelrod, Robert (1984), *The Evolution of Cooperation*, New York: Basic Books.

Bagus, Philipp, David Howden, Amadeus Gabriel and Eva María Carrasco Bañuelos (2016), "Mises and Montaigne: a comment", *History of Political Economy*, **48**, 733–40.

Bajari, Patrick and Steven Tadelis (2001), "Incentives versus transaction costs: a theory of procurement contracts", *RAND Journal of Economics*, **32**, 387–407.

Baker, George, Robert Gibbons and Kevin Murphy (2001), "Bringing the market inside the firm?", *American Economic Review*, **91**, 212–18.

Baker, George, Robert Gibbons and Kevin Murphy (2002), "Relational contracts and the theory of the firm", *Quarterly Journal of Economics*, **117**, 39–84.

Baker, George, Robert Gibbons and Kevin Murphy (2011), "Relational adaptation", accessed December 2, 2018 at http://web.mit.edu/rgibbons/www/BGM%20Relnl%20Adapt%20Nov%2013.pdf.

Barone, Enrico (1908), "The Ministry of Production in the collectivist state", repr. 2009 in Friedrick Hayek (ed.), *Collectivist Economic Planning*, Auburn, AL: Ludwig von Mises Institute (2009), pp. 245–90.

Baxter, William (1977), "Posner's antitrust law: an economic perspective", *Bell Journal of Economics*, **8**, 609–19.

Beard, T. Randolph and Michael Stern (2008), "Continuous cross subsidies and quantity restrictions", *Journal of Industrial Economics*, **56**, 840–61.

Belsley, Michael (1996), "The Vatican merger defense: should two Catholic hospitals seeking to merge be considered a single entity for purposes of antitrust merger analysis?", *Northwestern University Law Review*, **90**, 720–87.

Bergstrom, Theodore (2002), "Evolution of social behavior: individual and group selection", *Journal of Economic Perspectives*, **16**, 67–88.

Bingham, Richard (1998), *Industrial Policy American Style*, New York: M.E. Sharpe.

Bingham, Richard and Maria Papadakis (1998), "Industrial policy for new technologies: pitfalls and foibles", in Richard Bingham (ed.), *Industrial Policy American Style*, New York: M.E. Sharpe.

Black Hills Power, Inc. (2002), "Form 10-K 2001", SEC EDGAR website, accessed December 2, 2018 at https://www.sec.gov/edgar.shtml.

Blake, Robert (1952), *The Private Papers of Douglas Haig, 1914–1919*, London: Eyre & Spottiswoode.

Bloom, Allan (1990), "Rousseau – the turning point", in Allan Bloom (ed.), *Confronting the Constitution*, Washington, DC: AEI Press, pp. 211–34.

Borkin, Joseph and Charles Welsh (1943), *Germany's Master Plan*, repr. 1960, New York: Duell, Sloan and Pearce.

Bowles, Samuel and Herbert Gintis (2011), *A Cooperative Species: Human Reciprocity and Its Evolution*, Princeton, NJ: Princeton University Press.

Branstetter, Lee and Mariko Sakakibara (1998), "Japanese research consortia: a microeconometric analysis of industrial policy", *Journal of Industrial Economics*, **46**, 207–33.

Branstetter, Lee and Mariko Sakakibara (2002), "When do research consortia work well and why? Evidence from Japanese panel data", *American Economic Review*, **92**, 143–59.

Brătianu, G.I. (1927), *Actes des Notaries Génois de Péra et de Caffa de la Fin du Treizième Siècle (1281–1290)*, Bucharest: Cultura națională.

Bull, Clive (1987), "The existence of self-enforcing implicit contracts", *Quarterly Journal of Economics*, **101**, 147–59.

Byrne, Eugene (1916), "Commercial contracts of the Genoese in the Syrian trade of the twelfth century", *Quarterly Journal of Economics*, **31**, 128–70.

Campbell, Stephen, Stephanie Shipp, Tim Mulcahy and Ted Allen (2009), "Informing public policy on science and innovation: the Advanced Technology Program's experience", *Journal of Technology Transfer*, **34**, 304–19.

Chang, Connie, Stephanie Shipp and Andrew Wang (2002), "The Advanced Technology Program: a public–private partnership for early stage technology development", *Venture Capital*, **4**, 363–70.

Clark, John B. (1912), "The possibility of competition in commerce and industry", *Annals of the American Academy of Political and Social Science*, **42**, 63–6.

Coase, Ronald (1937), "The nature of the firm", *Economica*, **4**, 386–405.

Coase, Ronald (1960), "The problem of social cost", *Journal of Law and Economics*, **3**, 1–69.

Cohen, Wesley M. and John P. Walsh (2000), "R&D spillovers, appropriability and R&D intensity: a survey based approach", draft report, Advanced Technology Program.

Commons, John (1934), *Institutional Economics*, vol. 1, repr. 1989, New Brunswick, NJ: Transaction.

Constable, Olivia (2003), *Housing the Stranger in the Mediterranean World*, Cambridge: Cambridge University Press.

Contractor, Farok J. and Wonchan Ra (2002), "How knowledge attributes influence alliance governance choices: a theory development note", *Journal of International Management*, **8**, 11–27.

Corey, E. Raymond (1997), *Technology Fountainheads: The Management Challenge of R&D Consortia*, Cambridge, MA: Harvard Business School Press.

Cress, Donald (ed.) (2011), *Jean-Jacques Rousseau: The Basic Political Writings*, 2nd edn, Indianapolis, IN: Hackett.

Crocker, Keith and Scott Masten (1988), "Mitigating contractual hazards: unilateral options and contract length", *RAND Journal of Economics*, **19**, 327–43.

Crocker, Keith and Scott Masten (1991), "Pretia ex machina? Prices and process in long-term contracts", *Journal of Law and Economics*, **34**, 69–99.

Crocker, Keith and John Morgan (1998), "Is honesty the best policy? Curtailing insurance fraud through optimal incentive contracts", *Journal of Political Economy*, **106**, 355–75.

Crocker, Keith and Kenneth Reynolds (1993), "The efficiency of incomplete contracts: an empirical analysis of Air Force engine procurement", *RAND Journal of Economics*, **24**, 126–46.

Crockett, Sean, Vernon Smith and Bart Wilson (2009), "Exchange and specialisation as a discovery process", *Economic Journal*, **119**, 1162–88.

Crowley, Thomas and Thomas Lowery (2000), "How warm was the Medieval Warm Period?", *Ambio*, **29**, 51–4.

D'Aspremont, Claude and Alexis Jacquemin (1988), "Cooperative and noncooperative R&D in duopoly with spillovers", *American Economic Review*, **78**, 1133–7.

Davidson, Russell and James G. MacKinnon (1993), *Estimation and Inference n Econometrics*, New York: Oxford University Press.

De Roover, Raymond (1963), "The organization of trade", in M.M. Postan, E.E. Rich and Edward Miller (eds), *The Cambridge Economic History of Europe*, vol. 3, Cambridge: Cambridge University Press, pp. 42–118.

DeBreu, Gerard (1951), "The coefficient of resource utilization", *Econometrica*, **19**, 273–92.

Demsetz, Harold (1969), "Information and efficiency: another viewpoint", *Journal of Law and Economics*, **12**, 1–22.

Demsetz, Harold (1995), *The Economics of the Business Firm*, Cambridge: Cambridge University Press.

Demsetz, Harold (1997), "The firm in economic theory: a quiet revolution", *American Economic Review*, **87**, 426–9.

Demsetz, Harold (2011a), "The problem of social cost: what problem? A critique of the reasoning of A.C. Pigou and R.H. Coase", *Review of Law and Economics*, **7**, 1–13.

Demsetz, Harold (2011b), "R.H. Coase the neoclassical model of the economic system", *Journal of Law and Economics*, **54**, S7–S13.

Dixit, Avinash (2004), *Lawlessness and Economics: Alternative Modes of Governance*, Princeton, NJ: Princeton University Press.

Dixit, Avinash (2009), "Governance institutions and economic activity", *American Economic Review*, **99**, 5–24.

Dominiak, Adam and Jean-Phillipe Lefort (2015), "'Agreeing to disagree' type results under ambiguity", *Journal of Mathematical Economics*, **61**, 119–29.

Duguid, Shona, Emily Wyman, Anke F. Bullinger, Katharina Herfurth-Majstorovic and Michael Tomasello (2014), "Coordination strategies of chimpanzees and human children in a stag hunt game", *Proceedings of the Royal Society*, **281**, 1–9.

Dyer, Jeffrey, Benjamin Powell, Mariko Sakakibara and Andrew Wang (2007), "The determinants of success in R&D alliances", *Academy of Management Proceedings* (1), 1–6.

Edwards, Jeremy and Sheilagh Ogilvie (2012), "Contract enforcement, institutions, and social capital: the Maghribi traders reappraised", *Economic History Review*, **65**, 421–44.

Engels, Friedrich (1892), "Socialism: utopian and scientific", repr. 1978 in Robert Tucker (ed.), *The Marx-Engels Reader*, 2nd edn, New York: W.W Norton, pp. 681–717.

Falkenhayn, Erich von (1919), *General Headquarters 1914–1916 and its Critical Decisions*, London: Hutchinson.

Farrell, Joseph (1987), "Information and the Coase Theorem", *Journal of Economic Perspectives*, **1**, 113–29.

Faure-Grimaud, Antoine and Thomas Mariotti (1999), "Optimal debt contracts and the single-crossing condition", *Economic Letters*, **65**, 85–9.

Favier-Dubois, Cristian (2007), "Soil genesis related to medieval climatic fluctuations in southern Patagonia and Tierra del Fuego (Argentina), chronological and paleoclimatic considerations", *Quaternary International*, **162–3**, 158–65.

Feldman, Maryann and Maryellen Kelley (2003), "Leveraging research and development: assessing the impact of the U.S. Advanced Technology Program", *Small Business Economics*, **20**, 153–65.

Ferrell, Robert (1998), *Dear Bess: The Letters from Harry to Bess Truman, 1910–1959*, Columbia, MO: University of Missouri Press.

Flamm, Kenneth and Sadao Nagaoka (2007), "The chrysanthemum meets the eagle", *Issues in Science and Technology* (Fall), 70–77.

Flood, Merrill M. (1952), "Some experimental games", Research Memorandum Rm-789, RAND Corporation, Santa Monica, CA.

Fong, Glenn R. (1998), "Follower at the frontier: international competition and Japanese industrial policy", *International Studies Quarterly*, **42**, 339–66.

Freedman, David A. and Stephen C. Peters (1984), "Bootstrapping an econometric model: some empirical results", *Journal of Business & Economic Statistics*, **2**, 150–58.

Fudenberg, Drew and Jean Tirole (1992), *Game Theory*, Cambridge, MA: MIT Press.

Fudenberg, Drew, David Levine and Eric Maskin (1994), "Folk theorem with imperfect public information", *Econometrica*, **62**, 997–1039.

Gale, Douglas and Dean Lueck (2003), *The Nature of the Farm: Contracts, Risk and Organization in Agriculture*, Cambridge, MA: MIT Press.

General Accounting Office (GAO) (1995), "Performance measurement, efforts to evaluate the Advanced Technology Program", GAO/RCED-95-68, May, Washington, DC.

General Accounting Office (GAO) (1996), "Measuring performance: the Advanced Technology Program and private-sector funding", GAO/RCED-96-47, January, Washington, DC.

General Accounting Office (GAO) (2000), "Advanced Technology Program: inherent factors in selection process could limit identification of similar research", GAO/RCED- 00-114, April, Washington, DC.

Gibbons, Robert (2005), "Four formal(izable) theories of the firm?", *Journal of Economic Behavior and Organization*, **58**, 200–245.

Goeree, Jacob and Charles Holt (2001), "Ten little treasures of game theory and ten intuitive contradictions", *American Economic Review*, **91**, 1402–22.

Goitein, Shlomo (1967), *A Mediterranean Society: The Jewish Communities of the Arab World as Portrayed in the Documents of the Cairo Geniza*, vol. 1, Berkeley and Los Angeles, CA: University of California Press.

Goitein, Shlomo (1973), *Letters of Medieval Jewish Traders*, Princeton, NJ: Princeton University Press.

Goldberg, Victor (1985), "Price adjustment in long-term contracts", *Wisconsin Law Review*, 527–43.

Goldberg, Victor and John Erickson (1987), "Quantity and price adjustment in long-term contracts: a case study of petroleum coke", *Journal of Law and Economics*, **30**, 369–98.

Gordon, Scott (1978), "Should economists pay attention to philosophers?" *Journal of Political Economy*, **86**, 717–28.

Green, Edward and Robert Porter (1984), "Noncooperative collusion under imperfect price information", *Econometrica*, **52**, 87–100.

Greif, Avner (1989), "Reputation and coalitions in medieval trade: evidence on the Maghribi traders", *Journal of Economic History*, **49**, 857–82.

Greif, Avner (1993), "Contract enforceability and economic institutions in early trade: the Maghribi traders' coalition", *American Economic Review*, **83**, 525–48.

Greif, Avner (1994), "Cultural beliefs and the organization of society: a historical and theoretical reflection on collectivist and individualist societies", *Journal of Political Economy*, **102**, 912–50.

Griliches, Zvi (1979), "Issues in assessing the contribution of research and development to productivity growth", *Bell Journal of Economics*, **10**, 92–116.

Griliches, Zvi (1992), "The search for R&D spillovers", *Scandinavian Journal of Economics*, **94** (supplement), 29–47.

Grindley, Peter C. and David J. Teece (1997), "Managing intellectual capital: licensing and cross-licensing in semiconductors and electronics", *California Management Review*, **39**, 8–41.

Grindley, Peter C., David C. Mowery and Brian Silverman (1994), "SEMATECH and collaborative research: lessons in the design of high-technology consortia", *Journal of Policy Analysis and Management*, **13**, 723–58.

Grossman, Sanford and Oliver Hart (1986), "The costs and benefits of ownership: a theory of vertical and lateral integration", *Journal of Political Economy*, **94**, 691–719.

Hansen, Alvin, Francis Boddy and John Langum (1936), "Recent trends in business cycle literature", *Review of Economics and Statistics*, **18**, 53–61.

Hansmann, Henry and Reinier Kraakman (2000), "The essential role of organization law", *Yale Law Journal*, **110**, 387–440.

Hart, Oliver (1995), *Firms, Contracts and Financial Structure*, Oxford: Oxford University Press.

Hart, Oliver (2003), "Incomplete contracts and public ownership: remarks, and an application to public–private partnerships", *Economic Journal*, **113**, C69–C76.

Hart, Oliver (2008), "Reference points and the theory of the firm", *Economica*, **75**, 404–11.

Hart, Oliver and John Moore (1990), "Property rights and the nature of the firm", *Journal of Political Economy*, **98**, 1119–58.

Hart, Oliver and John Moore (2008), "Contracts as reference points", *Quarterly Journal of Economics*, **123**, 1–48.

Hausman, Jerry A. (1978), "Specification tests in econometrics", *Econometrica*, **46**, 1251–72.

Hills, J.D. (1919), *The Fifth Leicestershire, 1914–1919*, Loughborough: Echo Press.

Hobbes, Thomas (1651), *Leviathan, or the Matter, Forme and Power of a Commonwealth Ecclesiasticall and Civil*, repr. 2014, Whithorn: Anodos Books.

Hoff, Karla (1994), "The second theorem of the second best", *Journal of Public Economics*, **54**, 223–42.

Hovenkamp, Herbert (2005), *Federal Antitrust Policy: The Law of Competition and Its Practice*, 3rd edn, Eagan, MN: Thomson West.

Hubbard, R. Glenn and Robert Weiner (1991), "Efficient contracting and market power: evidence from the U.S. natural gas industry", *Journal of Law and Economics*, **34**, 25–67.

Hunt, Edwin and James Murray (1999), *A History of Business in Medieval Europe, 1200–1550*, Cambridge: Cambridge University Press.

Hurwicz, Leonid (1969), "On the concept and possibility of informational decentralization", *American Economic Review*, **59**, 513–24.

Hurwicz, Leonid (1972), "On informationally decentralized systems", in C.B. McGuire and Roy Radner (eds), *Decision and Organization*, Amsterdam: North-Holland, pp. 297–336.

Hurwicz, Leonid (1977), "The design of resource allocation mechanisms", in Kenneth Arrow and Leonid Hurwicz (eds), *Studies in Resource Allocation Processes*, Cambridge: Cambridge University Press, pp. 3–37.

Idelson, Holly (1996), "Advanced Technology Program caught in tug of war", *CQ Weekly Online*, March 2, 550–52.

Jaffe, Adam (1998), "The importance of 'spillovers' in the policy mission of the Advanced Technology Program", *Journal of Technology Transfer*, **23**, 11–19.

Jaffe, Adam (2008), "The 'science of science policy': reflections on the important questions and the challenges they present", *Journal of Technology Transfer*, **33**, 131–9.

Jensen, Michael and William Meckling (1976), "Theory of the firm: managerial behavior, agency costs and ownership structure", *Journal of Financial Economics*, **3**, 305–60.

Johnston, Jack and John Dinardo (1997), *Econometric Methods*, 4th edn, New York: McGraw-Hill.

Joskow, Paul (1985), "Vertical integration and long-term contracts: the case of coal-burning electric generating plants", *Journal of Law, Economics, and Organization*, **1**, 33–80.

Joskow, Paul (1987), "Contract duration and relationship-specific investments: empirical evidence from coal markets", *American Economic Review*, **77**, 168–85.

Joskow, Paul (1988), "Price adjustment in long-term contracts: the case of coal", *Journal of Law and Economics*, **31**, 47–83.

Kalbfleisch, John D. and Ross L. Prentice (2002), *The Statistical Analysis of Failure Time Data*, 2nd edn, Hoboken, NJ: Wiley.

Katz, Michael (1986), "An analysis of cooperative research and development", *RAND Journal of Economics*, **17**, 527–43.

Kawabata, Yasunari (1951), 'The Master of Go', *Shincho*, repub. 1981, *The Master of Go*, New York: Perigee Books.

Kedar, Benjamin (1976), *Merchants in Crisis: Genoese and Venetian Men of Affairs and the Fourteenth Century Depression*, New Haven, CT: Yale University Press.

Keller, Charles (2004), "1000 years of climate change", *Space Research*, **34**, 315–22.

Klein, Benjamin, Robert Crawford and Armen Alchian (1978), "Vertical integration, appropriable rents and the competitive contracting process", *Journal of Law and Economics*, **21**, 297–326.

Klette, Jakob, Jarle Moen and Zvi Griliches (2000), "Do subsidies to commercial R&D reduce market failures? Microeconometric evaluation studies", *Research Policy*, **29**, 471–95.

Koopmans, Tjalling (1957), *Three Essays on the State of Economic Science*, New York: McGraw-Hill.

Kreps, David and Robert Wilson (1982), "Rational cooperation in the finitely repeated prisoners' dilemma", *Journal of Economic Theory*, **27**, 245–52.

Lacker, Jeffrey and John Weinberg (1989), "Optimal contracts under costly state falsification", *Journal of Political Economy*, **97**, 1345–63.

Laidlaw, Frances (1998), "ATP's impact on accelerating development and commercialization of advanced technology", *Journal of Technology Transfer*, **23**, 33–41.

Lane, Frederic (1964), "Investment and usury", *Explorations in Entrepreneurial History*, **2**, repr. 1965 in F.C. Lane, *Venice and History*, Baltimore, MD: Johns Hopkins University Press, pp. 56–68.

Lane, Frederic (1973), *Venice, a Maritime Republic*, Baltimore, MD: Johns Hopkins University Press.

Lange, Oskar (1937), "On the economic theory of socialism: part two", *Review of Economic Studies*, **4**, 123–42.

Lange, Oskar (1938), "On the economic theory of socialism", repr. 1964 in Benjamin Lippincott (ed.), *On the Economic Theory of Socialism*, New York: McGraw-Hill, pp. 57–143.

Lange, Oskar (1967), "The computer and the market", in C.H. Feinstein (ed.), *Socialism, Capitalism, and Economic Growth*, Cambridge: Cambridge University Press, pp. 158–61.

Lanjouw, Jean and Josh Lerner (2001), "Tilting the table? The use of pre-liminary injunctions", *Journal of Law and Economics*, **44**, 573–603.

Lanjouw, Jean and Mark Schankerman (2001), "Characteristics of patent litigation: a window on competition", *RAND Journal of Economics*, **32**, 129–51.

Lehn, Kenneth and Michael Sykuta (1997), "Antitrust and franchise relo-cation in professional sports: an economic analysis of the Raiders case", *Antitrust Bulletin*, **42**, 541–63.

Lenin, Vladimir (1917), *The State and Revolution*, repr. 1970, Foreign Language Press.

Lerner, Abba (1946), *The Economics of Control*, New York: Macmillan.

Libecap, Gary and Steven Wiggins (1984), "Contractual responses to the common pool: prorationing of crude oil production", *American Economic Review*, **74**, 87–98.

Link, Albert, David Paton and Donald S. Siegel (2005), "An econometric analysis of trends in research joint venture activity", *Managerial and Decision Economics*, **26**, 149–58.

Llewellyn, Karl (1931), "What price contract? An essay in perspective", *Yale Law Journal*, **40**, 704–51.

Locke, John (1689), *The Second Treatise of Government and a Letter Concerning Toleration*, repr. 2002, New York: Dover Publications.

Lombardo, Antoniolo and Raimondo Morozzo della Rocca (eds) (1953), *Nuovi Documenti del Commercio Veneto dei Secoli XI–XIII*, Venice.

Lopez, Robert (1943), "European merchants in the medieval Indies: the evidence of commercial documents", *Journal of Economic History*, **3**, 164–84.

Lopez, Robert (1951), "Nuove Luci sugli Italiani in Estremo Oriente prima di Colombo", *Studi Colombiani*, Genoa: Convegno Internazionale di Studi Colombiani, pp. 337–98.

Lopez, Robert (1955), "Venezia e le Grandi Linee dell-Espansione Commerciale nel Secolo XIII", *La Civiltà del Secolo di Marco Polo*, Florence: Sansoni.

Lopez, Robert (1971), *The Commercial Revolution of the Middle Ages, 950–1350*, Englewood Cliffs, NJ: Prentice-Hall.

Lopez, Robert and Irving Raymond (eds) (1955), *Medieval Trade in the Mediterranean World*, New York: Columbia University Press.

Lyons, Bruce (1995), "Specific investment, economies of scale, and the make-or-buy decision: a test of transaction cost theory", *Journal of Economic Behavior and Organization*, **26**, 431–43.

MacKinnon, James (2006), "Bootstrap methods in econometrics", Economics Department Working Paper 1028, Queen's University, Kingston, ON.

MacKinnon, James G. (2002), "Bootstrap inference in econometrics", *Canadian Journal of Economics*, **35**, 615–45 (pp. 632–3).

MacNeil, Ian (1974), "The many futures of contracts", *Southern California Law Review*, **47**, 691–816.

MacNeil, Ian (1978), "Contracts: adjustment of long-term economic relations under classical, neoclassical, and relational contract law", *Northwestern University Law Review*, **72**, 853–905.

Majewski, Suzanne and Dean Williamson (2004), "Incomplete contracting and the structure of R&D joint venture contracts", in Gary D. Libecap (ed.), *Intellectual Property and Entrepreneurship*, Bingley: Emerald Group, pp. 201–28.

Marx, Karl (1848), "The victory of the counter-revolution in Vienna", repr. 1977 in *Marx/Engels Collected Works*, vol. 7, New York: International Publishers, pp. 505–6.

Marx, Karl (1872), *Das Kapital: Kritik der Polischen Oekonomie*, Hamburg: Otto Meissner, pp. 813–22.

Marx, Karl (2018), "Afterword to the German edition of *Capital* (1873)", *Capital: A Critique of Political Economy*, vol. 1, Champaign, IL: Modern Barbarian Press, pp. 10–15.

Marx, Karl and Frederick Engels (1848), *Manifesto of the Communist Party*, repr. 1969 in *Marx-Engels Selected Works*, vol. 1, Moscow: Progress Publishers, pp. 98–137.

Maskin, Eric (2008), "Mechanism design: how to implement social goals", *American Economic Review*, **98**, 567–76.

Masse, Bruce, Jolie Liston, James Carucci and J. Stephen Athens (2006), "Evaluating the effects of climate change on environment, resource depletion, and culture in the Palau Islands between AD 1200 and 1600", *Quaternary International*, **151**, 106–32.

Masten, Scott (1988), "Equity, opportunism, and the design of contractual relations", *Journal of Institutional and Theoretical Economics*, **144**, 180–95.

Masten, Scott (2009), "Long-term contracts and short-term commitment: price determination for heterogeneous freight transactions", *American Law and Economics Review* **11**, 79–111.

Masten, Scott and Keith Crocker (1985), "Efficient adaptation in long-term contracts: take-or-pay provisions for natural gas", *American Economic Review*, **75**, 1083–93.

Mauquoy, Dimitri and Keith Barber (1999), "Evidence for climatic deteriorations associated with the decline of *Sphagnum imbricatum* Hornsch. ex Russ. in six ombrotrophic mires from northern England and the Scottish Borders", *The Holocene*, **9**, 423–37.

Medvedev, Roy (2004), "European writers on their meetings with Stalin", *Russian Politics and Law*, **42**, 78–92.

Merges, Robert (1996), "Contracting into liability rules: intellectual property rights and collective rights organizations", *California Law Review*, **84**, 1293–393.

Milgrom, Paul, Douglas North and Barry Weingast (1990), "The role of institutions in the revival of trade: the law merchant, private judges, and the champagne fairs", *Economics and Politics*, **2**, 1–23.

Modigliani, Franco and Merton Miller (1958), "The cost of capital, corporation finance and the theory of investment", *American Economic Review*, **48**, 261–97.

Moore, John (1992), "The firm as a collection of assets", *European Economic Review*, **36**, 493–507.

Morozzo della Rocca, Raimondo and Antoniolo Lombardo (eds) (1940), *Documenti del Commercio Veneziano*, Rome: Istituto Storico Italiano per il Medio Evo.

Mowery, David and Nathan Rosenberg (1989), "New development in U.S. technology policy: implications for competitiveness and international trade policy", *California Management Review*, **32**, 107–24.

Mowery, David, Joanne Oxley and Brian Silverman (1998), "Final report: the role of knowledge spillovers in ATP consortia", Advanced Technology Program, Washington, DC.

Müller, A.L. (1974), "The physiocratic theory of value", *South African Journal of Economics*, **42**, 312–24.

Myers, Stewart (1977), "Determinants of corporate borrowing", *Journal of Financial Economics*, **5**, 147–75.

Myers, Stewart and Nicholas Majluf (1984), "Corporate financing and investment decisions when firms have information that investors do not have", *Journal of Financial Economics*, **13**, 187–221.

Nakasone, Yasuhiro (1983), "Toward a nation of dynamic culture and welfare", *Japan Echo*, **10**, 12–18.

Nash, John (1950), "The bargaining problem", *Econometrica*, **18**, 155–62.

Nash, John (1953), "Two-person cooperative games", *Econometrica*, **21**, 128–40.

National Science Board (NSB) (1998), *Science & Engineering Indicators – 1998*, NSB 98-1, Arlington, VA: National Science Foundation.

Neill, Thomas (1949), "The Physiocrats' concept of economics", *Quarterly Journal of Economics*, **63**, 532–53.

Nevitt, Jonathan and Gregory R. Hancock (2001), "Performance of bootstrapping approaches to model test statistics and parameter standard error estimation in structural equation modeling", *Structural Equation Modeling*, **8**, 353–77.

North, Douglas (1991), "Institutions", *Journal of Economic Perspectives*, **5**, 97–112.

Nunn, Patrick (2012), "Disruption of coastal societies in the Pacific Islands from rapid sea-level fall about AD 1300: new evidence from northern Viti Levu Island, Fiji", *Journal of Coastal Conservation*, **16**, 199–209.

Ogilvie, Sheilagh (2014), "The economics of guilds", *Journal of Economic Perspectives*, **28**, 169–92.

Olson, Mancur (1965), *The Logic of Collective Action*, Cambridge, MA: Harvard University Press.

Ordeshook, Peter (1986), *Game Theory and Political Theory*, Cambridge: Cambridge University Press.

Orr, Daniel and Paul MacAvoy (1965), "Price strategies to promote cartel stability", *Economica*, **32**, 186–97.

Ostrom, Elinor (2000), "Collective action and the evolution of social norms", *Journal of Economic Perspectives*, **14**, 137–58.

Oxley, Joanne (1997a), "Appropriability hazards and governance in strategic alliances: a transaction cost approach", *Journal of Law, Economics and Organization*, **13**, 387–409.

Oxley, Joanne (1997b), "Hazards and governance in strategic alliances: a transaction cost approach", *Journal of Economics and Organization*, **13**, 387–409.

Pareto, Vilfredo (1896), *Cours d'Economie Politique*, Lausanne: F. Rouge.

Pareto, Vilfredo (1897), *Cours d'Economie Politique*, 2nd edn, Lausanne: F. Rouge.

Pareto, Vilfredo (1909), *Manuel d'Economie Politique*, Paris: V. Giard and E. Brière.

Perelman, Michael (1994), "Retrospectives: fixed capital, railroad economics and the critique of the market", *Journal of Economic Perspectives*, **8**, 189–95.

Petrin, Amil and Kenneth Train (2003), "Omitted product attributes in discrete choice models", NBER Working Paper 9452, National Bureau of Economic Research, Cambridge, MA.

Pirenne, Henri (1925), *Medieval Cities*, Princeton, NJ: Princeton University Press.

Porter, Robert (1983), "A study of cartel stability: the Joint Executive Committee, 1880–1886", *Bell Journal of Economics*, **14**, 301–31.

Powell, Jeanne (1998), "Pathways to national economic benefits from ATP-funded technologies", *Journal of Technology Transfer*, **23**, 21–32.

Pribram, Karl (1937), "The notion of 'economic system' underlying business-cycle analysis", *Review of Economics and Statistics*, **19**, 92–9.

Pribram, Karl (1951), "Prolegomena to a history of economic reasoning", *Quarterly Journal of Economics*, **65**, 1–37.

Pryor, John (1983), "Mediterranean commerce in the Middle Ages: a voyage under contract of commenda", *Viator*, **14**, 133–94.

Radner, Roy (1980), "Collusive behavior in noncooperative epsilon-equilibria of oligopolies with long but finite lives", *Journal of Economic Theory*, **22**, 136–54.

Rivers, Douglas and Quang H. Vuong (1988), "Limited information estimators and exogeneity tests for simultaneous probit models", *Journal of Econometrics*, **39**, 347–66.

Robertson, D.H. (1923), *The Control of Industry*, London: Nisbet and Company.

Röller, Lars-Hendrik, Ralph Siebert and Mihkel Tombak (2007), "Why firms form (or do not form) RJVs", *Economic Journal*, **117**, 1122–44.

Roosevelt, Franklin (1942), "Message from the President of the United States transmitting recommendations relative to the strengthening and enforcement of anti-trust laws", *American Economic Review*, **32** (supplement), 119–28.

Rosenberg, Nathan (1960), "Some institutional aspects of the Wealth of Nations", *Journal of Political Economy*, **68**, 557–70.

Rousseau, Jean-Jacques (1755), *Discours sur l'Origine et les Fondements de l'Inégalité parmi les Hommes* (*Discourse on the Origin and Foundations of Inequality among Men*), Amsterdam: Marc Michel Rey.

Rousseau, Jean-Jacques (1765), *Discours sur l'Economie Politique* (*Discourse on Political Economy*), Geneva.

Rubin, Paul (2003), "Folk economics", *Southern Economic Journal*, **70**, 157–71.

Ruegg, Rosalie and Irwin Feller (2003), "A toolkit for evaluating public R&D investment: models, methods, and findings from ATP's first decade", July, National Institute of Standards and Technology, Gaithersburg, MD.

Sakakibara, Mariko (1997), "Heterogeneity of firm capabilities and cooperative research and development: an empirical examination of motives", *Strategic Management Journal*, **18**, 143–64.

Sakakibara, Mariko (2001), "The diversity of R&D consortia and firm behavior: evidence from Japanese data", *Journal of Industrial Economics*, **49**, 181–96.

Sakakibara, Mariko (2003), "Knowledge sharing in cooperative research and development", *Managerial and Decision Economics*, **24**, 117–32.

Salanié, Bernard (1997), *The Economics of Contracts*, Cambridge, MA: MIT Press.

Sampson, Rachelle (2004), "Organizational choice in R&D alliances:

knowledge-based and transaction cost perspectives", *Managerial and Decision Economics*, **25**, 421–36.

Saussier, Stéphane (2000), "Transaction costs and contractual incompleteness: the case of Electricité de France", *Journal of Economic Behavior and Organization*, **42**, 189–206.

Scarf, Herbert, with Terje Hansen (1973), *The Computation of Economic Equilibria*, New Haven, CT: Yale University Press.

Schabas, Margaret (2007), *The Natural Origins of Economics*, Chicago, IL: University of Chicago Press.

Schacht, Wendy (2009), "The Technology Innovation Program", Congressional Research Service Report for Congress, June 29.

Schwartzman, Jack (1990), "Henry George and George Bernard Shaw: comparison and contrast: the two 19th century intellectual leaders stood for ethical democracy vs. socialist statism", *American Journal of Economics and Sociology*, **49**, 113–27.

Seager, Henry and Charles Gulick Jr. (1929), *Trust and Corporation Problems*, New York: Harper and Brothers.

Sewall, Hannah Robie (1901), "The theory of value before Adam Smith", *Publications of the American Economic Association*, **2**, 1–128.

Sherman, John (1890), *Trusts: Speech of Honorable John Sherman of Ohio delivered in the Senate of the United States, Friday, March 21, 1890*, Washington, DC: s.n.

Shulman, Daniel (2006), "Matsushita and the role of economists with regard to proof of conspiracy", *Loyola University Chicago Law Journal*, **38**, 497–505.

Siegel, Donald, Charles Wessner, Martin Binks and Andy Lockett (2003), "Policies promoting innovation in small firms: evidence from the U.S. and U.K.", *Small Business Economics*, **20**, 121–7.

Simon, Herbert (1951), "A formal theory of the employment relation", *Econometrica*, **19**, 293–305.

Simon, Herbert (1991), "Organizations and markets", *Journal of Economic Perspectives*, **5**, 25–44.

Skyrms, Brian (2004), *The Stag Hunt and the Evolution of Social Structure*, Cambridge: Cambridge University Press.

Smith, Douglas (1996), "The intracorporate conspiracy doctrine and 42 U.S.C. section 1985(3): the original intent", *Northwestern University Law Review*, **90**, 1125–84.

Smith, Vernon (2007), *Rationality in Economics: Constructivist and Ecological Forms*, Cambridge: Cambridge University Press.

Sorin, Sylvain (1992), "Repeated games with complete information", in Robert Aumann and Sergiu Hart (eds), *Handbook of Game Theory with Economic Application*, vol. 1, Amsterdam: North Holland, pp. 71–107.

Spence, Michael (1984), "Cost reduction, competition, and industry performance", *Econometrica*, **52**, 101–21.

Staudohar, Paul (1978), "Player salary issues in Major League Baseball", *Arbitration Journal*, **33**, 17–21.

Stegner, Wallace (2007), *Discovery! The Search for Arabian Oil*, Vista, CA: Selwa Press.

Stigler, George (1964), "A theory of oligopoly", *Journal of Political Economy*, **72**, 44–61.

Tadelis, Steven (2002), "Complexity, flexibility, and the make-or-buy decision", *American Economic Review*, **92**, 433–7.

Taylor, Fred M. (1929), "The guidance of production in a socialist state", *American Economic Review*, **19**, 1–8.

Taylor, Frederick W. (1911), *The Principles of Scientific Management*, New York and London: Harper & Brothers Publishers.

Taylor, Frederick W. (1947), *Scientific Management*, New York: Harper.

Teece, David J. (1986), "Profiting from technological innovation: implications for integration, collaboration, licensing and public policy", *Research Policy*, **15**, 285–305.

Telser, Lester (1972), *Competition, Collusion, and Game Theory*, Chicago, IL: Aldine Atherton.

Thompson, John B. (2010), *Merchants of Culture*, Cambridge: Polity Press.

Thorelli, Hans (1955), *The Federal Antitrust Policy*, Baltimore, MD: Johns Hopkins Press.

Topkis, Donald M. (1998), *Supermodularity and Complementarity*, Princeton, NJ: Princeton University Press.

Townsend, Robert (1979), "Optimal contracts and competitive markets with costly state verification", *Journal of Economic Theory*, **21**, 265–93.

Tucker, Robert (ed.) (1978), *The Marx-Engels Reader*, 2nd edn, New York: W.W Norton.

Verburg, Rudi (2012), "The rise of greed in early economic thought: from deadly sin to social benefit", *Journal of History of Economic Thought*, **34**, 515–39.

Vidulich, Paola (ed.) (1976), *Duca di Candia: Quaternus Consiliorum (1340–1350)*, Venice: Il Comitato ed.

Von Mises, Ludwig (1951), *Socialism: An Economic and Sociological Analysis*, repr. 2009, Auburn, AL: Ludwig von Mises Institute.

Werden, Gregory (2004), "Economic evidence on the existence of collusion: reconciling antitrust law with oligopoly theory", *Antitrust Law Journal*, **71**, 719–800.

West, Joel (1996), "Utopianism and national competitiveness in technology rhetoric: the case of Japan's information infrastructure", *The Information Society*, **12**, 251–72.

Williamson, Dean (2009), "Organization, control, and the single entity defense in antitrust", *Journal of Competition Law and Economics*, **5**, 723–45.

Williamson, Oliver (1971), "The vertical integration of production: market failure considerations", *American Economic Review*, **61**, 112–23.

Williamson, Oliver (1973), "Markets and hierarchies: some elementary considerations", *American Economic Review*, **63**, 316–26.

Williamson, Oliver (1974), "The economics of antitrust", *University of Pennsylvania Law Review*, **122**, 1439–96.

Williamson, Oliver (1975), *Markets and Hierarchies: Analysis and Antitrust Implications*, New York: Free Press.

Williamson, Oliver (1976), "Franchise bidding for natural monopolies – in general and with respect to CATV", *Bell Journal of Economics*, **7**, 73–104.

Williamson, Oliver (1979), "Transaction cost economics: the governance of contractual relations", *Journal of Law and Economics*, **22**, 233–61.

Williamson, Oliver (1985), *The Economic Institutions of Capitalism*, New York: Free Press.

Williamson, Oliver (1988), "Corporate finance and corporate governance", *Journal of Finance*, **43**, 567–91.

Williamson, Oliver (1990), "A comparison of alternative approaches to economic organization", *Journal of Institutional and Theoretical Economics*, **146**, 61–71.

Williamson, Oliver (1991), "Comparative economic organization: the analysis of discrete structural alternatives", *Administrative Science Quarterly*, **36**, 269–96.

Williamson, Oliver (1995), "Chester Barnard and the incipient science of organization", in Oliver E. Williamson (ed.), *Organization Theory*, New York: Oxford University Press, pp. 172–206.

Williamson, Oliver (1996a), "Revisiting legal realism: the law, economics, and organization perspective", *Industrial and Corporate Change*, **5**, 383–420.

Williamson, Oliver (1996b), *The Mechanisms of Governance*, Oxford: Oxford University Press.

Williamson, Oliver (1999), "Revisiting legal realism: the law, economics, and organization perspective", in Glenn R. Carroll and David J. Teece (eds), *Firms Markets and Hierarchies*, New York: Oxford University Press, pp. 197–234.

Williamson, Oliver (2005), "The economics of governance", *American Economic Review*, **95**, 1–18.

Wilson, Woodrow (1889), *The State: Elements of Historical and Practical Politics*, Lexington, MA: D.C. Heath and Company.

Winter, Sidney (1987), "Knowledge and competence as strategic assets", in D. Teece (ed.), *The Competitive Challenge*, Cambridge, MA: Ballinger, pp. 159–84.

Wooldridge, Jeffery M. (2002), *Econometric Analysis of Cross Section and Panel Data*, Cambridge, MA: MIT Press.

Wren, Daniel (1980), "Scientific management in the USSR with particular reference to the contribution of Walter N. Polakov", *Academy of Management Review*, **5**, 1–11.

Yang, Bao, Jinsong Wang, Achim Brauning, Zhibao Dong and Jan Esper (2009), "Late Holocene climatic and environmental changes in arid Central Asia", *Quaternary International*, **194**, 68–78.

Zachariadou, Elizabeth (1983), *Trade and Crusade: Venetian Crete and the Emirates of Menteshe and Aydin (1300–1415)*, Venice: Hellenic Institute of Byzantine and post-Byzantine Studies.

Zhang, Justin and Tian Zhu (2000), "Verifiability, incomplete contracts and dispute resolution", *European Journal of Law and Economics*, **9**, 281–90.

Zhu, Tian (1999), "Contingent versus noncontingent contracts", *Journal of Economic Research*, **4**, 87–99.

Zhu, Tian (2003), "Specific investments, flexible adaptation, and requirement contracts", *Economic Inquiry*, **41**, 299–304.

Case Law

Addyston Pipe & Steel Co. v. United States 85 F.271 (6th Circuit 1898)
Arizona v. Maricopa County Medical Society 457 U.S. 332 (1982)
Blomkest Fertilizer v. Potash of Saskatchewan 203 F.3d 1028 (8th Circuit 2000)
Broadcast Music Inc. v. Columbia Broadcasting System, Inc. 441 U.S. 1 (1979)
Calculators Hawaii Inc. v. Brandt Inc. 724 F.2d 1332 (9th Circuit 1983)
Chicago Professional Sports LP v. National Basketball Association 95 F.3d 593 (7th Circuit 1996)
Citizen Publishing Company v. United States 394 U.S. 131 (1969)
City of Mt. Pleasant v. Associated Electric Cooperative, Inc. 838 F.2d 268, 276 (1988)
Copperweld Corp. v. Independence Tube Corp. 467 U.S. 752 (1984)
CostCo Wholesale Corporation v. Maleng 522 F.3d 874 (9th Circuit 2008)
C-O-Two Fire Equipment Co. et al. v. United States 197 F.2d 489 (1952)
Dagher v. SRI, 369 F.3d 1108, 1118 (9th Circuit 2004)
Discon Inc. v. NYNEX Corp. 93 F.3d 1055 (2nd Circuit 1996)
Don Williams v. I.B. Fischer Nevada 999 F.2d 445 (9th Circuit 1993)
Federal Trade Commission v. Owens-Illinois, Inc. 681 F.Supp. 27 (1988)

Federal Trade Commission v. University Health, Inc. 938 F.2d 1206 (11th Circuit 1991)

Fleischman v. Albany Medical Center 728 F.Supp.2d 130 (2010)

Freeman v. San Diego Association of Realtors 322 F.3d 1133, 1148–49 (9th Circuit 2003)

HealthAmerica Pennsylvania Inc. v. Susquehanna Health System 278 F.Supp.2d 423, 428 (2003)

Hospital Corporation of America v. Federal Trade Commission 807 F.2d 1381 (7th Circuit 1986)

Iain Fraser v. Major League Soccer, LLC 284 F.3d 47, 58 (1st Circuit 2002)

In re Baby Food Antitrust Litigation 166 F.3d 112 (3rd Circuit 1999)

Jack Russell Terrier Network of Northern California v. American Kennel Club, Inc. 407 F.3d 1027 (US Circuit 2007)

James McCoy Smith v. Pro Football Inc. 593 F.2d 1173 (DC Circuit 1979)

John Mackey v. National Football League 543 F.2d 606 (8th Circuit 1976)

Joseph E. Seagram and Sons v. Hawaiian Oke and Liquors 416 F.2d 71, 82 (9th Circuit 1969)

Kiefer-Stewart Co. v. Joseph E. Seagram and Sons 340 U.S. 211 (1951)

Knutson v. Daily Review Inc., 548 F.2d 795, 801 (1977)

Levi Case Company, Inc. v. ATS Products, Inc. 788 F.Supp. 428 (1992)

Los Angeles Memorial Coliseum Commission v. National Football League 726 F.2d 1381 (9th Circuit 1984)

Malcolm Weiss v. York Hospital 745 F.2d 786 (3rd Circuit 1984)

Murphy Tugboat Company v. Shipowners & Merchants Towboat Co. 467 F.Supp. 841, 859–60 (1979)

National Society of Professional Engineers v. United States 435 U.S. 679 (1978)

New York v. Saint Francis Hospital, Vassar Brothers Hospital and Mid-Hudson Health 94 F.Supp.2d 399 (2000)

Petruzzi's IGA v. Darling-Delaware Company 998 F.2d 1224 (3rd Circuit 1993)

Robert M. Bogan v. Northwestern Mutual Life Insurance Company 953 F.Supp. 532 (1997)

Rothery Storage & Van Co. v. Atlas Van Lines, Inc. 792 F.2d 210 (DC Circuit 1986) 71

San Francisco Seals, Ltd. v. National Hockey League 379 F.Supp. 966 (1974)

Socony-Vacuum Oil v. United States 310 U.S. 658 (1940)

Superior Models v. Tolkien Enterprises 1981 WL 40556, 211 U.S.P.Q. 876 (1981)

Thomsen v. Western Electric Co., 512 F.Supp. 128, 133 (1981)

Timken Roller Bearing v. United States 341 U.S. 593, 598 (1951)

United States v. Apple Inc., 952 F.Supp.2d 638 (S.D.N.Y. 2013)

United States v. General Motors 121 F.2d 376 (7th Circuit 1941)

United States v. General Motors Corporation, 121 F.2d 376 (7th Circuit 1941)
United States v. Yellow Cab 332 US 218, 228 (1947)

Statutes

America COMPETES Act 2007
Bayh–Dole University and Small Business Patent Act 1980
Hart–Scott–Rodino Antitrust Improvements Act 1976
National Cooperative Research & Production Act 1993
National Cooperative Research Act 1984
National Industrial Recovery Act 1933
Omnibus Trade and Competitiveness Act 1988
Sherman Antitrust Act 1890
Stevenson–Wydler Technology Innovation Act 1980

Author index

Subject index

Case law index